IN SEARCH OF
LANDFALL

ALSO BY PATRICK RICHARDSON

Reports from Beyond: A Journey through Life to Remote Places
(Ultima Thule Press, 2008)

PRAISE FOR *REPORTS FROM BEYOND*

'Patrick Richardson is an authentic traveller, who is intrepid, curious and endlessly resourceful. He writes about his unusual and adventurous journeys with
eloquent zest, with an eye for the revealing, quirky detail, with an open mind
and a carefully controlled lyricism. Like the best travel writers, he does not only
journey through faraway places; he also journeys through his own imagination.
He well understands danger, strangeness, difference and contingency; and he
knows that the exotic is not necessarily glamorous. He is a master.'

HARRY REID, AUTHOR AND FORMER EDITOR OF *THE HERALD*

'This is a record of the most sustained travelling I have ever come across. On
tiny budgets, over forty years Patrick Richardson has probably seen more remote parts of the world than any other traveller. He is not looking for funny
stories or opportunities to advertise himself; he merely seeks to be there, to
see, to look, to listen and to witness. Cities generally leave him cold; it is to the
rural, the village, the road, mountain and desert that he is drawn. These reports
are at times almost melancholy, openly admitting to suffering, deprivation and
isolation as much as to exultation. We, the readers, peek over his shoulder into
the dizzying multiplicity of our planet. He has endeavoured to bring it all back
home in this remarkable book.'

ANDREW GREIG POET, NOVELIST AND MOUNTAINEER

'Patrick Richardson's travelogue and memoir is a joy to read. It takes you back
to the time when travel was something we did for its own sake and the world
was all to be discovered. Reading his fluid and evocative prose is like going
down that dusty road again, not knowing where we'll be tomorrow.'

PETER IRVINE, MBE, JOURNALIST AND AUTHOR OF *SCOTLAND THE BEST*

IN SEARCH OF
LANDFALL

THE ODYSSEY OF AN
INDEFATIGABLE ADVENTURER

Patrick Richardson

ULTIMA
THULE
PRESS

First published in Great Britain in 2014 by Ultima Thule Press

www.insearchoflandfall.com

ISBN 978-0-9558448-1-2

British Library Cataloguing-in-Publication Data
A catalogue record for this book is available on request from the British
Library

AUTHOR'S NOTE
To protect their privacy, identies of certain people in this book have
been changed, along with some place names. All photographs by the author,
unless otherwise acknowledged.

Typeset by Tom Gorham
Printed and bound by Clays Ltd
Cover design by Jim Hutcheson

*This book is in memory of my mother and my father, who gave
me the inestimable gift of life,
and for Gabriella*

here, just some water,
there amidst the trees
the sea!

Sogi

Contents

BOOK I

Endless Horizons

'Who's this?' my mother's mother, Eva, a staid Presbyterian matron with grey hair in a bun, demanded accusingly when she opened the door of her Victorian flat in Corstorphine, one of Edinburgh's most respectable suburbs.

'Timothy, my husband,' my mother retorted as bold as brass. She had just returned from London with my father, instead of the man she had been engaged to – and my grandmother had been eagerly expecting to greet – less than two months previously. My grandmother, the strait-laced daughter of the factor to the Duke of Northumberland, was so scandalised that she slammed the door in their faces, and they spent the night under a hedge in a field at the foot of wooded Corstorphine Hill.

My father had a shilling in his pocket.

The start of my parents' relationship eight years before my extraordinarily eventful life began had been highly dramatic. When my mother, Rosemary, was twenty-three, her best friend in the Scottish capital had been Mona, a fellow journalist whom she had met while employed on a women's magazine in London. After my mother mentioned that she was going back down south for the weekend and was looking for somewhere to stay, Mona had suggested that her family, who lived in Dulwich, might put her up. It was shortly before the Second World War, and my mother – a buxom, vivacious, energetic woman – had been engaged to a debonair volunteer infantry officer with a well-paid job at Austin Reed, the prestigious tailors. She had no sooner arrived at the house, an impressive six-bedroom Victorian villa, than she noticed a shy, good-looking, dark-complexioned young man smoking a pipe as he exercised his parents' huge, black-and-white Great Dane on the neatly mown lawn. Lean, with wavy black hair, he was Mona's twenty-one-year-old brother, Timothy, who had also been a journalist before being made redundant and penniless due to the looming conflict. Undeterred, my mother had fallen head over heels in love with him. Then, six weeks later, a month after war was declared, they had been married in Hampstead Town Hall Registry Office in a civil ceremony so secretive the only other people present were my mother's best friend, the well-known poet and writer Hubert Nicolson, and a passer-by in the street whom they asked to act as second witness.

The repercussions were far-reaching. Eva disapproved so strongly of her daughter's 'disgraceful and inexcusable behaviour' that she wouldn't speak to my mother for a year; Ethel, my father's mother, accused her recently acquired daughter-in-law of being a 'scarlet woman' and forbade the newly-wed couple to cross her doorstep ever again. For the next few months, while they were seeking jobs, they lived in cheap digs in Kilburn High Road in London, where there was only a gas ring to cook on and two twin beds; in the evenings, because they had so little money, they ate pie and chips. Eleven months passed, during which my mother, who had been carrying twins, had a miscarriage. Neither of my parents was overly put out, as they found the prospect of having two additional mouths to feed in such uncertain times daunting. Indeed – so my sister alleged, to my astonishment, half a century later – my mother might, by repeatedly having hot baths, have even tried to induce it. Irrespective of what happened, my mother, an intrepid and in-domitable woman who had swum in the river at close-by Lindfield in Sussex virtually up to the day the twins were due, speedily recovered.

Her fearlessness had first shown itself in childhood. When she was five, her father, an altruistic, kind-hearted doctor, had taken her on a brief flight in an open-air Tiger Moth biplane with Sir Alan Cobham, at the time a world-famous long-distance aviation pioneer.

Five years afterwards, neighbours rushed to let her parents know that she was playing on the six-inch-wide ledge outside the third floor of their elegant Georgian house in Edinburgh, oblivious of the thirty-foot drop to the pavement. Three years later, her father had been horrified when, on a cruise with her to Madeira, he had spotted her balancing perilously on rail-ings at the stern, directly above the propellers. Then, in the mid-1930s, soon after he died, an appreciative patient bequeathed her a legacy of £1,000. Without further ado, she packed her typewriter, cashed the cheque and an-nounced to her horror-struck mother that she was going to the continent to 'write some articles'.

She spent six months travelling by herself to Budapest, Vienna, Venice and Palermo in Sicily – a remarkably courageous thing for any woman to do at the time, when Mussolini was at the height of his power, far less one

of barely twenty.

Shortly after the miscarriage, the call-up was announced. Like his father, a pacifist and a hard-line communist in the First World War, not to mention the first salaried general secretary of the National Union of Journalists and the president of the International Federation of Journalists, my father believed in non-violence.

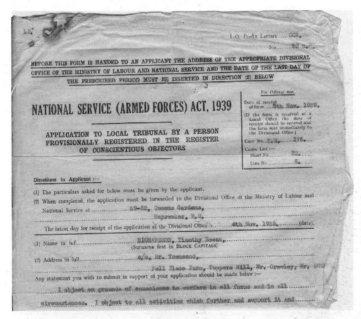

The tribunal responsible for hearing conscientious objectors listened attentively when he informed them that, since his schooldays at Alleyn's College, Dulwich, where he had declined to join the Officer Training Corps, he had refused to kill another human being. To my mother's huge relief, they granted his claim for exemption and gave him three options: go to prison, drive an ambulance, or do agricultural labour until the war ended. He chose the third, and three weeks later he found himself in a minuscule flat in East Grinstead in Sussex, from where he started working on various farms.

Within a few weeks, my mother joined him. To their amazement, he encountered little hostility towards pacifists, although some farmers could be abrasive. On one farm, he was sacked for asking for the new minimum wage; on another, he was summarily dismissed for taking a pint of the farmer's milk for his cat. The regional labour exchange forced my mother to accept a post as a stenographer in an office, where she hated the ambitious, backbiting businessmen, malicious tittle-tattle and scandalmongering. After a while, my father was offered a post as head cowman on a farm three miles away in the depths of the countryside. Initially they dithered, as both of them had previously lived only in towns. But at length they decided to take it, because along with it went Upper Sheriff Cottage, one half of an attractive, half-timbered black-and-white house.

Apart from her being able to give up her job, it also meant that they would have free wood, free milk and, with food rationed, would be able to grow their own vegetables.

In the heart of the Weald – a more bucolic place it would be difficult to imagine – the cottage was practically surrounded by fields and woodlands, and to reach it you had to get off a bus in the middle of a forest, descend a steep hill and cross a tiny bridge over a brook. Every morning, my father rose at 5 a.m. and irritably kicked his unreliable second-hand motorbike into life before he drove up the hill to work. It was extremely arduous. Every day, for fifteen hours, he had to muck out byres, milk cows and make hay. During the damp winters, he had to tramp through mud, shivering with cold and soaked to the skin. At night, when he was exhausted, he had to go on fire-watch. But despite having been blessed with an iron constitution, he had so many mystifying chills and bouts of what appeared to be flu that my mother worried that he had rheumatic fever, although it was actually brucellosis, a disease contracted from cows, from which he sporadically suffered for the next thirty years. There were occupational hazards, too. One evening, after he had finished his day's labour, he jumped down onto bales of straw and the prong of a pitchfork went right through his foot. Then, shortly afterwards, an oncoming army lorry forced him and his motorbike off the road into a ditch, a crash that left him with a scar on his chin for the rest of his life.

In the early days of their marriage, my mother, who called my father 'Fox', or 'Foxy', and my father, who called my mother 'Bibi', adored each other.

She loved his toned body, his dark brown eyes bright with intelligence, his long lashes, his straight nose, his sensitive mouth, his pearly teeth, his slim hips, his straight back and his sinewy legs.

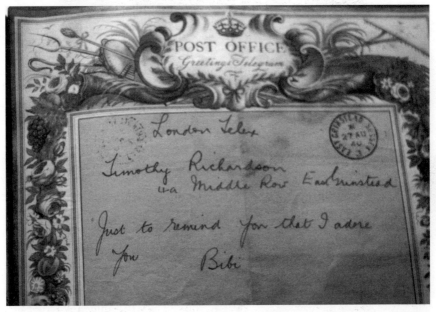

He had a keen brain and, although he could be temperamental and as stub-born as a mule, he was great fun to be with. Besides being an unselfish lover, he was helpful in the house, where he prepared meals and washed the dishes, and every night he carried up chocolate biscuits and milk, her favourite treat, to her in bed. He, for his part, loved her pretty face, her sensuous lips and mouth, her pert nose, her lustrous black hair and her voluptuous figure. And, crucially, she shared his values and beliefs, such as the abolition of capital punishment, independence for India, the establishment of a minimum wage and nationalisation. In fact they could scarcely bear to be apart, and when they were, he wrote her – for such a reticent, undemonstrative man – astonishingly passionate letters.

Although living there was hard, as there was no electricity and instead of having a bath they had to boil kettles to wash in the sink, it wasn't long until they fell in love with life at Upper Sheriff Cottage. In the riotous, luxuriant garden butterflies flittered. In the morning, when the air smelled fresh and sweet, they could hear cocks crowing and the soft squish of cows going to be milked. Spring, when the hedgerows were laden with wild roses, was singularly beautiful. In the woods, rampant rhododendrons and carpets of bluebells made vivid splashes of vermilion. Cuckoos called, dewy meadows were carpeted with buttercups, and orchards were weighed down with pear, apple and cherry blossom. Bees buzzed outside thatched cottages draped with japonica, horses grazed in lush green paddocks, and my parents heard nightingales sing as they had never heard them sing before. At intervals, as they sat wrapped in each other's arms on the upper deck of a bus after an evening out in nearby East Grinstead, she felt that the countryside looked so magical that she almost wept at the beauty of the lengthening shadows over the woods, the mantle of mist cloaking the downs and vales, the glorious vistas falling away to the horizon, the sliver of the waning moon, the hooting of owls and bats flitting against dusky barns, and the murmuration of starlings in the star-spangled sky.

For all that, before she first came across my father, my mother had had innumerable admirers and at least three serious suitors, and, although she idolised my father, she continued to have an eye for other men. Furthermore, she was unusually emancipated for the times and she even occasionally wondered what a polygamous relationship would be like, until she dismissed the notion as being potentially ruinous for their marriage. All the same, halfway through the war, and a year after my sister was born, their marriage ran into difficulties – only they knew why – and she was alleged to have had an affair with Karl, a handsome, blue-eyed, six-foot-two German prisoner

of war who worked on a neighbouring 'open' farm. Again, not a living soul apart from my parents and Karl knew whether there was any substance to the rumour, although, after my mother died, I discovered that she had sold my sister's christening mug – one of their most treasured possessions – to raise enough money to take him down to Brighton by train for the day.

In later years, though, when I questioned my father about it, he retorted brusquely: 'I don't know, I was too busy to notice.'

In truth he had been so desperate he had gone to Mona and asked her what to do.

'Tell her it's either him or you,' came the reply.

My father did confront my mother, who, as a consequence of whatever was said, opted for him, because presently life in sylvan Sussex resumed its peaceful, uneventful course.

There were interruptions, naturally. One weekend, hounds of the local hunt came crashing into their garden, and their dog, a lovable brown Cocker spaniel called Dinah, was so terrified that she bolted. My mother, who hated hunting, was so incensed that she chased her for a mile across fields until she found her at the local railway station, where she picked her way over live electric rails to rescue her. On another occasion, when she was pushing my two-year-old sister who, like my father, had very dark hair, in her pram down a country lane, a German V-2 rocket, or 'doodlebug' as they were called, exploded in a field a hundred yards away. Then, towards the conclusion of the war, she and my father, on hearing the approaching thunderous drone, craned their necks every evening to watch wave upon wave of four-engined RAF Lancaster, Halifax, Liberator and Flying Fortress bombers darken the sky as they set off to raid Germany.

Before then, my father had told my mother that, if they had a child, he wanted to have a daughter exactly like her, and she had told him she wanted to have a son exactly like him. Now, blissfully unaware of the dire consequences such fixed preferences would have, their wish was granted; a year after hostilities ceased, I was born in a maternity hospital in East Grinstead. Like most mothers, mine considered her children to be the best-looking in the world, although an early photograph of me depicts a grinning, simian infant with jug-handle ears sitting bolt upright in a pram.

For the next four years, my parents lived harmoniously in the cottage. Twice a year, my grandmother, who had come round to her daughter jilting a dapper volunteer infantry officer in favour of an unemployed left-wing conscientious objector, made the 450-mile journey down to stay with them. There, she showered them with gifts, most of which – especially the cushions embroidered with baby rabbits and toadstools – were the antithesis of their taste. Regrettably, I have no recollection of life in Sussex at all, and I have to depend on photographs to build up a picture of it. Another of these depicts me as a two-year-old infant in a red toy fire engine in a garden ringed with hollyhocks, while a third – of which for a long time I was thoroughly embarrassed – depicts a podgy toddler with blond, curly hair standing amongst daffodils in a Saxon churchyard.

In Sussex, there was invariably plenty for my parents to do. There was

the garden, where my father built a chicken run and a hen house, and grew beans, beetroot, blackcurrants, cabbage, carrots, lettuce, onions, parsnips, peas, potatoes, rhubarb, shallots, spinach and tomatoes. There were parish fêtes, where my mother once entered me – attired in a mackintosh, to represent the British summer – in a fancy dress competition. Pursued by their two faithful cats and their kittens, they went for walks in the woods, where she picked armfuls of foxgloves and honeysuckle for the cottage, or they rambled across fields sprinkled with violets and cowslips, where she collected hay for the kittens' litter. Lindfield, a village of half-timbered, black-and-white Elizabethan houses, had a reed-fringed duck pond with swans, and an immaculately rolled cricket pitch on the village green, where, every Saturday, there was the thwack of willow on leather and men in cream flannels bellowed 'Howzat!' Cuckfield was a pleasant market town whose fair had a beautiful nineteenth-century merry-go-round. West Hoathly was a hamlet consisting of thatched cottages, a thirteenth-century Saxon church with panoramic views down over the drowsy Weald, and a Tudor pub called the Cat, which allowed children inside for lemonades.

But the place they loved the most was the lake at Horsted Keynes. Every Sunday, after lunch at the local pub, they freewheeled their bicycles down past a tiny church and two whitewashed cottages to the lake. Practically encircled by impenetrable woods, it was exceedingly secluded, and there my mother picked primroses and violets in a dappled glade before she spread their rug and opened her picnic basket under a tree whose branches dangled low over the warm, limpid water. Summers in Sussex can be hot, so they sunbathed idly on the mossy bank or swam off a rickety landing stage to a wooden raft.

Later they said that, their poverty notwithstanding – at the start, my father earned a mere thirty shillings a week – their years in Sussex were the happiest of their lives. Naturally, my mother at times was nostalgic for her job as a journalist or homesick for Edinburgh. She missed her mother. She missed eating vanilla ice creams in cafés overlooking Princes Street. She missed watching ferries at South Queensferry, she missed the salty tang of the sea and the swooping seagulls, and she missed watching trains rumble across the rust-red Forth Bridge. But in Sussex she loved the lazy, sun-drenched, seemingly never-ending days. She loved being able to go barelegged and cycle everywhere, she loved the balmy air with its odour of jasmine or mint, and she loved the country lanes and pastures speckled with yellow primroses and cowslips. And, first and foremost, she was deeply fulfilled by her children.

My father, on the other hand, loved the tough, physical labour and digging in his vegetable patch. He loved working with animals, with which – because he was gentle with his hands – he had a natural affinity. He loved wearing his khaki shorts and open-necked shirt, and feeling the wind in his hair when he rode his motorbike. And the two of them had such fun together, above all when chasing each other round the kitchen with spoons, a game whose only rule was that afterwards the winner, the person who made the other laugh the loudest, could do whatever he or she liked to the loser … But my father was a very intelligent man and, with a growing young family to support, he didn't want to spend his life as a cowman. Be that as it may, after the war, because of the stigma attached to pacifists, he couldn't find other employment and had to continue on the farm.

Eventually, four years later, he managed to be accepted as a student by an agricultural college in Edinburgh. There, my parents rented the Victorian flat of my grandmother, who went to live with her sister in a bungalow in Blackhall. On the first floor above a bustling thoroughfare, our new home had a gloomy drawing room with half-drawn claret curtains, aspidistras at the window, and a chintz ottoman, chaise-longue and armchairs grouped round the fireplace. Opposite, there was a loudly ticking antique grandfather clock, a Steinway grand piano and a mahogany sideboard with photographs and silver fencing trophies won by my long-dead Irish grandfather. There was only one bedroom, with glazed door panels that you couldn't see through, so my sister and I slept in twin bunk beds in a fusty cupboard in the hall redolent with resin, Brasso, wax polish and turpentine. At the rear of the flat was a snug scullery overlooking a communal back green.

It was here, in the winter of 1950, that I became conscious for the first time that I existed. One fading November afternoon, when I was four, and I was petrified by the cawing of rooks in the gargantuan oak tree in the back green, I found myself in the pantry next to the sink. It was pitch-dark, and I can still vividly recollect how claustrophobic I felt, until I emerged to see the glow of the seemingly permanently lit coal fire. But even more vividly imprinted in my memory was the day when I was playing near the sideboard, where afternoon tea was being laid for my uncle, a benevolent, bespectacled doctor visiting us from Australia.

'Patrick,' my mother burst out, 'for goodness sake, take your train out of the kitchen! How can I cut sandwiches with all your toys cluttering up the place?'

As I stood up, I stumbled against the sideboard and accidentally spilled a newly brewed pot of tea over my face. For a split second, it felt as if I had been stung by myriads of infuriated bees, and my first reaction was to claw at the skin of my crimson, blistered cheeks, until, as quick as a flash, my uncle, who had been nearby, grabbed my hands.

'Oh my God, my God!' my mother shrieked as, blinded by scalding water, I lay screaming on the floor.

With my uncle still pinning my arms to my body, I was rushed, siren wailing, by ambulance to hospital. Four days sped by in a blur of bandages, starched white sheets, polished linoleum corridors and anxious faces peering down at me. But it was my uncle's prompt action that prevented me from being physically scarred for life.

Six months after we arrived from England, I attended my first primary school, where I had my initial taste of the harsh world outside my grandmother's flat. A five-minute walk away, it was down a tranquil side street in Corstorphine village, which included a fifteenth-century church, a public library and a leafy park with tennis courts and swings. Although I was only five, on my first day my nerves were jangling, as I had heard rumours that newcomers were dragged to outside lavatories in the playground to have their heads flushed down the toilet. As I had feared, I had to undergo the ordeal, although, to my relief, it was less traumatic than I had imagined. Far more unnerving was morning assembly. Every day, the school lined up in orderly, disciplined ranks in the playground. There, the headmaster, a squat, bald man with a pot belly the size of a beer barrel, addressed the school, and the Union Jack was raised on a flagpole. Then, after we had sung the national anthem, he jotted down the names of the latecomers, whom he belted with his 'Lochgelly special', a thick brown strap, which he so obviously revelled in using.

The school itself was a cheerless Victorian building with labyrinthine wooden corridors, and from day one I took care to tuck myself away behind creaking desks carved with initials at the back of the classroom to avoid being sent to him to be beaten. Like many children, I found learning to write the alphabet extremely difficult. I also recall discovering what I perceived to be a weird species called 'girls' in the class. One was called Janey, and for some reason I resolved to make her my girlfriend. As was to be expected, I didn't have the faintest clue what having a girlfriend meant, so, believing it was the kind of thing you did with your girlfriend, I wrote her a poem. Because I couldn't think of what to say, I adapted a nursery rhyme I knew. My version went: 'Three blind mice, three blind mice, take down your knickers and slide on the ice ...'

Years later, when I was eleven, I had my first interview for a private school and recited it ingenuously to the examining panel. I didn't get in.

In the beginning, I stood on the sidelines during the morning interval at primary school, looking on enviously as the other boys played football. I couldn't fathom why I was excluded and, although I presumed this befell all newcomers, it was the first time I became conscious that, somehow, I was an outsider, a feeling that has pursued me my entire life. By and by, I was given a game, although, when the captains picked two teams, I was the last to be selected. Then, at lunch, all the pupils stampeded to the adjoining grocery shop, where we frittered away our dinner money on brown malt loaves, which were all the rage at the time.

Soon I made my first friend, one of four children of an impoverished family who lived round the corner. Squashed into a ground-floor flat at the foot of Corstorphine Hill, they attended Holy Cross Academy, a Catholic school. They wore threadbare green uniforms and, although I didn't know what being Catholic meant, I already sensed that they were regarded as being different from most people. My new friend and I would play on a swing dangling from a mammoth bough of the oak tree in the back green, which spiked railings divided according to the 'stair'.

To the right of the green was an eight-foot-high, ivy-covered wall behind which was our dentist's detached Edwardian villa. I detested going there, understandably, and my mother insisted on accompanying me into the dentist's room, so she later disclosed, to ensure that I didn't 'get up to any mischief'.

After a few years, appalled by the headmaster's reign of terror, my parents transferred me to another local primary. Housed in a low modern complex, its headmaster had a reputation as a humane, liberal-minded man. Once more, I tucked myself away at the back of the class, trying to put as much distance as I could between my teacher and myself. A lofty, skeletal-looking man with a Roman nose, a deathly pallor and deep-set eyes, he had strands of wispy, ash-grey hair combed back over his skull. Unfortunately for me, my scholastic career as a serial miscreant was just beginning. First I was ejected from the choir for misbehaving while we practised Handel's 'Largo'. Then there was my inattentiveness in his class, which, along with my inability to differentiate between the spelling of 'there' and 'their' in my English essays – which weren't at all bad – he obviously found exasperating.

At last, I joined a snaking queue of other children waiting to be beaten. This consisted of receiving up to six of the belt on one hand, with exceptionally badly behaved children receiving six on each hand. It was excruciatingly painful, especially if it went beyond the wrist, which in theory it wasn't supposed to do. Nevertheless, I suffered in silence, until one evening, after I had received six of the belt, my mother detected a red weal disappearing up my sleeve.

'What on earth's that?' she asked.

I rolled up my sleeve and showed it to her.

'In God's name, how did you get that?' she cried, mortified. Neither of my parents believed in corporal punishment, and the only time in my life my mother ever hit me – across the back of the legs with a bamboo cane – she was so remorse-stricken that she never forgave herself. Now, she was so furious after I explained I had been punished for not paying attention in class that the following day she stormed down to confront the headmaster.

'Are you aware of the punishment being meted out in your school just for being inattentive in class?' she demanded. 'I know my son's no angel, but even so I find six of the belt utterly excessive.'

Rooted to the spot by the force of her onslaught, he gave her his word that he would order his deputy to keep his use of the belt to the minimum. She also wrote a letter of complaint to the city's director of education, from whom she received a written apology in which he confirmed that if belting went beyond the wrist teachers ran the risk of being prosecuted. Even so, the whole episode only made her all the more determined to get me into an independent – and hopefully more liberal – school the minute I passed the entry test.

Meanwhile, I continued playing football in the playground, where, together with the other boys, I was in awe of 'Horny', the nickname of James Horn. With his neat, tight curls he already looked a small, middle-aged man, although he was only eight years old, but his consummate dribbling earned him a status bordering on the mythical. I for my part was merely a scrapper, but how thrilled I was when I was given a fluorescent-green jersey to wear; I had been selected as the reserve team's goalkeeper! Not only that; during the annual sports day, I won the 100-yard sprint and the high jump. For all that, I primarily look back on the games for how, wanting just to be like the other boys, I was ashamed of my by now grossly overweight mother as she proudly looked on. I never forgave myself for that day, when, rather than pretending not to recognise her, I ought to have been eternally grateful for her indefatigable determination to protect me from sadistic primary school teachers.

It wasn't until I was seventeen that I learned from my parents that my

English teacher was actually Scotland's greatest living poet; not only that, he had been both a pacifist and a conscientious objector during the Second World War. Four years afterwards, while I was crossing George Square, the leafy, cobbled campus of Edinburgh University, I caught sight of a man with hollow eyes and skin drawn so tightly over his skull that, to me, his face looked like a death mask. It was Norman McCaig, who had just been appointed fellow in creative writing. Unable to resist the temptation to take my revenge, I decided to confront him.

'You're Norman McCaig, aren't you?' I enquired ingenuously.

A faint smile flitted across his face. 'Yes, I am,' he answered, perhaps expecting to hear some flattering comment.

'I remember you!' I remarked tersely. 'When I was seven, you used to belt me because I was inattentive in class and couldn't spell.'

It may be my imagination, but his face paled before I walked on. Nonetheless, if I imagined it was the end of the affair, I was mistaken. After he died, three decades later, Catherine Lockerbie, the distinguished literary editor of the *Scotsman*, devoted half a page to his obituary. In the first of two contributions, one of the paper's chief correspondents wrote how 'watching him work a classroom was a reminder of his Brodie-esque ability to charm and enthuse'. In the second, she herself wrote: 'A generation of Scottish schoolchildren will fondly recall his visits to their classrooms, the twinkle gleaming reassuringly from beneath the patrician brow. How sadly he will be missed!'

Scarcely able to believe what I was reading, I wrote her a two-page letter, describing my experience at my primary school and informing her that, on the contrary, every seven-year-old child in my class had feared him like the plague. 'No,' I concluded, 'he won't be missed, not by this contributor, at least.'

A week later, I received a letter from her. In it, she wrote that she could appreciate how greatly he must have hurt me for me to feel so wounded after all those years. 'However,' she went on, 'given his subsequent generosity and encouragement for budding writers, for whom he had unfailingly kept an open house, I hope in your heart you can bring yourself to forgive him for what were surely his youthful excesses. What's more, I feel confident that, if he were alive, this is what he would want you to do.'

Profoundly touched, I felt that she was right, and it was time to let go of my smouldering resentment.

Once Mr McCaig's beatings ceased, things calmed down for me and there were few signs of the tumultuous events that were to be such a feature of my adult life. After my father graduated from agricultural college, he applied for various jobs in Scotland. At length, frustrated by continual rejections, he successfully applied for one in Kenya. The family was on the point of emigrating, and he had even bought our tickets from Southampton to Mombasa, when Mau Mau guerrillas started their struggle for independence from Britain. Deterred by reports of 'atrocities' against European settlers, he cancelled our passages and redoubled his efforts to obtain employment in Scotland until the agricultural subsidiary of a powerful international corporation offered him a post in its publicity department.

Apart from establishing his respectability in my grandmother's eyes, this provided a good salary that enabled my parents to buy their first house. It was considerably overdue, as the hall cupboard had become far too cramped for my sister and me. I can still vividly conjure up my first sight of the new house. Situated only a mile from my grandmother's flat, it was the first of a row of bungalows before undulating countryside began to the west. The bungalows were concrete, box-like buildings in a bleak, treeless street, but, to my sister and me, the house was paradise. I was only nine years old, and the dining room, with its three windows overlooking the back garden, seemed positively palatial in comparison to my grandmother's kitchen, while the back garden itself, with its newly mown striped lawn, looked like how we imagined a court at Wimbledon.

For an hour, my parents stood chatting on the lawn, until we were invited to bowls of strawberries and delicious rich cream on a table at the bottom of the garden. But I was lost to everything and everyone. I was in raptures at the prospect that all this might shortly be my territory. I could jump up and down on the lawn, which felt so bouncy it was like being on a trampoline. I could creep round the seven-foot-high hedge that ran along the side of the house to the front garden. And I could hide in the thick rhododendrons and dense foliage that protected the lawn from the next-door neighbours, where, like some jungle explorer, I could mount expeditions with my bow and arrow to repel intruders – other small boys – rash enough to venture into my new empire.

We moved in. Now, when I look back on it, all the days in summer seemed, as so often in childhood, to be long and sunny. Stupendous white clouds ballooned in dreamy aqua-blue skies, and I practically lived in the garden. There were countless things to do there. On Sundays, we picnicked on a rug at the foot of the rockeries, where my mother, who loved cooking, laid out an array of mouth-watering sandwiches and savouries. Twice a year, my father stood on a chair and clipped the hedge, while I swept up the cuttings on the pavement. I helped him hoe the vegetable patch at the side of the house. When he mowed the lawn, I helped him empty cuttings onto an ever-growing compost heap in the bottom right-hand corner. I played with my football, and if the ball bounced into the garden of the neighbours, I wriggled through the fence to retrieve it before they could shout at me. My sister and I knocked a tennis ball over a net my parents had strung across the lawn.

Best of all was the yellow, ex-RAF inflatable dinghy our parents bought for us, whose tubular walls were as hard as concrete, but where we had the time of our lives diving into the icy, three-foot-deep water. A snaking hose supplied water to it, and I took endless delight in turning its high-pressure jet on unsuspecting blackbirds or torpid cats. When deflated, it was stored underneath the dining room in the cellar, the entrance to which was a knee-high wooden door. Inside, you had to be careful not to hit your head on gas and electricity pipes attached to the low concrete ceiling. But how I relished rooting about there! There were disused lawnmowers, disembowelled horsehair cushions, pots of paint and glue, and tea chests containing moth-eaten clothes. There were the remains of mahogany cabinets and mounds of mildewed books. There were corroded bicycles with flat tires and gears and lamps that never functioned. At the far wall there was a gaping hole in the brick foundations, but I was exceedingly wary of going through it; beyond, it was as black as a coal pit and, by my candle, all I could make out were chunks of masonry, brick and tiles on the ground. Moreover, I was terrified my candle might go out and that someone, thinking no one was inside, might lock the cellar door, so cutting off the chink of light, my lifeline to the outside world, and leaving me entombed for ever.

For years, my father cultivated the rockeries in the back garden, until he allowed them to be overrun with weeds. To me, with their plants, shrubs and mauve lupins, they resembled Lilliputian mountain ranges. These provided ideal cover for my toy tin Red Indians who besieged toy wagon trains trundling across the grassy plains – the lawn – below. They would sweep down from behind rocks and, amid blood-curdling cries and whoops, valiantly battle troops of cavalry three times their strength. I invariably sympathised with the former, and viewed the columns of metallic settlers as trespassers into uncharted territory where only buffalo – and on Sundays, lawnmowers – roamed. First and foremost, I prized Big Chief Sitting Bull, who sat cross-legged and imperturbable on a craggy ledge in the rockeries, puffing on his pipe outside his wigwam – an up-ended polystyrene cup.

One birthday, I received a model cowboy town. Consisting of a two-foot-long, brown and sulphur-yellow wooden walkway with a saloon, barber's, bank, Wells Fargo office and sheriff's jail, almost immediately it was staging rowdy bar-room mêlées, bank robberies and stagecoach hold-ups. Not far away from where I played with it in the garden, underneath a shady rowan tree in the corner by the hedge, there was a mound I named Boot Hill. This housed the grave of our first dog, which had been with us in Sussex. For five years after she died, the family placed a vase of fresh violets, pansies and daisies on top of her lovingly tended grave, until bracken, brambles and time swallowed it up. Sherry left behind her daughter, Brandy, an equally lovable brown Cocker spaniel, who had equally large, doleful eyes and floppy ears the size of paddles. At intervals, on going into the kitchen, I was puzzled to discover that up to seven diminutive replicas of her had emerged from nowhere and lay snuggled up to her, and one of my most wretched childhood memories is of my father, after failing to obtain homes for them, drowning them on Sunday evenings in the kitchen sink.

My mother was a child who never grew up, and consequently adored everything to do with children. When my sister and I were infants, she had loved to tuck us up and lull us to sleep with bedtime stories and nursery rhymes; decades afterwards, I could still recite many of them by heart. As soon as I got home from primary school, she would sit down with me in a corner of the sitting room in readiness for *Children's Hour* on the radio. After a few minutes, a soft, comforting female voice asked, 'Are you ready, children? Then we'll begin …' But, most of all, my mother enjoyed giving children's birthday parties.

She was peerless at organising games, of which she had an apparently infinite repertoire. At the parties she would have up to thirty infants hold hands and go round and round in circles while she recited 'Twinkle, Twinkle, Little Star'. Following that, we played pass the parcel and the egg and spoon race, until we ended with pass the orange, to find which team was the quickest at passing the fruit held under your chin without using your hands.

As well as parties and games, she loved festivals. A week before Easter, she got out her paintbrush and paint box and spent hours and hours decorating hard-boiled eggs. They were miniature works of art and, although I was very young, on Easter Day it pained me to see the intricately painted turquoise, pink, mauve, orange and pale green shells crack and disintegrate when my sister and I rolled them down a grassy slope between the rockeries. But Easter was special in more ways than one. After we received our enormous chocolate Easter eggs, we had the traditional lunch of roast lamb with mint sauce, roast potatoes and vegetables. Then, in the afternoon, we had high tea, which consisted of a daffodil-yellow Easter cake with candles, egg sandwiches and hot-cross buns.

In November, before the Halloween party, my father leaned a ladder against a wall in the kitchen and scrambled through a hatch in the ceiling to fetch the Halloween decorations, contained in two tea chests in the loft. Within hours the dining room would be garlanded with paper witches on broomsticks, grinning cardboard skeletons, and turnip lanterns that my sister and I had hollowed out. After the party began, the children would gorge themselves on plates of home-made pies and cheese and cress sandwiches, before we dooked for apples in a tin tub. After Halloween came Guy Fawkes Night, when the flames of our bonfire illuminated the back garden, and the evening resounded to the whoosh of Catherine wheels, firecrackers and rockets.

Nevertheless, the biggest event of the year was undoubtedly Christmas. Already, by November, my mother would spend her entire evening writing Christmas cards to her seemingly countless friends or wrapping presents to their children, an unenviable, time-consuming task as every Christmas she received over 150 cards. Before long, as the great day itself drew near, she and my father bought a ten-foot-tall Christmas tree that my father stabilised with bricks in a tub wrapped in red crepe paper before he erected it in front of the sitting room window. Then, once more, he climbed the ladder to the loft,

this time for the Christmas decorations, and soon the tree would be dripping with silver tinsel, fairy lights, angels, candles and dozens of gold baubles.
On the shelf near my father's chair my mother constructed the annual crib,
complete with model figures of Jesus and Mary and the Three Wise Men.
Above, there was a German advent calendar, with a window to be opened
daily until Christmas Eve.

Every Christmas Eve we attended the carol service at St Mary's Cathedral, the soaring, nineteenth-century Gothic church near the West End. In
those days, the nights invariably seemed to be crystal clear and frosty, with
ever-receding constellations of shining stars, and crisp snow carpeting the
hushed, deserted streets. Usually we tried to obtain seats in the three back
rows, so that we could leave early, which we sometimes did. Generally, my
sister and I sat between our parents; I was so small my legs didn't touch the
ground, and all I could see of the service were the stockings or trousers of the
congregation in front of me. My mother, who had a beautiful voice, loved
to sing the carols and when every now and then I stole a glance at her, she
had tears in her eyes. When the service was over, we would linger to chat
to her friends. Then, after we emerged from the imposing western doors
out into the sooty night, we crunched through the snow to the echoing,
equally cathedral-like Caledonian railway station at the West End. There, we
viewed the model railway at the foot of a thirty-foot Christmas tree. It was
amazingly realistic, with stations, level crossings, sidings, tunnels, junctions,
embankments and cuttings. Afterwards, we ambled along Princes Street to
the tree on the Mound. Donated every year to Edinburgh by the Norwegian
government in gratitude for Scotland's support during the Second World
War, it was even taller than that in the Caledonian. I preferred it, as it was
decorated with hundreds of white lights, unlike the multi-coloured ones in
houses on the way home.

Once back in the bungalow, my mother hung red-and-white stockings at
the foot of our beds in the bedroom that I shared with my sister. For the most
part, agog in the hope of catching Santa Claus and his reindeer coming down
the chimney, I could scarcely sleep for excitement. We never did, of course,
but to our delight we awoke in the morning to discover the stockings bulging with stickers, crayons, pencils, notebooks, stencils, erasers, bars of chocolate, liquorice sticks and bags of sweets. After breakfast, when my mother
had tuned into carols sung by the choir of King's College, Cambridge, on

the radio, my sister and I hurried through impatiently to the sitting room to receive our presents. We received dozens of them, because my mother had so many friends, and before long the floor would be strewn with heaps of crumpled wrapping paper. While we opened the presents, my mother noted down which of us had been given what and by whom, to ensure we wrote our thank-you letters. If we received money, we had to keep a meticulous tally of how much; the vast majority of her friends were unstinting in their generosity, and we received up to £40 or £50 each, a prodigious sum at the time, especially to a child. The sole exception to this was my grandmother's sister. A snobbish, pretentious woman whose wealth was based on farms her husband owned in the Borders, she lived in an Edwardian mansion in leafy Barnton, Edinburgh's most desirable suburb. Even so, she was our meanest relative; every Christmas, her grey Bentley swept up to our front door and a chauffeur in spotless livery haughtily delivered her Christmas present – a Mars bar each – to my sister and me.

At 1 p.m. it was time for the sumptuous, three-course lunch. Still, what I looked forward to before all else was my mother's home-made Christmas pudding. The same ritual inevitably accompanied it; my mother, sister and I would draw the curtains, and my father would sprinkle the Christmas pudding with brandy from a bottle before he took it out to the hall. Then he knocked on the door and carried it back into the dining room, where, in a whoosh of flames, he lit it on the table, the signal for my sister and I to vie for the lucky silver sixpences my mother had hidden in it. When the meal was finished we lounged around the table, lighting sparklers, throwing streamers and pulling crackers containing miniature plastic toys and jokes on slips of paper. Then we would don paper hats and tell the jokes before we adjourned to watch the Queen's speech on television in the sitting room. There, my parents dozed by the fire, and my sister and I played with our new toys. But Christmas could be stressful because of our expectations, and by evening we were all often irritable, and my mother so worked up that her nose bled.

The following day, Boxing Day, the family took the bus to the Christmas pantomime at the King's or the Lyceum theatre. There, my mother normally bought the best seats in the house, in the first three rows, and we stuffed ourselves with three boxes of Quality Street chocolates. My first pantomime, if my memory serves me well, was *Jack and the Beanstalk*, which my mother clearly enjoyed as much as my sister and me. Latterly the pantomimes became ever more overblown, and nearly all the bawdy gags, most of which were aimed at the adults, went over my head. It didn't matter; along with the other children, I loved shouting 'Behind you!' as the crocodile crept up on Captain Hook in *Peter Pan*, or 'Oh, yes you are!' and 'Oh, no you're not!' at the three Evil Sisters in *Cinderella*.

Apart from giving parties for children, my mother also threw a wildly successful one every New Year for fifty of her friends. Mostly, they were surgeons, teachers and QCs, although there were other people from less exalted walks of life. Before the party began, there were feverish preparations as we hoovered the carpets, tidied the beds and checked the food on the table, which would be laden with sausage rolls, cheese-and-onion dips, chicken sticks, salmon and turkey sandwiches, chipolata sausages, and fruit salad and cream. All at once, the doorbell would ring, and soon the dining room was so bursting with guests it was impossible to move. My mother was a marvellous hostess, because she so loved people. The life and soul of the party, she went round introducing guests to each other, and most of them got on so famously that within thirty minutes everyone was engaged in stimulating conversations or laughing and joking. I, on the other hand, hated whenever she dragged me across to introduce me to her friends. Both my father and I were shy and, to avoid having to chat to people, we kept refilling their glasses from wine bottles on the sideboard, or we hung about the table, nibbling vol-au-vents. As time wore on, everybody donned party hats; then, at midnight, the party reached its climax and my mother positioned herself at the head of a throng before they conga'd from room to room, rocking with laughter.

The first book I read was *Little Black Sambo,* which had colour illustrations of a boy seated under a mango tree, waiting for the fruit to fall. I also fell in love with the *Thomas the Tank Engine* series about a locomotive with a chubby florid face and his friends, two coaches called Annie and Clarabel. But two other books I found profoundly unsettling. The first was *Alice in Wonderland,* with Tenniel's drawings of Alice, the macabre duchess and caterpillars with human expressions.

The second was our original 1917 copy of *Struwwelpeter,* the German children's book by Heinrich Hoffman. Its sadistic, illustrated stories about what befell badly behaved children, for instance 'Little Suck-a-Thumb', a boy who refuses to cease sucking his thumbs and has them snipped off by a tailor with mammoth scissors, scarred my psyche. This was because, for the first five years of my life, I sucked my own thumb so much that a wart grew under the nail and had to be painfully removed in the Royal Infirmary.

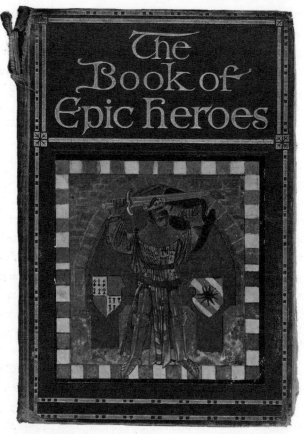

As I grew older, my taste in books, of course, evolved. Like nearly all boys, I was an avid reader of comics. Then, when I was ten, I began reading my father's *Just William* books, a set of faded red hardbacks he had had since he was a child. It wasn't long before I was addicted to the stories of the naughty eleven-year-old schoolboy with the tousled hair who was eternally getting into scrapes or terrorising his elder sister, his parents and a seemingly inexhaustible number of terrifying, indestructible aunts; little did I know the disastrous effect these stories were soon to have on me. Apart from these, I was gripped by the *Book of Discovery* series, which consisted of *The Book of Myths*, *The Book of Inventions* and *The Book of Epic Heroes*. My grandfather had given these to my father when he was a boy, and inside each was inscribed 'To Timmy, 1927'. They had once been handsome hardbacks with dark green covers embossed with gold lettering, but now they were scuffed and dog-eared. Nevertheless, I implored my father to let me have them, but he refused, until several years later he capitulated and gave them to me as a birthday present. My favourite was *The Book of Epic Heroes*, as I identified with Roland, the French hero who blew his horn as he made his final defiant stand against the Vascones during the Battle of Roncevaux Pass.

I was similarly passionate – again like innumerable boys in those days – about trains, and one of my greatest wishes throughout my childhood was to receive an electric railway set as a Christmas or birthday present from my parents. To my great regret, they could never afford one, and I had to make do with a clockwork train set instead. Still, I pursued my interest in other ways. Periodically, my mother took me to the railway bridge in Princes Street Gardens to wave at drivers of the steam locomotives that still pulled the trains. They were unfailingly good-humoured, and leaned out of their cabs and hooted their whistle before we were enveloped in clouds of cindery smoke. Every so often, I went trainspotting by myself to Waverley Station, where I stood on wet, draughty platforms, fastidiously noting engine types and numbers in my notebook. At intervals, as a treat, my parents took my sister and me by train to seaside resorts in Fife. As we rumbled noisily over the gigantic rail bridge, I stood on my seat and hurled pennies out of the window, a long-established ritual regarded as a bringer of good luck. But one trip above all is branded in my memory. My mother had loved water since childhood, and on Ely beach, after she rolled down her stockings to go for a paddle, as she always did when she was by the sea, I became separated from her. I don't know who was more frantic with worry, and I can clearly recall flinging myself into her arms once we found each other an hour later.

In addition, during the summer holidays, the family took the train to North Berwick, a seaside town with ochre roofs twenty-five miles away in East Lothian. I preferred it to those in Fife and, like many children, relished building sandcastles in an unavailing attempt to hold back the incoming tide, although, when I was very young, I was frightened of the thousands of tiny mounds made by sandworms on the beach.

My mother loved animals – she didn't even flinch if bees or wasps landed on her – so another of the family's favourite trips was to Edinburgh Zoo.

One weekend, when we were halfway up the hillside on which it is spread out, we approached the hippopotamus enclosure.

'What a pong!' my mother exclaimed, holding her nose.

I had never heard the word, so I assumed she was referring to some monstrous animal I hadn't seen. From that day on, whenever we approached the compound, I entreated them to let me see the 'pong', and couldn't work out why they burst out laughing. Nearby, bordering the reptile houses, were bushes where my mother told my sister and me that, when she was a child, she had caught a glimpse of a fairy. It was a claim she maintained her whole life, along with a belief in the supernatural that she inherited from her Irish relatives, the vast majority of whom professed to believe in leprechauns.

But my insatiable passion was for the sea. It began when my parents gave me a gorgeous outsize hardback called *The Book of Ships* that they had bought in an antiquarian bookshop. Inside were superb drawings of all the famous tea clippers, along with paintings and photographs of the *Titanic*, the *Olympic* and the *Lusitania*, three of the biggest liners ever built.

Over the following two years, my focus changed and I became fascinated by naval ships, notably British battleships of the Second World War. At one time, I could recount the history of every one of them, as well as those of Germany and Japan. But my love of ships led to one of the most embarrassing moments of my childhood. One day, my mother took me to Navy Day at Rosyth, the naval base directly in the lee of the Forth Bridge, when the public was allowed to board visiting warships. I so enjoyed exploring the decks of HMS *Ark Royal,* the successor to my favourite aircraft carrier, that we returned the following year. This time we had the opportunity to go down into a submarine. I was first to clamber down the conning tower, where smartly uniformed members of the crew were waiting to assist the public. My mother was next, but her hips were so wide that she became jammed, and the more she descended the higher her skirt rode up her thighs. The sailors were convulsed with laughter, although I was so mortified I didn't know where to look. My mother, on the other hand, was totally unruffled; when she arrived at the foot of the conning tower, she beamed so disarmingly at the sailors it was as if nothing had happened.

My father did his best to be a good father and – amazingly – I can't remember him ever meddling in my life or offering me guidance. Nor did he ever lose his temper with me, far less scold, chastise or spank me. The result was that, for nearly a decade, we were very close. He took me down to the docks in Leith, where his firm had an office, to see cargo ships unload gigantic bales of imported esparto grass. Although he had detested sports since he was a child, from time to time he took me to Tynecastle stadium to attend football derbies between Heart of Midlothian and Hibernian, the team I supported because, being of Catholic and Irish origin, they were the underdogs. When I was eight, he also taught me how to play chess, which we played at least twice a week for the next nine years. Not only that; every Saturday morning he and I took the bus down to the indoor swimming baths at Portobello, a run-down suburb on the Firth of Forth.

Right on the seafront, from where the triangular volcanic cone of Berwick Law was plainly visible, the baths were housed in a two-storey, red-brick Victorian building, with black metal turnstiles and, in the foyer, display cases laden with silver swimming trophies and sepia photographs of Edwardian men with twirled, upturned moustaches, bushy side whiskers and long johns. At the time, there were two pools, one for men and one for women. To begin with, I was so reluctant to go into the water that my mother had to come down and take me into the showers for women, where I can still see myself standing, gazing awestruck at these peculiar beings with two pendulous bags – breasts – sagging down their front. Nevertheless, within a month I was playing contentedly in the shallow end of the baths for men, while my father, a powerful swimmer, swam twenty lengths of breaststroke followed by another twenty, kicking like a frog, on his back.

Afterwards, we climbed the stairs to the canteen for bacon rolls or went outside to the seafront, where I bought tuppenny packets of aniseed balls from a nearby kiosk with my Saturday pocket money. A few yards away, a circle of stiff, long-in-the-tooth women sang 'Stand up, Stand up for Jesus!' to the accompaniment of a Salvation Army brass band. Then we idled along the promenade, past neglected cafés, gaudy amusement arcades and flaking fish and chip shops. The beach itself, whose seaweed-encrusted breakwaters buried in the sand looked like backbones of prehistoric beasts, still lured pasty-faced, working-class holidaymakers from Glasgow in the summer. During the summer there would be children building sandcastles or going for donkey rides, along with men flying kites and dogs chasing footballs. But in the winter, when there was a slate-grey sky and a slate-grey sea, it was very desolate, with only seagulls wheeling close to the shore, and solitary, doleful-looking people walking their dogs along the promenade.

At the end, to the west, was Portobello's outdoor swimming pool. Situated not far from grimy factories and Edinburgh's sewage plant, it had been built in the mid-1930s in art deco style, and was renowned for its two-foot-high artificial waves and its gargantuan size – it could hold 1,200 swimmers and accommodate 6,000 spectators. Off and on, if the weather was sunny, our whole family went there at weekends. There, I would frolic in the waves and challenge myself to climb to the top of the white diving tower with its three, progressively higher springboards. At length, I succeeded in reaching the highest one, but the world below was in such a spin that it was several years before I could summon up the courage to take what appeared to be a suicidal, death-defying leap off it. However, the temperature of the pool's salt water, which was heated by steam from the adjoining power station and was never more than twenty degrees, combined with the inclement summers, meant the pool's fate was sealed when the era of low-cost air travel abroad began and, lamentably, it was demolished in the 1970s.

On the way home, my father and I usually found seats at the front of the top deck of the bus, as it was coming straight from the nearby terminus. There, my father lit up one of his Four Square cigarettes, which along with Senior Service were his favourite brand. One lunchtime, the bus, which seemed to be going very fast, was approaching traffic lights at the West End, and I can still see an amorphous shape being drawn inexorably towards us as if by a magnet. It was a woman crossing the road, and there was a sickening thud before the bus shuddered to a halt; the bus had knocked her down. Later it turned out she had died in hospital, and my father was called to give evidence at an inquest, but even though he testified the bus had been speeding, to his disgust the driver was acquitted.

My mother had legions of best friends, many of whom were either teachers of art or artists. There was the art teacher at St George's School, a statuesque woman with a droll expression, a deep breathy voice and thick spectacles whom my sister and I loved for her mischievous sense of humour and whose pupils so adored her that many of them stayed in touch with her for decades. There was Margaret Glass, an art teacher at a rough secondary state school, a lovable, bumbling woman whose shabby clothes were usually covered with hairs from her two mangy black Labradors and who looked as if she didn't have two pennies to rub together, although she was unfailingly generous and her father had been a highly regarded painter as well as president of the Royal Scottish Academy. There was the spry, twig-like, seventy-year-old woman who lived alone on the other side of the Dean Bridge whose father had also been president of the Royal Scottish Academy. There was the tiny, atrophied artist and sculptor who wore towering green or purple frizzy wigs, along with spectacles the size of saucers, and who every Edinburgh Festival held one-woman shows of critically praised paper cuts that poured from her studio opposite St Mary's Cathedral. There was the petite, highly strung sculptor who spoke in staccato sentences, smoked like a chimney, and lived in a grandiose New Town house where her husband, a turgid lawyer, had a reputation for being rude to guests at their dinner parties.

Besides her best friends, my mother had dozens of other friends. There was the well-spoken, middle-aged proprietor of a thriving travel agency, who periodically took us for an outing in his beautiful, racing-green Jaguar or invited us to his red sandstone villa near the Botanic Garden. There was her friend who lived in a small castle halfway up Corstorphine Hill before she and her son moved to a Victorian villa on the seafront in North Berwick; subsequently, he gained notoriety as an incorrigible philanderer before he emigrated to the Caribbean and set up a scuba-diving business. There was the convivial, black-haired Jewish hospital consultant with a hooked nose who made my mother laugh like a drain at our parties. There was the upper-class woman and her husband, an eminent QC, both of whom spoke with tortured vowels, and who also lived opposite St Mary's Cathedral in the West End. There was a pint-sized patron of the arts and her husband, a plain-speaking, opinionated headmaster of Falstaffian proportions who delighted in arguing at parties with anyone prepared to debate with him.

A few of my mother's friends I associate with the traumas of childhood. First, when I was six, there was the affair with the spindly, brittle woman who was as thin as a scarecrow and babysat periodically for our parents. She had a flat chest and a hatchet face, and both my sister and I disliked her strident manner and shrill, rasping voice. One evening she whacked us across our knees with a ruler, so afterwards we complained to our mother, who questioned her about what had happened. She alleged – falsely – that we had been rude to her, although my mother didn't believe her and never invited her to babysit again. From that time onwards, whenever she visited us, my sister and I scuttled quickly to our bedroom.

Another distressing experience I associate with Enid, my mother's best friend for over sixty years. They had known each other since they were seven, when my mother's Catholic father, whom she idolised, had sent her to board at the Convent of the Sacred Heart at Craiglockhart in Edinburgh. Both she and Enid had loathed it and, to entertain themselves, at midnight they used to career on a wooden tray down the carpet of the convent's impressive main stairway. This had continued until one night they made such an ungodly racket that they awoke the nuns, who punished them severely. Now Enid lived in Ayr with her two sons and husband, who had presided over the family's ailing photography business, but intermittently they drove through to Edinburgh, where our family piled into their car, a classic, open-topped Alvis. One Sunday, when I was seven, they took us down to North Berwick. While everyone was picnicking on the beach, I fell into the open-air paddling pool; although it was only two feet deep, I hadn't yet learned to swim, and I floundered hysterically as my mother raced to rescue me.

That same year, during the summer holidays, our family took the bus with Margaret Glass to go camping in the Trossachs. To our dismay, after three days, we all developed diarrhoea and had to pack up the tents prematurely. The entire return journey I struggled to control my bowels, because the bus had no toilet, and after it dropped us off in Corstorphine, I scurried up the hill, desperate to reach home before it was too late. Just as I turned the corner to our house, dark brown liquid began trickling down my legs and, burning with shame, I cried plaintively as I waited for my mother to arrive and open the front door.

My mother also loved her Irish relatives. Being so gregarious and talkative herself, she identified strongly with them. Her affinity with Ireland, however, irrefutably originated with her love for her father, William Frost.

A solidly built man with fleshy features, a scrub of white moustache and thinning hair brushed straight back over his head, he was from County Clare, where his parents had owned a modest country estate. Close by lived an entire clan of Frosts, one of whom had written *The History and Topography of the Country of Clare*, for decades commonly acknowledged to be the definitive account of the county. The Frosts claimed they were descended from sailors of the Spanish Armada shipwrecked off the Irish coast, where they had intermarried with the natives. They were also ardent Republicans, and even claimed to be related to the Irish patriot James Connolly, who was born in Edinburgh, and whom the British executed by firing squad in 1916 for his role in the Easter Uprising in Dublin. In later years, I called in on my mother's favourite first cousin, who lived in Dublin. By that time, although she was an infirm, shrunken woman in her eighties, she was still in

full command of her faculties, and I could scarcely believe my ears when she still espoused her support for the IRA, who, in an act of unforgivable barbarity, had just blown up twenty-seven innocent men, women and children in the Omagh bombing atrocity.

My mother's father, who fenced and played hockey for Ireland, had studied medicine there. Afterwards, he had felt duty bound to run the family estate, until, aged thirty, he had come over to Edinburgh to study for a postgraduate degree in gynaecology at the university. One morning, as he was hurrying to lectures, he observed a young girl crossing the leafy Meadows, together with her four sisters. It was my seventeen-year-old grandmother on her way to school in adjoining George Square. He was so taken with her that, despite being thirteen years older, he found a pretext to introduce himself, and courted her for several years before she accepted his proposal of marriage.

Once he had graduated, he built up a successful medical practice and by and by he bought a magnificent house in Moray Place. In the grandest square in the Georgian New Town, each of its four storeys had four floor-to-ceiling astragal bay windows separated by fifteen-foot-tall Doric columns, and the steps leading up to the front door were flanked by decorative, nineteenth-century black gas lamps.

Here, in 1915 – in a house that, years later, was presented to the Queen for use as a grace and favour residence – my mother was born.

Like the majority of well-to-do people at the time, her parents had a cook and servants, and a sepia photograph of my mother depicts her, aged three and muffled in furs, posing with the chauffeur on the running boards of their stylish convertible parked outside.

Another photograph shows her father standing, attired in a tweed suit with a watch chain looped across his waistcoat, on a shoot with wealthy friends. But he was, at the same time, a principled, humane man with a sympathetic bedside manner, and he often treated his poorer patients, who worshipped him, for free.

Then, during the Great Depression, the practice's fortunes waned and, as he himself was forever ill, the family was forced to move to Melville Street. A less exalted address in the West End of Edinburgh, in the shadow of St Mary's Cathedral, the house was nevertheless huge and in an eminently desirable part of town.

At the time my mother was so enthralled with Wendy, the girl in *Peter Pan* by J.M. Barrie, that she named a cupboard in the basement her 'Wendy' house. She also so identified with Peter that she fantasised that she, like him, could fly, and it was only after she had launched herself off the bottom shelf that she found she was sadly mistaken. At length, the family had to move yet again, this time to a house near Donaldson's Hospital, the crenellated Gothic palace that later became the National School for the Deaf. By the time her father died aged sixty, after an operation for gallstones, his finances had so collapsed that he apologised in his will for leaving his wife as good as penniless.

She, too, routinely took to her bed during their thirty-year marriage, claiming to suffer from minor ailments, but most of these vanished, a sign possibly of how dysfunctional their marriage had been, after his death.

In those days, Edinburgh seemed an altogether different world. When we lived in my grandmother's, almost directly opposite on the corner was a high-quality, family-owned grocer's that reeked of rare teas, freshly ground aromatic coffee, figs and newly caught game. Two doors along was a 'ladies' shop where old-fashioned mannequins were adorned with frumpy blouses. Next to them, amputated wooden hands pointed from Lingerie to Haberdashery, where the prices of lace tablecloths, napkins and doilies were rounded to a halfpenny of every pound. When we moved to the bungalow, milk floats hauled by hulking Clydesdale horses delivered bottles every day to our doorstep. Every month, men with sooty faces and blackened caps rode along the street on their carts, shouting 'Coal, coal!' In spring, swarthy gypsies parked their caravans in a lay-by near Cammo woods, to the west. In Princes Street, cream-and-maroon double-decker trams clanged noisily past venerable, outdated emporiums such as Forsyth's and Jenners. Once in a while, 'Onion Johnnies', whom I assumed had cycled all the way from Normandy, pedalled past the Scott Monument with strings of onions dangling from their handlebars.

About this time, the family started going on summer holidays to the village of Bamburgh in Northumberland. There, we lodged with a kindly, stooped elderly woman who almost had a moustache. She lived in a row of honey-coloured cottages up virtually the only street from the impressive Norman castle.

Opposite, in the middle of the village, was a copse of contorted trees where rooks squabbled in their nests day and night. During the holidays we would rise at dawn and pick mushrooms in mist-swathed fields near a hill-ock two miles before Budle Bay. Afterwards, my father accompanied me to a little hump-backed bridge over the main east coast railway line to watch the London-Edinburgh express thunder by in clouds of ashen smoke. Every so often, I attempted to play tennis with an angelic-looking ten-year-old girl dressed in tennis whites and white socks whose parents also regularly went to Bamburgh on holiday, and who, along with my own parents, smiled proudly as she and I scampered around the public grass courts at the foot of the castle. If the weather was miserable, we had afternoon tea in Ye Olde Bake House, twenty yards down from our cottage. It was cosy and quaint, with chintz curtains, tablecloths and cushions, and served home-baked scones and strawberry tarts.

If it was sunny, we picnicked in sand dunes overlooking the beach, on the other side of the castle. There, shielded from the bracing wind, we watched six-foot breakers crash down on the vast, empty beach that sweeps all the way to Seahouses, a fishing village three miles down the coast. One afternoon, an hour after my father had gone swimming, I glanced up from my colouring book and espied him, two hundred yards offshore, gesticulating towards us. I thought he was enjoying himself, so I waved back and returned to my cray-ons. Half an hour later he re-emerged, exhausted, and told us that each time he had tried to swim ashore the notorious undertow had carried him out to sea. Increasingly desperate, he had become weaker and weaker, and, unable to attract attention, he had trod water until the tide turned, and he eventually succeeded in staggering back onto the beach.

The following year, my mother passed her driving test. I can still recall how excited my sister and I were when, as the summer holidays approached, my parents purchased their first car. A pale blue-and-white Hillman Imp, it was the family's pride and joy and it opened up thrilling new possibilities. However, because they didn't have enough money to take us abroad, which scarcely anybody did at that time anyway, they took us to a Butlins holiday camp in Yorkshire. But the start of the holiday was nerve-racking. A short distance before Filey we began driving up one of the steepest hills in Britain. It was a one-in-three gradient and my mother, who had practically no driv-ing experience, couldn't put the car into first gear, and stalled it time and again. The rest of the family criticised her roundly, but at least she had passed her test, unlike my father, who expressed no interest in learning to drive.

It wasn't my mother's only misadventure when driving the Hillman. The following year we travelled to Bunbeg in Ireland for our summer holidays. At the time, County Donegal was still intensely rural and abounded with braying donkeys, thatched cottages and wrinkled women in black. Bunbeg itself was an enchanting – or so it seemed to me – Gaelic-speaking fishing village with a single street that terminated in a small harbour. There we stayed in a white, two-storey house owned by the local bank manager, with whose wife my mother had become friends in Edinburgh, where she was a housemistress at the exclusive St George's School for girls. One day, as we were driving along the edge of precipitous cliffs, my parents had a furious argument. The longer they argued the more upset my mother became, and the more upset she became the faster she drove until we were doing over eighty miles an hour. Paralysed with fear, my sister and I cowered in the back. For a millisecond, I considered throwing myself out of the car or trying to seize the ignition keys until I realised both plans were impractical; if I did the former, I would probably kill myself, and if I did the latter there would be a struggle, she would lose control at the wheel, and we would plummet hundreds of feet to the sea. Fortunately, the situation was resolved by the car screeching to a halt, whereupon my father jumped out, slammed the door and strode off into the distance, until we picked him up, four miles further on.

When I wasn't devouring books about the navy, trainspotting or playing chess with my father, I mucked around with my friend, a skinny, cheeky scamp with matchstick legs, tousled ginger hair and ginger freckles who lived with his divorced mother in a bungalow near the parish church. She was equally sharp and angular – her legs were like a stork's – and, with her painted fingernails and thick lipstick, she regarded herself as genteel and ladylike. One Sunday, my mother suggested the four of us should go for a walk across the Pentland Hills, which overlook Edinburgh. They aren't exactly a stroll, as they are five hundred feet high and consist of boggy moorland. Be that as it may, my friend's mother turned up, to our disbelief, in stilettos; we had barely set off before they sank into the waterlogged ground, and we had to turn back.

Afterwards, I became friends with a boy with a gap between his two front teeth who looked the image of a youthful J.F. Kennedy and lived in one of the working-class sandstone tenements that climb a dead-end street off Corstorphine Road. Round the corner from his house there was a knotted oak tree reputed to be two hundred years old. Opposite was the Duchess café, which had the biggest selection of confectionery for miles around, with jar upon jar of sweets, including soor plums and lemon sherbets, my favourites. Although his house was near our bungalow, it felt like another planet, but that didn't bother me, and I went for tea every other Saturday in his parents' snug kitchen.

We were perpetually up to some escapade or other. Every Wednesday evening, we took the bus down to Portobello baths, where we took immense pleasure in provoking the lifeguards. In Corstorphine, we scaled a high wall to steal crab apples from the orchard of the manse. We played marbles and we went hunting for conkers. We took our 'guiders' – crude wooden contraptions with four wheels and a steering rope we had cobbled together – and careered up and down the 'bumps', brackish nearby marshland. We cycled with jam jars to the Caledonian Canal at Ratho to fish for minnows or collect frogs' spawn, or down to a narrow road that runs along the Firth of Forth where, to look grown up, we smoked straws, as we were too young to buy cigarettes.

Some of our pranks were positively foolhardy. Intermittently, we crept into the goods yard at Haymarket station and stole detonators, which we placed on the main railway line to Glasgow, hoping the expresses that pounded past a few feet away would make them explode. One Guy Fawkes Night, we lit a packet of squibs and thrust them through the letterbox of an inoffensive grey-haired woman whose house looked out onto the 'bumps'. Fortunately, we didn't set her house alight, but she was so irate she telephoned the police, who, somehow, found out we were the culprits. Our parents were notified and we had to report to the local police station where we were firmly reprimanded and warned of the direst consequences if it occurred again.

At the top of the road from our house there was a broken-down farm, before it was demolished and replaced by a petrol station. Until then, there was nothing to stop us from wandering through barns to an inner farmyard, where there were piles of disused farm machinery, and horses poked their noses out of stables. Further up from the farm, the road sliced through cornfields bordered with rosehip hedges, until it reached the top of Corstorphine Hill. From here you could see the Firth of Forth and, on the opposite side, the Ochil Hills; on a cloudless day you could even pick out the foothills of the Highlands. To the west, fields sloped down to Cammo woods, where, supposedly protected by feral dogs, a mad woman called the 'Old Woman of Cammo' was reputed to live in a haunted house. But although we roamed endlessly through the neighbouring countryside, we never caught a glimpse of her. However, one December, when our family was clambering over a fence to steal mistletoe for our Christmas tree, we heard the sound of baying hounds. I hastily shinned up a tree while my parents and my sister beat an unseemly retreat across the fence.

On occasion, as another treat, my parents took my sister and me to the restaurant at Turnhouse airport. It was only three miles away, and to get there you took a country lane that climbed to a knoll called Cow Hill before it crossed an arterial road and passed a disused quarry. The airport was a low, contemporary, two-storey building, and inside it was light and airy. The restaurant was on the first floor, where there were far-ranging views down over the all but deserted runway, as there were scarcely any planes. I enjoyed going there, as the tables were set with spick-and-span tablecloths, polished cutlery and sparkling wine glasses, and the delicious three-course meals cost only seven and sixpence. On Saturdays, my mother deposited us at the Astoria Cinema in Corstorphine and the Pools Synod Hall in the West End for the afternoon matinee. These have long since gone, but in those days they were mobbed with exuberant little boys and girls who whooped and shrieked at every opportunity.

When I was very young, conditions in our house were basic. Still, my father hid a colossal, Excalibur-like sword – to defend us in case burglars broke in – underneath their bed in their room at the front of the house. Every Sunday evening, after my mother had deposited food for squirrels in the rapidly growing tree outside the back door, she washed me in the deep bathtub next to the kitchen sink. I invariably looked forward to it, as I revelled in being the focus of her attention and being lathered with soap. As time rolled by, and my father's salary increased, conditions improved and my parents bought Ercol tables and chairs, which were in vogue at the time. They also put up prints of three post-Impressionist paintings on the walls of the dining room. The first, by van Gogh, showed fishing boats drawn up on a beach. The second, by Manet, portrayed a daydreaming barmaid behind the counter of the bar of the Folies Bergère. The third, by Gauguin, depicted alluring Tahitian girls in Western Samoa; never in my wildest dreams did I imagine that, forty years later, I would travel there myself. In addition, the dining room contained our bookshelves, most of which were chock-a-block with bleached red hardbacks of the Left Book Club, which my father had acquired in the 1930s. However, the only book that interested me was *Ulysses* by James Joyce, because I had overheard my parents discussing its 'sexy passages'. But although I left no stone unturned, they had hidden it so well I could never find it.

On Friday evenings, my sister and I attended the Brownies and the Cubs respectively at the local parish church, where, like the other boys, I coveted the badges you earned if you mastered specific skills. This lasted until one day the pack went on a camping trip to Perthshire. My heart was in my mouth, as it was rumoured that first-timers were 'blackballed', a self-explanatory initiation rite involving the use of Kiwi shoe polish. As I had feared, I was held down, kicking and shouting, by older boys who stormed into my tent as soon as we set up camp. This time, in contrast to my first day at primary school, I hated the experience so much that I never returned to the Cubs.

Our neighbours were a motley crew. There was the obliging middle-aged couple who lived in the house opposite. She was an unprepossessing, careworn woman who wore dowdy clothes and a headscarf the whole year round. He was a six-foot-two, scrawny, sad-eyed man with a lugubrious face and mournful eyes that, along with his frayed black suit and black Homburg, reminded me of an undertaker. Two houses along were a middle-aged couple whose son, although he was three years older than me, I became friendly with, and who subsequently became my sister's first boyfriend. Opposite them, on our side of the street, were a family with three daughters. From time to time I played with the youngest, who had freckles and hair the colour of carrots. At the time, that struck me as a perfectly natural thing to do, and I can still recall feeling that playing with her wasn't equivalent to playing with boys, and maybe should entail something else, although what exactly I wasn't sure. Halfway along there was the sour, prune-faced, crabby old woman who wore a raincoat and a transparent plastic headscarf irrespective of the weather. Initially all the children in the street detested her, although she gradually softened and we even grew to like her. Lastly, fifty yards up the road there lived the manager of Heart of Midlothian Football Club. In those days, the club was so successful that it twice won the Scottish league, but he was almost never at home.

In the beginning, I saw a good deal of my sister, Rosemary. She was a lovely-looking child, with dark hair, hazel eyes, long eyelashes and a gap between her two upper front teeth that gave her a very appealing look.

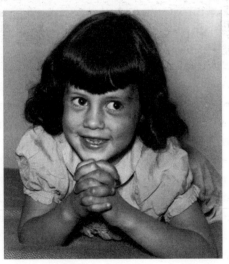

For several years, like many children, both of us wet the bed and bit our nails. We also shared a bedroom, or the 'nursery' as my parents called it, where we played with her Edwardian doll's house or pushed each other on our beautiful, black-and-white, nineteenth-century wooden rocking horse. Outside, we fed our pet rabbit in its hutch near the hedge and I skipped with her on the pavement, until I realised both were activities boys didn't do. In the summer, we splashed in the paddling pool and knocked a tennis ball over a net stretched across the back lawn. Occasionally, we cycled to the public courts in the park facing Corstorphine School, while, in winter, we built snowmen in the back garden.

For all that, like most brothers and sisters, we fought a lot, chiefly about whose turn it was after meals to wash, dry or tidy away the dishes in the kitchen. A few years later our paths began to diverge, and she and the three daughters who lived along the road whiled away hours bouncing up and down on their pogo sticks on the pavement outside our house, or whirling their hula hoops around their waists, both of them fads for prepubescent girls in those days. Then, when she reached puberty, my father spent two months converting the loft into my bedroom. After that, because we attended different schools and had different friends, our paths crossed less and less, apart from at meals or on holidays.

To help pay for our school fees, my mother took a part-time job as secretary to the governor of Saughton Prison. For several years she enjoyed it, as she liked the people, especially the jolly chief steward, with whom she worked. As a result, our house was deserted when my sister and I got back from school, and whoever arrived home first had to put on the fire. This entailed stacking firelighters up in a pyramid, putting coal on them and lighting a match. To begin with, I couldn't get the fire to light, but eventually I succeeded, especially if there was kindling. Then, after some time, it was replaced by a gas fire, which you had to ignite with a gas poker. This was supposed to make it easier, although I was exceedingly wary of the whole process, because I was scared to death I might blow up the house.

When I was seven, I became conscious of events in the outside world. I can still hear the modulated tones of the newsreader's voice in 1953 as he gave the first live commentary on the Queen's coronation on our first television set, or the excitement at the news that Hillary and Tensing had conquered Mount Everest. There were other memorable milestones. In 1956, there was

the Suez crisis, when Britain and France invaded Egypt in their inglori-
ous attempt to regain control of the Suez Canal, expropriated by Colonel
Nasser. There was the invasion of Hungary by the Soviet Union. There was
the scandal surrounding Commander Crabb, the Royal Navy frogman who,
during the state visit to Britain by Marshal Bulganin and Nikita Khrushchev,
the Soviet leaders, vanished without trace when undertaking a reconnaissance
mission around a Soviet cruiser in Portsmouth harbour. Who had authorised
him? Had he been captured alive and spirited back to the Soviet Union? Or
was his the headless body discovered fourteen months later? These questions
intrigued me, along with half the British populace. But above all I can still
see the launch of the Russian Sputnik, the first satellite to circle the earth,
and hear its melancholy beep-beep-beep from outer space. The next year, I,
like everybody, was heartbroken to learn that Laika, the little dog blasted into
space on Sputnik 2 to study weightlessness, died after seven days in orbit.

Seeds of Rebellion

All too soon, my years of childhood innocence ended. Three years after moving into our new house, I succeeded at my second attempt in being accepted by George Watson's College, one of the city's best private schools. A stupendous neoclassical pile with a separate, equally palatial junior school, it had four boarding houses, a stadium for rugby and athletics, tennis courts, an indoor swimming pool, a gym and about a dozen rugby and cricket pitches.

Initially I was placed in one of the three top classes, but still heavily under the influence of the *Just William* books, I had come to believe school existed exclusively for my entertainment, and masters were there solely to be made fun of. Soon, in imitation of Bill and Ben, the Flowerpot Men, characters in a popular children's television programme at the time, I was clowning about with two new friends in the seemingly never-ending marble corridors crying 'Weed, weed!' In the class of my bungling mathematics master I flicked chewed paper pellets at the ceiling to see if I could get them to drop onto the heads of unsuspecting pupils. In the class of my Latin master, a buffer with a blubbery, pockmarked face, bulbous nose and rheumy eyes, I fired paper darts at his back when he was at the blackboard. But although the school had a liberal educational ethos compared with my two primary schools, there were other teachers, such as the steely French master who prided himself in thrashing anyone foolish enough to misbehave in his class. Worst of all was the deputy headmaster, who was responsible for discipline and had an even more terrifying reputation with the belt.

The masters weren't the only targets of my oafish misbehaviour. Midway during the second term an olive-skinned, fourteen-year-old refugee from Hungary, whose father was a nuclear physicist, joined the class. A cultivated and thoughtful boy, when he first set foot in the UK he knew only three words in English: 'yes', 'no' and 'abstain', from listening illicitly to UN debates on *Voice of America* radio. Not surprisingly he quickly became our form master's favourite. In revenge, the class, myself included, shamefully bullied him. One lunchtime, three of us took bags of mashed potato from the dining hall. Then, while he was drinking from a drinking fountain down steps near the gym, we called out his name and, when he looked up, emptied them on his face. Our bullying, however, hopefully didn't mark him for life; years later he became a highly successful West End theatre director.

Of course, my misconduct came at a price. One day when I was up to the usual tomfoolery in chemistry class, I was on the point of hitting a South African boarder on the head with my chemistry book, when he turned round abruptly, saw me, and instinctively lashed out with his fist, smashing several of my front teeth. They were acutely painful, because many of the nerves were exposed. For months my mother had to take me to the Dental Hospital to have them filed down, and I could only drink lukewarm liquids through a straw. That wasn't all. In my exams at the end of the year my marks in biology, physics and chemistry didn't even reach double figures. My sole redeeming feature was that, to everyone's amazement, I won the school's chess championship, an improbable achievement given that I received five per cent – the lowest ever recorded – in my exam in mathematics, the discipline with which chess is principally associated.

And worse was to come. That spring, I went with the school for a two-week trip to Lake Thun in Switzerland. It was the first time I had travelled abroad, and I was heavily under the spell of my room-mates, the infamous

Nicol twins. One Friday, during an outing to Lake Maggiore in Italy, just across the border, the three of us were caught stealing cuckoo clocks in a jeweller's and it was only the intervention of the gym master that prevented the police from being called. When I arrived home, as expected, I was admonished severely by the newly appointed headmaster, who cautioned my distraught mother that if anything similar happened again I would be expelled.

The warning didn't have the slightest impact on me. Four months later, I stole some short-playing 78s from the afternoon 'sale' that 4C was holding in the tuck shop. That evening, I was listening to one of them – 'Telstar' by the Tornados, I will never forget – in the loft when I was swept by a wave of guilt. Intent on returning them the following morning, I set off ahead of time to school, where I sped to 4C's classroom before anybody arrived. I was depositing the records on the table when the door opened and the head boy marched in.

'Richardson, the headmaster wants to speak to you,' he said, to my horror.

'Why?' I enquired, feigning innocence. 'What've I done?'

'Yesterday, you were seen stealing records from 4C's sale in the tuck shop,' he stated coldly.

Being summoned to the headmaster's luxuriously carpeted, book-lined study off the echoing marble entrance hall was, up to that point, one of the most nerve-racking experiences of my life. It is difficult to convey what a remote, God-like figure he was. Every morning, after the bull-like music master stilled the orchestra with his baton, the head boy swung open the doors of the assembly hall. This was the signal for 1,000 pupils, prefects and the entire staff to rise, until the headmaster, wearing his black gown, swept in imperiously and mounted steps to his throne-like chair in the centre of the imposing stage. That wasn't the only reason he was held in such awe. A few years earlier, he had had a formidable reputation as the dynamic headmaster of one of England's most distinguished independent schools, before, still in his early forties, he had taken on the challenge of trying to stamp his mark on ours, the largest private school in Scotland.

Now I stood quaking in front of him as he sat writing a report behind his impressive mahogany desk. After what seemed a lifetime, he looked up and broke the unbearable silence. 'Richardson,' he proclaimed in his restrained, magisterial voice, 'you are suspended forthwith, pending expulsion, unless your parents can persuade me otherwise. You may go.'

The following day, my mother, at her wits' end once again, dashed to the school and spent an hour imploring him to reconsider his decision until, swayed by her forceful personality, he finally relented.

'Very well,' he proclaimed, 'but only because your son had the sense to return the records before he was confronted with what he had done. This indicates to me that he has at least developed a conscience since he was caught stealing cuckoo clocks in Italy. Nor do I overlook the fact that, despite his shameful academic record, he is the school chess champion at the implausible age of thirteen. Nevertheless, as that is his sole saving grace, let it be firmly understood this is his last chance.'

Although I now took care to heed his warning, at the end of my second year my exam results were again so abysmal that, in addition to having to repeat the year, I was demoted to the bottom class. The class, 2C, was a dumping-ground for the year's misfits, and teaching us must have been a nightmare. Our English master, a horsy-looking man with a long face, was a rangy Englishman in his thirties who was younger than many of the other masters. Moreover, he was soft-spoken and tolerant, and, unusually for the school, was one of the new generation of masters in the early 1960s who refused to resort to corporal punishment. Most of the class consequently viewed him as hopelessly lenient, and played practical jokes on him they would never have dreamed of with more discipline-oriented masters. One morning, before he entered the classroom, we balanced the legs of his table on the edge of his dais so that it would topple over when he plonked his corrected jotters down. Sure enough, it did. His face went as white as chalk and, after our hoots of derision had died down, he wouldn't permit the class to leave the room until the culprits owned up. For forty-five minutes we sat in awkward silence, until, as nobody owned up, he was forced to dismiss us. I felt sorry for him, although I was piqued at the way he continually awarded the top marks for our essays to a studious-looking friend of mine with horn-rimmed spectacles, as I regarded my work as equally good.

Nor did the local boys I became friendly with, each of whom vied to be more reckless than the next, help my school performance. There was our jaunty, cavalier leader who, despite being at a state school – something the rest of us looked down on – attracted the lion's share of the local girls thanks to his good looks, swashbuckling demeanour and strapping physique, plus the fact he played rugby for Edinburgh Schools. There was the gangling boy with a shambling gait who attended Edinburgh's most expensive day school and responded so willingly to our egging him on to ever greater acts of buffoonery that we all suspected he wasn't quite right in the head. There was ginger-haired Billy and his friend David, both of whom had been at Watson's junior school since they were five. But there any similarity between them ended. Billy, like myself, was in the bottom class while David was in the top class, and – although he was only in his fourth year – was in the first XV and in the cricket first XI. As a consequence, Billy was subtly possessive of his prestigious friendship with David, and kept undermining my attempts to be friends with him, whom I much preferred. Nobody could have predicted that he would later drop dead on a golf course, aged thirty-two.

However, none of the gang, unlike myself, allowed their foolhardiness outside school to interfere with their studies within it. Much of the time we loafed about, blowing cigarette rings and spitting, both of which were regarded as being 'cool'. We had four topics of conversation: whether we could 'get a ride' or 'go all the way' (have sexual intercourse) with girls: pop music; sport; and, first and foremost, playing cards for money. The minute the parents of one of us went out for the evening, he rang the others to arrange a game of three-card brag, a version of poker. We were also in the Scouts, and every Friday evening, the minute it was over and the scoutmaster had left for the night, we drew the velvet curtains across the stage in the church hall, where we gambled away ever increasing amounts of our pocket money. This lasted until one evening, to our horror, the scoutmaster's face peered round the curtain unexpectedly; returning to fetch something he had left behind, he was so incandescent with rage that we were all expelled on the spot.

But the church was the site of a far more formative event. In my bedroom in the loft, I revelled in my new-found privacy and many a time I lay awake at night, listening to the sad, distant wail of goods trains as they rumbled through the darkness. Then, when I was thirteen, my hormones had started to change, my vocal cords had begun to deepen, and I'd had the first signs of facial hair. Within six months, I had discovered that if I stretched out naked in front of the electric fire I could experience incomprehensible stirrings in my loins. A short while afterwards, I and my friend with whom I had gone swimming, only faintly aware of what we were doing, had masturbated each other in our cubicles at Portobello baths. Not long afterwards, a black-haired boy at school, who everybody said looked my double, and I had also begun fondling each other underneath our desks at the back of the French class. Now, in the church, I was to have my first sexual intercourse with a girl.

Although she was barely fifteen, she'd already had sex with everyone in our gang except myself. One evening, wanting to get in on the act, I telephoned her and invited her to meet me. She readily agreed, and three days later we met in the church's coal cellar, the only place we were sure we wouldn't be interrupted. There, on top of a pile of black slag, I fumbled around with her in the semi-darkness, not knowing what to do until she guided me into her. In spite of it being a neither comfortable nor pleasurable experience, our trysts continued for a number of weeks until, one Saturday night, after my parents had gone out, I invited her to our house. We were writhing naked on the sitting-room carpet when I was horror-struck to hear a key turn in the front door. It was my parents returning prematurely, so we flung on our clothes and I shoved her bra and knickers underneath the settee as she scrambled up to the loft, from where she made a hasty exit across the roof. When my parents came in and sat down on the sofa, little did they suspect what was beneath them. Meanwhile, I sat there, ostensibly absorbed in a television programme, although my heart was pounding like a piston.

Not much later, I was eating at the table in the dining room when I decided to stop speaking to my father – permanently. I had no inkling why, since we hadn't had an argument; indeed we never did. But the signs had been there for some time. I had started to defeat him at chess, and after we began playing for trivial sums of money he had lost so much he refused to play me any more. Furthermore, we had ceased going to the baths or football matches together. In retrospect, it is easy to figure out why I behaved as I did: not talking to my father was a way of creating an identity for myself and, in Freudian terms, rebelling against him. Moreover, it was the end of the 1950s, when rock and roll burst onto the scene and, for the first time, teenagers were discovering the notion of youthful rebellion.

My father couldn't understand my aversion towards him, yet, because it wasn't his style to talk about personal relationships, he never attempted to ascertain the reason for it. Then, a year later, I began speaking to him again. This time it had to do with my changing relationship with my mother. When I was younger, I had of course enjoyed the companionship of my father, although she had been, well, the hub of my universe, and someone who had unceasingly supported me. But after the initial euphoria of their marriage had evaporated, they had begun having frequent arguments. More often than not these were about money – he accused her of being a spend-thrift – and some had been very physical; I still see myself, at the age of eight, clambering onto his back crying 'Leave her alone, leave her alone!' as they grappled with each other in the dining room.

She was, however, a hefty woman who, physically, at least, gave as good as she got. Once, during one of their arguments, she pushed him so violently against his aquarium in the sitting room that, to their consternation, the glass shattered and gallons of water and dozens of expensive Siamese fighters, neon tetras and angelfish, my father's pride and joy, cascaded onto the carpet.

But now, as I had become increasingly critical of her, their roles had reversed, and I more and more resented having to sit next to her in the dining-room, while it was taken for granted that my sister's place was beside my father. There were several reasons for my irritation. At the table in the dining-room, I was annoyed by the noise she made eating and drinking. In public, I was embarrassed by the way she made such a loud fuss whenever she had to queue to be served. Moreover, I was beginning to marvel at the beauty of the female body, and, as she sometimes weighed anything up to eighteen stone, her flabby arms and awesome thighs troubled me. But mostly I had become conscious of how volatile she was becoming compared to my father, above all during their rows, when she became ever more emotional while he remained collected, self-controlled and dispassionate.

What I didn't know, however, was that her outbursts were her only defence, given his rationality and command of the English language, against his withering attacks on her size. Nor did I know to what extent this was linked to her deep-rooted emotional problems. These, as so often is the case, had begun when she was very young.

A plump only child, she had already been chubby when her father, whom she worshipped of course, sent her to board at the Convent of the Sacred Heart. Unable to comprehend how he could do this to her, she had wept continuously and tried to stow away in the boot of his car when he took her back there after she had spent blissful weekends at home. In real-ity she was too young to understand that he only sent her to the convent because, as its doctor, he received a significant reduction in its fees, the only way he could think of to provide her with a first-class education. Nor did it help that classmates called her 'Zeppie', after the gigantic German airship, *Graf Zeppelin*, while the head nun, Mother Maud, whom she abominated, even made her stand in a corner wearing a dunce's hat on which was written 'I am a hippopotamus'.

Then, when she was sixteen, her father had died after years of ill health. She was stricken with grief, understandably, although she had jumped for joy when her mother, unable to pay the convent's fees, had sent her as a day pupil to one of the city's less expensive private schools. Even so, it wasn't long until Eva had insufficient money for even this, so my mother had had to leave school when she was seventeen and go to London to try to obtain a job in journalism.

By the time she first set eyes on my father six years later, she was, of course, already quite large. But despite her size, he was so infatuated with her, as she was his first, and last, girlfriend, that he declared it merely meant there was more of her to love. After my sister and I were born, however, he had little by little withdrawn from her sexually and emotionally. Perhaps he never regained his trust in her after what did – or didn't – happen between her and the German POW. Perhaps, as happens with men in some marriages, he no longer perceived her as a woman but as a mother. Perhaps it was the boredom of marriage, where familiarity so often breeds contempt. Perhaps, as a consequence of her size, she no longer attracted him sexually. In any event, this had set off a vicious circle: the more he withdrew from her, the more she ate; the more she ate, the larger she became; and the larger she became, the more he withdrew from her.

She herself endlessly maintained that her obesity was partly caused by an under-active thyroid gland, and the amount she ate was, in fact, never enough to explain her size. Naturally, she was constantly trying to diet, but she no sooner lost several pounds than she regained them. As a result, owing to her vulnerability and emotional personality, she had become the family scape-goat. This only made her eat all the more, until, when her weight approached twenty stone, she was finally admitted to hospital. Her stay was a disaster. On the second day, she was putting on her make-up when a coarse woman in the adjacent bed sniggered at her and, probably envious of my mother's charm, good looks and educated voice, announced loudly to the rest of the ward, 'Wi' a face like yours, I widnae bother.'

My mother was a powerful, resolute woman, but she also suffered from lack of self-esteem caused by my father's remorseless attacks on her size. She was so distressed that she telephoned for a taxi and, still in her nightdress, discharged herself from the hospital before she arrived home, weeping inconsolably.

Of course, I wasn't always misbehaving during my formative teenage years. At my mother's insistence, every week I went for afternoon tea with Eva, who had moved back into her flat after my parents bought their first house. For long such a beautiful woman, she was by now a portly, grey-haired figure, with spectacles, tweeds and a fox-skin stole. She also spoke with a North-umberland 'birr', a curious, guttural pronunciation, above all of the letter 'r', which her forebears argued was proof the family had a long lineage dating back to the Vikings who had settled in that county. Although, to me, she looked as if she had for time immemorial been extremely old, I enjoyed visiting her. Whenever I climbed the stairs to her first-floor flat, the table in the homely kitchen was set with lace doilies, bone china crockery, plates of home-made cheese and cucumber sandwiches, and tasty cakes. I even liked her Lapsang Souchong tea, which I thought tasted of bacon and which she poured from a dainty silver teapot.

When my grandmother wasn't fussing over me, she was forever dusting, polishing or pushing her carpet sweeper around. But most of the time she seemed to live at the sink, where she scrubbed clothes on an old-fangled wooden scrubbing board before she wrung them on a prehistoric-looking wringer. Above, a pulley suspended from the ceiling was constantly groaning with voluminous pink knickers, pink corsets and pink petticoats. Even so, she had a weekly 'help', who had started service with her and her husband at the age of twelve, and, after he died in 1934, my grandmother, who lived by herself for another thirty years, kept her on. She treated her as a friend, and, whenever I climbed the stairs to her flat, I would come across them tut-tutting about the 'atrocious weather', the 'disgraceful cost of living' and the 'deplorable lateness of the trams'. After Eva died, my mother also employed her, and by the time my mother died, she had been 'serving' the family for over seventy years.

By now my father had grown to respect my grandmother on account of her staunchly held Scottish Presbyterian principles, with which, predict-ably enough, he disagreed. My mother's relationship with her, on the other hand, was periodically fraught. Over time, when my grandmother became a frail, lovable old woman, she became exceedingly forgetful; one evening, she telephoned, panic-stricken, to say she had lost her wedding ring, merely to phone an hour later to say that she had discovered it on her finger. Her eye-sight also deteriorated so badly that she could only hobble with the aid of a white stick. Regardless, my mother used to hurry her along brusquely; in fact she found her so irritating that once she even hit her over the head with a shoe. Yet when Eva had to move into a private nursing home my mother was extraordinarily attentive; after my grandmother was diagnosed with cancer at the age of eighty-eight, my mother did everything in her power to have her cured, and was broken-hearted when she died.

Apart from going to my grandmother's, I visited 'Auntie' Minnie and 'Auntie' Janey, two of my grandmother's four sisters. Then both in their seventies and attired in black apart from their high, starched Edwardian white collars, they lived in a semi-detached house halfway up Corstorphine Hill, which began only fifty yards round the corner from my grandmother. I enjoyed going there, too, as, apart from Meissen figurines of a shepherd and a shepherdess, the house was running over with knick-knacks that included two Victorian porcelain piggy banks, one a Black Sambo and the other a Chinaman who both rolled their heads and lifted their hands to their mouth when pennies were deposited on their palms. After the oldest of the sisters died, my mother encouraged me to visit her younger sister, who had gone to live in a nursing home in a shady, leafy street near my school. Incontestably the family's favourite 'auntie', she was an endearing, still very alert woman with twinkling eyes and a deeply puckered face, but by then I considered visiting her a chore.

In addition, I regularly met my mother, at her request, for coffee in one of the cafés on Princes Street. There she delighted in showing me off to her friends in my smart maroon school blazer and grey flannels, although I continually dreaded that my pals would see me and think I was a 'mother's boy'. We went to Fullers, a café whose prodigious bay windows on the first floor commanded a stunning view up to the castle, and McVitie's, an old-fashioned café at the West End, whose doorman I disliked owing to his military-style cap and uniform. Once, I was rude to him, and my mother demanded I apologise. I refused until, after she threatened to withhold my pocket money, I reluctantly said I was sorry.

The most noteworthy event outside school came one summer, when my mother talked my father, whose salary had grown steadily, into taking us on the family's first holiday abroad. This was a major feat, as my father was a singularly unadventurous man who had resisted going anywhere apart from Bamburgh or Ireland, while she, of course, had already travelled widely. Not surprisingly my sister and I were jumping with excitement as we set off in our latest car, a second-hand green Riley with stylish tail fins and luxurious leather seats, to drive to northern Spain.

The holiday, though, got off to a distinctly inauspicious start. On the way down to Dover, we dropped in on my father's mother, Ethel, in Staines in Middlesex. There she lived in the Priory, an impressive but dilapidated Victorian house which, because it had belonged to some well-known film producers, had had camera tracks running around the now jungle-like, rambling back garden, where there had also been a small film studio. My grandmother had never forgiven my parents for eloping, and now, most likely at the urging of my mother, who invariably preferred reconciliation to conflict, they were visiting her for the first time in twenty years. Instead of having tea with everybody else in the shadowy, oak-panelled library, I opted to go for a swim in the swimming pool. It was obviously only used once in a blue moon, as it was half-covered with water lilies, and my grandmother had omitted to tell me that, at the sides, the water was only three feet deep. After I dived in off the springboard, I hit my head on the bottom, and the local doctor had to be called to put six stitches in my forehead. Then, the following day, we broke our journey in Sussex, where my parents called in on friends whom they had known since their days at Upper Sheriff Cottage. Eager to appear grown up, and egged on by my grinning father, I downed two pints of the potent local cider whereupon I was sick over their carpet.

Despite that, after we stopped in Bordeaux in south-west France to have my stitches removed in a hospital, I loved the journey. Close at hand, on the coast, was Les Landes, where we pitched our new, family-sized tent in a campsite in pine forests behind the dunes. Every morning I flirted with the fourteen-year-old daughter of a French family in the neighbouring tent, before I cavorted in the six-foot-high breakers that roll in from the Bay of Biscay. In the evenings, we drove to restaurants deep in the forest, where we had delicious, three-course menus de jour for only seven francs. Further down the coast was San Sebastian and Basque fishing villages in Spain, where bandy-legged, hardy little men wearing black berets spilled out of smoky bars, and red-white-and-green Basque flags fluttered from buildings.

In fact we were so enamoured with the Basque country that we returned there for the next two years, before we continued south to Andalusia. The trips, for all that, were again marked by incidents. One night, when we were camping on a rise overlooking a bay near Zarauz, my father was awakened at midnight by a suspicious noise. Armed with a hammer, he had to chase away a prowler who, my father was convinced, had shadowed my sister, by now an attractive, well-proportioned eighteen-year-old. Then there were the episodes with the car. Shortly before our third holiday in Spain, I had passed my driving test in Edinburgh, but after I had pestered my mother to allow me to take it for a spin, I had promptly crashed it into a parked Land Rover. Mercifully, I had suffered only bruises and there had been minimal damage to either car, but from that day on she forbade me to drive it again. Now, however, she admitted just outside San Sebastian that she was so exhausted that she was almost falling asleep at the wheel, so she finally yielded when I volunteered to take over. It was another calamitous lapse of judgement; twenty minutes later, I knocked a cyclist off his bicycle and, after she made sure he wasn't injured, she took over at the wheel before we fled.

El Rompido in Andalusia was a blinding white village close to the Portuguese border. It was very Spanish, with only holidaymakers from the nearby industrial town of Huelva on the beaches. I for my part didn't find these particularly appealing, but my parents fell in love with them and the area so much that, intending to build a house with money invested by my increasingly financially astute father, they bought a small plot of land in Cartaya, where land was ridiculously cheap, right on the coast. There were other reasons. My mother had become so ashamed of her body that she contrived to hide it whenever someone photographed her; here, on the beaches, where there were so many other overweight women, she felt thoroughly at home, as no one noticed her in her bulging swimsuit. My father, on the other hand, liked the beaches because so few foreign tourists – whom he despised – visited them. It was the start of his love affair with Spain; indeed, with his swarthy skin, sunglasses, *puro* (cigar) and black Basque beret, he looked more Spanish than the Spanish, although, fifty years later, the only Spanish words he had learned were *por favor* (please), *la cuenta* (the bill) and *una cerveza* (a beer).

El Rompido, though, proved to be the last family holiday. After my sister and I left home, in the late 1970s my mother persuaded him to go to the Cyclades islands in Greece. At the time, they were still relatively off the beaten track, and he was so taken by them that, yet again, he wouldn't go anywhere else except there or back to Spain. Frustrated, she continued to accompany him, but that didn't dampen her wanderlust. After they sold the plot of land in Andalusia, as they were spending so much time in the Greek islands, over the next decade she travelled by herself to Morocco, Poland and the Soviet Union, almost as daring destinations for a single woman in the 1980s as Mussolini's Italy had been in the 1930s.

Long before then, my rebelliousness at school took on a nonconformist dimension. This unquestionably had to do with my parents. My father, besides being a pacifist since his schooldays, was also an atheist and a steadfast communist, stances he had inherited from his father, who was so influential that when he died several newspapers, including *The Times*, carried a comprehensive obituary devoted to 'Red Richardson'.

My mother, too, possessed a strong dissenting streak, of course, and already, in Sussex, she had written in her diaries just how much she deplored 'the army, the police, Franco, strike-breakers and Conservatives'. Then, when my sister and I were in our early teens, she had started taking us every Sunday, most likely as a delayed reaction to her Catholic upbringing at the convent, to the Quaker meeting house at the West End. Now, as a consequence, I was exempted from morning prayers at school, and sat instead in the room for latecomers and Jews, listening to the sound of hymns drift across the grandiose entrance hall.

At the time, my new form master was also my English master. A delicate, sensitive man in his late forties with sallow skin and a soft, educated voice, his nickname was 'Drac', an abbreviation of Dracula, on account of his sepulchral black gown and the way he limped along the corridors. In truth his nickname did him an injustice; he was only lopsided because the Japanese had extracted one of his ribs while torturing him in a prisoner of war camp during the Second World War. Now he simply wished to be left in peace, and after he set us written exercises he sat behind his table inscrutably observing the class and massaging his mouth with the back of his hand.

It was in his class that I became friends with a tall, gangling boy with a commanding presence whose grandfather had been governor of the Bank of Rome in Addis Ababa, where he had been on first name terms with high-ranking officials in the court of Emperor Haile Selassie, and whose mother was a maverick Italian. Looking and speaking like Prince Charles, he was the most disreputable, but gifted, boy in the school, and totally impervious to what anyone thought of him. Nonetheless, because he wrote wildly imaginative compositions and was, with his booming, fruity voice, the undisputed star of the Dramatic Society, it was broadly recognised that he was too talented to be expelled, although, with his wanton disregard for authority, he at intervals skirted perilously close to it.

It was through him I became attracted to acting, and in the summer term I joined him in *The Caine Mutiny*. I was very nervous in my impersonation of Lieutenant Queeg, while he was a born actor and gave a bravura performance in the lead part. But far more formative was his influence on me politically. He made no bones of his communist beliefs, and before long we were going to meetings of the Young Communist League in drab, murky rooms at the top of Leith Walk. In addition, fearing a nuclear holocaust, he and I travelled down to London for a march of the newly formed Campaign for Nuclear Disarmament. It was merely the start of his picaresque life. Subsequently, he studied languages at Perugia University in Italy and Strasbourg in France before he married an Indian woman. Then he divorced her and married a Bulgarian woman who had been the erstwhile lover of President Zhukov of Bulgaria. For ten years they lived in Sofia before he divorced her, too. At length, he went to teach English in Saudi Arabia, where he met a Chinese woman whom he married, before they gravitated to China.

That year at school was ingrained in my mind for other events as well. The Cold War was at its height and once, during the Cuban missile crisis in 1962, the school's air raid sirens unexpectedly went off. I had no inkling it was simply a trial run, and when our class was urgently marshalled to bunkers behind the rugby pitches, I was afraid that it was the start of the Third World War. A short time later came the swimming gala. I was on the point of diving in to swim my leg of the fifty yards freestyle relay for my house when the throng of parents round the swimming pool heard the headmaster's measured voice announce through the loudspeaker: 'Unfortunately, I have exceedingly bad news to report. President Kennedy has just been assassinated in Dallas. The gala is therefore abandoned.'

There was a hush, followed by an almost palpable frisson of shock, whereupon the evening broke up in disarray.

One Thursday, one of my more conventional school friends invited me on a blind date with two sisters from North Berwick he had been introduced to recently. I accepted, and that Saturday night we met up with them outside a tutorial college on the Bridges where both of them were doing secretarial courses. My friend's date was called Frances; mine was called Julia. As long as I live I shall never forget the first time I set eyes on her. It was like looking at *The Birth of Venus*, the embodiment of female perfection, in Botticelli's masterpiece. Waiting on the corner, and wearing a short pink dress, was the most classically beautiful seventeen-year-old girl I had ever seen. She had the nose and high cheekbones of a Greek goddess, a completely unblemished complexion, exquisite white teeth, soft pink lips the colour of her dress, shoulder-length blonde hair, a slender body and long legs. My friend and I took the sisters to a party at his parents' house where I stood at the mantelpiece, spellbound by this vision, listening enraptured to her talk about her mentor, an ageing professor who encouraged her interest in Roman archaeology, and her love for poetry and the stage. These, I presumed, were no more than poses, as they struck me as implausible interests for such a ravishing girl to be so passionate about. But it was immaterial; although she was coquettish, and doubtless aware of her beauty through the flattery of admirers, she was also high-spirited and intelligent.

Before I knew what was happening, for the first time in my life, I was madly in love. Every weekend, I borrowed my parents' white Mini – their second car – and drove my friend down the road that snakes along the coast to North Berwick, where it transpired that she was not only in an amateur dramatic society but she did, indeed, have a friendship with an elderly, grey-haired man who had worked for Historic Scotland before he retired. Most Saturday evenings we had to go to the town's cinema, where her father, a gangly, skeletal-looking man, was the manager. On the main street, adjacent to the church, it was very much a family affair. Smartly attired in his white shirt, bow tie and black dinner jacket, her father welcomed patrons. Her mother, a small, unsophisticated woman with a perm and spectacles, sold tickets from behind the kiosk. Frances, who must have suffered from being in Julia's shadow, patrolled the aisles with a tray of ice creams, and Julia ushered people to their seats with her torch.

When the programme commenced, claret curtains parted and there were advertisements, whereupon the curtains closed again. For five minutes there was a lull and everyone sat eating ice creams and listening to the soaring melodies of Mantovani. At last, the curtains reopened and the film began. After the audience settled down, Julia and I canoodled in the back row. Then, when the film was over, we drove up the unfrequented road that wound up a cliff at the end of the east beach. To my frustration, Julia never allowed me to go beyond petting, as she wanted to keep herself for 'when I get married'. But I was reconciled to it, because she seemed so pure and virginal compared with the girl with whom I had had my first experience of sex in the coalbunker of the church.

When we weren't at the cinema, we strolled along the beach or sat holding hands on the rocks beyond the outdoor swimming pool, where we gazed at the sunset and watched breakers roll in from the sea. Every so often, we went to parties in the Yacht Club, a sandstone building bordering the swimming pool and the pocket-sized harbour, which in those days was still chock-full with fishing boats. Of course, we also went to her house, one of a row of Victorian villas behind the cinema. I got on well with her parents, who thought highly of me, notwithstanding my arguments about politics with her father, a simple, ultra-conservative man with a pronounced stammer.

'You're ... well a ... well a ... well ... nothing but a communist!' he would stutter after yet another heated discussion.

Besides being repelled by their half-bald, yapping Yorkshire terrier, I was flabbergasted by their insularity. One Saturday, Julia asked if they would like some of our takeaway pizza.

'I'm not eating that foreign muck!' her father blustered. 'I like well a ... well a ... well a ... plain, simple Scottish food!'

Julia regularly came back to our house, where my mother doted on her, while I harboured the suspicion that my father, like any hot-blooded man, secretly desired her. She and I would decamp up to the loft, the only access to which was a vertical wooden ladder in the hall cupboard. There, we fondled each other until we heard the door open.

'What are you two doing up there?' my mother, too plump to squeeze up through the narrow space, would call distrustfully. 'Come down this instant!'

We also went to parties of my local friends, none of whom could keep their eyes off her. It was partly through having such a breathtakingly beautiful girlfriend that, feeling humiliated at still being in the bottom class even though I had repeated yet another year, I started both to conform and buckle down to my studies. Every Sunday, I ironed my white shirt and grey flannels, and polished my black shoes. On the bus to school in the mornings, I surrendered my seat to old-age pensioners and mothers with infants. In class, my demeanour towards the masters was exemplary. I developed an interest in history, where I was unfailingly the first to answer the teacher's questions. In geography, little suspecting that the world's cultures and topography were to become my overriding passion in life, I worked conscientiously on my project, the Basques, under the approving eye of the bespectacled master whose prominent nose was responsible for his nickname 'Beaky'. And every afternoon, I went straight home to do three hours' homework.

My diligence paid off. In my exams at the end of the year, I came first in English, art and history – where I received the highest mark ever recorded – and I was promoted to a class streamed for the sixth form. Unconsciously, I had come to another vital decision. Apart from the Dramatic Society, the school had prospering literary and debating societies. In fact two of the latter's stars, David Steel and Malcolm Rifkind, both of whom were only a few years ahead of me, became leader of the Liberal Party and foreign secretary of Margaret Thatcher's Conservative government respectively. In addition, the headmaster, who had ambitious plans to consolidate the school's already long-established reputation for academic excellence, had just inaugurated the new, state-of-the-art music school, and one pupil even went to Moscow to study with Rostropovich, the incomparable cellist, before he became principal cellist of the London Symphony Orchestra.

Even so, the school placed paramount importance on sporting prowess, and it was predominantly the outstanding members of the rugby, cricket and hockey teams who were appointed prefects or, the acme of achievement, school captain. As a result, I had become increasingly interested in sports. After a short time, I was playing rugby for the third XV, and swimming and playing tennis for my house. Although the school didn't consider chess a sport, every year I also kept on winning the school championship. This, however, was greatly to the disgust of the chemistry master, who organised the chess club every Thursday. A middle-aged Englishman with a lisp and a walrus moustache, he had never forgiven me for my defeating him from day one, when I was thirteen. Worse, he had had to stomach that since my second year I had been captain of the school chess team, which won the Schools District Championship four years in succession. Indeed I demonstrated such promise – I never lost a match – that my parents wanted to enter me for the National Schoolboy Chess Championship, which I had an excellent chance of winning. All of us were disgruntled when the headmaster refused to give me permission, saying that it would only distract me from my studies.

Then came the March Hare, the annual mile race round the school and its grounds. Unknown to everybody, when school was finished, I had been training for it by going for a three-mile jog down to Cammo woods. Now, during the race, I kept in touch with the previous year's winner, the favourite who was the wing three-quarter for the first XV. Suddenly, as the final hundred yards loomed, I drew level at his shoulder. Then, to his astonishment and that of the huge waiting crowd, which included the headmaster, the masters and the rest of the 1,000-strong school, I inched in front of him before I collapsed across the finishing line.

The triumph was a sensation. The following morning, many of the prefects looked at me with new respect. In my Latin class, the teacher acclaimed me as the 'fastest runner in the school'. A week later, my new form master, a vain man who wore smart Italian suits and had a permanent suntan, asked to see me after school.

'Richardson,' he began, 'apart from your sporting achievements for Cockburn House, next year you will be in the first XV and you will run the mile for the athletics team. Furthermore, I understand that this year you are about to be presented with a special cup in recognition for being school chess champion five years in a row. I accordingly intend to propose that you be made a prefect.'

I was thunderstruck. He wasn't merely my form master and my French teacher but, at my parents' insistence, I had gone to him for extra-curricular Russian lessons. During these, I hadn't withheld my sympathy for the Soviet Union, though that didn't appear to have deterred him because, as good as his word, in my final year I was made a prefect. The prefects were like gods, and presently, revelling in my new-found authority, I was bawling at pupils not to run in the corridors. I patrolled the mid-morning and lunchtime queue for the tuck shop to forestall queue hopping. I instructed untidy pupils to tuck their shirts in their trousers. Once, I demanded a teenager have his lanky hair cut, as it was longer than regulations permitted. When he refused point-blank – the Beatles and long hair were just beginning to be in fashion – I ordered him to write out the Latin alphabet fifty times. When he didn't do those, I doubled them. When he didn't hand those in either, I reported him to the deputy headmaster, who beat him. Five days afterwards, when school had finished, I bumped into him at a bus stop round the corner.

'Richardson,' he hissed with a look of visceral hatred, 'you're a bastard, and one day I'll get you.'

I let it pass. The smartest turned-out prefect with my stainless white collars and neatly ironed grey flannels, my chest swelled with pride when I stood next to the head boy at lunch, and the headmaster smiled at me as he swept past in his black gown on his way to high table! And how proud I was when, for a week, it was my turn to stand at the lectern along from him on the gigantic stage and read the daily service to the entire morning assembly! But there was more. At the end of my last year, I won the class prize, the prize for writing and the Club of India prize for geography. As I crossed the stage to collect them from the headmaster, I wondered if he had ever conceived that the rebellious, thirteen-year-old pupil he had so nearly expelled six years earlier would undergo such a metamorphosis. At the school leavers' dance, I was the proudest boy in the assembly hall when all the boys and masters goggled at Julia, who, with her swept-up coiffed hair, svelte figure and orchid-coloured, backless Grecian-style gown, was the undoubted belle of the ball.

All the same, I couldn't help feeling disappointed. At dusk one evening, at the start of my final year, my local friends and I had been fooling around with some girls in a neighbouring hay barn when an enraged farmer brandishing a pitchfork had erupted out of a caravan. We had fled, as you might expect, but as I was easily the fastest runner, in the gathering gloom I had sprinted headlong into a barbed-wire fence. It had gouged deep wounds in my thigh, and now, whenever I tried to accelerate on the playing field, I pulled a muscle. The result, for me, had been disastrous. I'd had to give up playing rugby, and so failed to achieve one of my biggest goals, to play for the first XV. I had limped in last when I had attempted to run the mile for the athletics team, and I had even had to drop out of the March Hare race, so failing to defend my title.

Scholastically, I hadn't lived up to my potential either. Spurred on by my mother, who was highly ambitious for me, but against the advice of my teachers, I had sat the entrance exam for Oxford University. But even though I had applied to St Edmund's Hall, at that time one of the weakest colleges academically, I had only been placed on the reserve list. In my final exams, I had received only two As and two Bs, a mediocre result compared to the class dux, who, although he was three years younger than myself, had received six straight As. I had failed to win the history prize, which I had been expected to do, because of the critical essay I had written about Winston Churchill, the subject of that year's competition. For the first time in six years I had even been beaten by the only boy I had feared in the school's chess championship. But worst of all was the humiliation I felt at, as a consequence of repeating two years, not having reached the sixth form, despite being, at nineteen, the oldest boy in the school.

It was only as I made my way round the school, tearfully saying farewell to my masters, that it dawned on me that my sheltered world was at an end. Be that as it may, I wasn't wholly unprepared. Itching to leave home for fresh pastures, I had dumped Julia, who was broken-hearted, and applied to four universities in England. In those days, it was extremely unusual for anybody with Scottish qualifications to apply for universities south of the border. This, combined with my exam results, meant I was only accepted by Leeds, my fifth choice. Deciding what to study hadn't been straightforward, either. My entire childhood, influenced by my grandfather, who had been a doctor, I had aimed to be a surgeon. This ambition had lasted until I watched the first live BBC transmission of an operation, which showed the Queen's Surgeon with his hands in a mass of bloody intestines. Sickened, I had long since jettisoned the idea and now I opted to study history, politics and economics instead.

Casting off

Before university started, I set off on my first journey abroad by myself. This was to Israel, where I had volunteered – a fashionable thing to do at the time – to work for three months on a kibbutz. The journey by ship from Venice down the rugged Adriatic coast and through the sparkling Mediterranean was magical. The top deck was awash with idealistic youthful volunteers who were going to work on kibbutzim, too, and by day many of them played guitars and flirted with each other; at night we slept in our sleeping bags bathed by moonlight.

But Israel wasn't a pleasurable experience. The kibbutz, Kfar Hanassi, was in upper Galilee, near the Golan Heights.

It was shortly before the Six-Day War, and the Heights still belonged to Syria. One afternoon we were shelled, and everyone had to shelter in bunkers under the communal dining hall. Unluckily for the Syrians, their aim was so inaccurate that twenty Arabs in a settlement twenty miles into Israel were killed instead. Before every dawn I had to get up to shift irrigation pipes in orange orchards. The work was exceedingly wet, as I had to wade around for lengthy periods in flooded fields. Within a week I discovered the Wellington boots I had been given were too big, but to my annoyance the kibbutz ignored my requests for a smaller pair. There were other reasons to complain: the volunteers were housed in overcrowded shanty huts, and twice I awoke in the morning to find scorpions in my shoes. For all that, although we had to labour for ten hours a day without pay, we weren't granted the same privileges as native kibbutzniks, and we even had to pay for stamps for letters home.

Before long I detected an inflamed-looking streak shooting up my leg from a blister on my heel. When I went to the kibbutz doctor, he advised me to rest. Despite that, the secretary, a Glaswegian who supervised the volunteers, was adamant that I continue working. That weekend I was seriously worried, so I went by bus to Tel Aviv to consult a private doctor. He informed me that if I had delayed seeking medical advice any longer I could have had blood poisoning. Fuming, I returned to Kfar Hanassi, where, notwithstanding that I was pumped full of antibiotics, the secretary insisted I return to work in the orange orchards.

One humid evening, I was relaxing in the outdoor auditorium, engrossed in the weekly film on its twenty-foot screen. The film was a gripping Hollywood romance, and the main star had just declared 'I love ...' to his female lead when the soundtrack abruptly died.

'Patrick Richardson to reception,' a loudspeaker crackled.

When I got there, I was astonished to see my sister, who, quite fortuitously, had been a volunteer on a kibbutz near Safad, sixty miles away. After we chuckled at the mixed-up synchronicity on the screen, she elucidated what had happened.

'I finished on the kibbutz earlier than I expected, so I thought I'd look you up before I go to Jerusalem to visit Rachel,' she began, referring to the pen pal with whom she had corresponded since she was a teenager. 'The nearest the Safad bus comes to Kfar Hanassi is a crossroads a few miles away. So I phoned your kibbutz and told them I'd been working as a volunteer on a nearby kibbutz for three months and asked them to pick me up. But they wouldn't hear of it, so I had to walk. It was really hot, and it's taken me five hours to get here!'

The following morning, one of my days off, I received a message saying the secretary wanted to talk to me. As soon as I entered his office, I could see that he was furious. 'Don't you and your sister know it's strictly forbidden to enter the kibbutz after 5 p.m. without express permission!' he yelled. 'Do you realise she could've been shot?'

That hadn't occurred to me, although, after the episode with the Welling-ton boots, I was in no mood to be lectured. 'Well, it'd never have happened if the kibbutz had had the decency to pick her up!' I snapped. 'It would've taken you twenty minutes, but instead it took her five hours to walk here.'

At midday, still simmering with anger, my sister and I crossed over to the open-air swimming pool. There was still an hour before it closed for the day, but when we arrived, we found the lifeguard padlocking the gates.

'Hold on, we'd like to have a swim,' I said politely.

'You cannot. There is no one here, so I close early.'

'But we're here!'

'Not important, we are shut.'

We were standing looking nonplussed when the secretary chanced to pass by. I spelled out the situation to him. 'Look,' I added, 'we've both been working like slaves, and we need to relax. Can't you order him to let us in?'

For a second, there was a glint in his eye as it dawned on him this was his opportunity to gain his revenge. 'No!' he declared gleefully.

'Right!' I countered. 'I've had it up to here!'

We stalked back to my hut, where I stuffed my belongings into my ruck-sack, before my sister and I stormed off the kibbutz on its daily mini-bus to Jerusalem.

Two hours later, leaving my sister to continue on to meet her pen friend, I got off the bus and set off to explore Israel. I was hitchhiking round Lake Tiberius when I ran into a stocky, fast-talking Lothario with a goatee beard who was studying electronics at Birmingham University. As he too was travelling round Israel, we agreed to team up and, for a month, I could only look on enviously as he inveigled a stream of young women in youth hostels into his sleeping bag. After Lake Tiberius, we hitchhiked down through the Negev Desert to Eilat on the Red Sea. At the time, it consisted of only huts on a beach. On our second evening, we were invited to a party on the third floor of a half-completed block of flats. For some puzzling reason, the floor was flooded, presumably because of burst mains, and as I sloshed into the sitting room, where sofas were knee-deep in water, for the first and only time in my life I saw a bacchanalian orgy take place.

After I left the student from Birmingham, I met up with my sister, and we travelled up the coast to Acre. Late one balmy, moonless night we stopped to sleep on a beach near a hamlet. Before I got into my sleeping bag, I stripped off and went for a swim. Fondly imagining that I was swimming parallel to the beach, I swam backstroke for twenty minutes before I turned to do breaststroke. It was only then that, horror-stricken, I realised I had swum so far out I couldn't see the shore. For ten seconds I panicked until, to my overwhelming relief, I was able to make out the glimmer of the hamlet in the inky blackness.

A week afterwards, we took the express train from Athens to Munich. While we were passing through western Yugoslavia, peasants came round the compartments selling slivovitz. I had never heard of it, so I bought a bottle and by the time the train pulled into Munich I was so inebriated that I scarcely recognised which country I was in. Despite that, after we left the railway station my sister and I headed straight to the Hofbräuhaus, the city's well-known beer hall, where a Lederhosen-clad Bavarian brass band was playing. To the amusement of the vast throng in the seething hall, I clambered on to a table and sought to conduct it, until I fell off, hit my head on the ground and lost consciousness.

From the moment I set foot in Leeds, I disliked both it and its university intensely. I found the city grey, industrial and uninspiring, and although I liked having three cooked meals a day in Boddington Hall, one of the university's contemporary halls of residence in the leafy outskirts where I was staying, I felt the bulk of the undergraduates there were boorish, northern philistines studying engineering, who spent most of their spare time playing rugby or getting drunk. For the first two terms, my sole friend was a Jewish fresher with a nose like a scimitar and a strong Liverpudlian accent, who was studying dentistry. One Friday, he got back to discover that somebody, presumably an anti-Semite, had drilled a hole in his door, inserted the nozzle of the emergency fire hosepipe in it, and turned it on. When he managed to force the door open, he found all his lecture notes floating in a foot of water.

There was an official investigation, of course, but although everybody was positive that 'the Engines' (the nickname for those studying engineering) were to blame, nobody could prove it. My friend was devastated, unsurprisingly, and for me it was the last straw. Downcast and feeling socially isolated,

I resolved to transfer back to Edinburgh, whose university, which had been only my sixth choice, had also accepted me to study politics. That Easter, to ensure that I wasn't making another major mistake I travelled up to have a look at the politics department. I was browsing in its cramped library when I ran into an intellectual-looking student with a prominent forehead, spectacles and receding hair – Malcolm Rifkind. He was doing a postgraduate degree in political science. After I explained we had been at school together, I asked him what the politics department was like.

'Oh, superlative!' he boomed pompously.

In the interim, in my third term at Leeds, I had made friends with a group of third-year undergraduates in Boddington Hall. Mainly southerners studying English, at first they had regarded me as unfriendly and stand-offish, although, struggling to forge an identity for myself after leaving school, I was, in reality, simply lacking in confidence. They were interested in the arts, but they also knew how to enjoy themselves. At weekends, we piled into antiquated cars and went to parties. We drove to the Yorkshire Dales or close-by towns such as Ripon. Once, we went to the celebrated *Mystery Plays*, staged in ruins outside York Minster. Periodically, I attended the debates, which were dominated by the fiery, newly elected president of the students' union. His name was Jack Straw; I couldn't have known he, too, would become foreign secretary, this time in Tony Blair's Labour government from 2001 until 2006.

By the end of the third term, I was enjoying Leeds so much that I thoroughly regretted my decision to transfer universities. But it was too late to change my mind again, so I returned to Edinburgh where, after the summer, I went straight into second year. Before the term began, I found two students to share a shabby attic flat on the once-genteel eastern edge of the New Town. One was the sociable, wildly popular ex-head boy at my school, who had been captain of the first XV, as well as Scottish schoolboy 100-yard breaststroke swimming champion. The other was a mild-mannered thirty-year-old mature student at teacher training college with floppy hair and a baggy corduroy jacket with elbow patches. Rarely without a pipe clenched between his lips, he was fond of jazz and was amiable enough, although he was so lethargic that every so often I wanted to shake him.

Sartorially at least, I was still astonishingly conservative and every day I wore a navy-blue blazer, grey flannels and my old school tie to university. It wasn't long before I felt that I had made an awful blunder in dropping Julia. Through my mother, who had stayed in contact with her, I heard that, while I was in Leeds, she had had a series of short, unsatisfying affairs with young men interested mainly in sports cars and playing golf. Now, according to my mother, she was unattached, so I decided to invite her to a party I would hold at my flat, where I would try to win her back.

To my delight, she accepted my invitation. During the party, the flat was thronged with people and, as I was the host, I hardly caught a glimpse of her. At 10 p.m., when I tried to find her, I found the kitchen door jammed shut. After I managed to prise it open, I discovered her kissing my new flatmate, a six-foot-tall, upright Englishman with a turned-up nose, who had replaced my previous flatmate and was also at university. Irate, as I had told him about my plan beforehand, I flung him down the stairs and out of the front door. It was an act that was to backfire disastrously; Julia, aghast at my unwarranted behaviour, ran down to the street after him and they not only spent the night together, but they had a relationship for the next three months. If I assumed, however, it was the end of my love affair with Julia, I had another think coming; twenty years later she was yet again to play a pivotal role in my life, this time with nearly fatal consequences.

A few months later, at the start of the spring term, I began going out with Vanessa. We had known each other since we were teenagers, when we had both attended the Quaker meeting house, where her parents were friends of my mother. Even at that time, I had been aware of her as she and I and other teenagers entertained ourselves on the ground floor, until we joined the adults sitting in silence on rows of wooden benches upstairs. Practically as tall as myself, she was now a twenty-year-old who, with her short curly hair framing her almond-shaped face, was as pretty as a picture. She had taught for a year in Jordan before coming back to study English in Edinburgh, where she was still nostalgic for the Arabs, whom she had loved.

Now and then, we dropped in on her parents in a residential school for disturbed children where her father was headmaster. A rambling mansion tucked away in trees at the foot of the furrowed, windswept Pentland Hills, it was very eerie on miserable winter nights, with the pitiless wind soughing mournfully in the stark branches, and only a couple of lights piercing the Stygian darkness. Inside, her parents, both of whom were highly educated and as tall as lamp posts, and the rest of the family sat round a roaring log fire playing Scrabble, at which they all excelled. Six months afterwards, convinced, as I had been with Julia, that I could do better, I broke off with Vanessa, too. I had no sooner done so than she started going out with a beefy, six-foot-three student who had just been selected as wing three-quarter for Scotland's rugby team. Consumed with jealousy, I waited for their relationship to break up, but when it did, several months later, she made it abundantly clear that I'd had my chance and she was no longer interested in me.

During the summer holidays came what proved, in hindsight, to be the turning point of my life, when my sister and I were selected to go on a student expedition from Edinburgh overland by bus to India. Called Comex, an abbreviation of Commonwealth Expedition, it was organised by an ex-Indian army colonel whose dream was to 'break down the barriers that divide people in the Commonwealth'. In fact, three-quarters of the students who applied did so because, at only £50 each, it was an absurdly cheap way of getting to India, which was rapidly becoming fashionable even before the Beatles visited it the following year. The three-month expedition, whose patron was the Duke of Edinburgh, consisted of eleven self-financed buses from eleven British universities. Each had thirty students, selected for specific skills they could contribute to the group. Thus a student studying mechanical engineering was the mechanic, a student studying medicine was the doctor, and a domestic science student was the cook. I was studying politics, but was chosen to be one of the three drivers as I had five years' driving experience, more than anyone else excluding Ian and Gerry, the two other drivers. Before we set off, the three of us were given a two-week crash course in driving, and all the students approached commercial companies for donations in cash or in kind. The majority of them responded positively, and one company donated so many sacks of oats that we had porridge for breakfast the entire journey to New Delhi and back.

After we reached Asia Minor, we usually camped for the night in the middle of dry, barren plateaux. To begin with, obeying the colonel's orders – who, like not a few officers in the military, had socially conservative views concerning sexuality – men slept on one side of the bus and women on the other. Within days, however, wriggling bodies could be observed in sleeping bags as males and females paired off. After we set off, we seldom encountered the other buses owing to the vast distances involved, although every once in a while the expedition came together to stay on campuses of universities such as Istanbul, Chandigar and Rawalpindi. There, each bus put on a show representative of its regional culture for the host students; for example Edinburgh put on Scottish country dancing, and Bristol, distinguished for its Old Vic, staged an extract from a Shakespeare play. Notwithstanding these cultural activities, several of the buses had a notorious reputation, notably the one from Liverpool, whose students were infamous for smoking marijuana. Others drove too fast, and every so often a bus overtook us in clouds of dust, with cheering students hanging out of the windows.

It took us five weeks to reach New Delhi because, after the Turkish border with Persia – as Iran was called at the time – the road to India consisted of rutted tracks for thousands of miles. To stick to our schedule, we regularly had to drive for twelve hours a day and, if we were behind schedule, deep into the night. Each driver had his own navigator. Mine was a skittish, pint-sized, seventeen-year-old Pakistani boy whom all the women on the bus doted on and competed to have sit on their knee. To make us all laugh he affected a high-pitched, falsetto voice, but at night he sat silently beside me, scrupulously watching the track stretch away in the blackness; behind me, in the mirror, all I could see were two rows of nodding, bleary-eyed heads.

The journey to India is still indelibly etched in my mind. One morning, after we had camped in the desolate Anatolian plateau in Turkey, I woke up, frozen, in my sleeping bag. Suddenly, at the foot of snow-capped Mount Ararat, I made out dots approaching us on the long, forsaken road that darted as straight as an arrow to the east. As they approached, they metamorphosed into women wearing ankle-length turquoise and claret traditional costumes. They had earthen pitchers on their heads and, without glancing up, they scurried by until they again became barely visible dots on the long, forsaken road to the west. But a few of the memories I retain of the journey are less pleasant. In Kandahar, in southern Afghanistan, we stopped to buy some much-needed provisions. A seventeen-year-old Austrian girl, the youngest person on the bus, unwisely disregarded the colonel's advice for the females on the expedition to dress appropriately, and as she bent over to pack boxes into the boot, her miniskirt rode up her thighs. Within minutes, enraged men with bushy black beards gathered with stones in their hands, and we all had to leap on board and make a rapid exit.

One of the highlights was the Khyber Pass. The previous night, while waiting for armed guards to accompany us through the parched, lawless mountains, we had slept on the rooftops of hospitable villagers. After our escort turned up at midday we set off, and soon tribesmen armed to the teeth were careering past us on top of garishly embellished lorries. As we headed ever further into the pass, all three drivers took turns at the wheel. Ian, a stolid, bespectacled Scotsman, was an already vastly experienced driver, because part of his mechanical engineering course had involved operating two-ton lifting equipment in the Amazon. Gerry and I, on the other hand, had difficulty double-declutching, which you had to do to engage the gears. To my dismay, I found myself at the wheel as we headed into the most dizzying descent, and, although I didn't show it, I was petrified the brakes would fail and we would topple into the abyss. Nevertheless, monitored assiduously by Ian, I managed to steer the bus to the foot of the pass without incident.

When we finally reached New Delhi, the expedition drove in a regal procession down India Gate to Gandhi's tomb, where we laid wreaths. Then we were introduced to Indira Gandhi, the prime minister of India.

A serene, dignified-looking woman, she shook hands with myself and all 328 students and, smartly dressed in my blazer and tie, I watched on as she was introduced to the youngest member of the expedition. Then, a week later, we split up for a month to travel throughout India. Sadly, when the bus from Durham University was in a horrific accident in Yugoslavia, the expedition's journey back to Britain was marred by tragedy. As an approaching crane drove by, the twenty-three-year-old student driving the bus heard an ear-splitting crash. When he turned round, he saw that all fourteen students on the left-hand side of the bus had been decapitated. Paralysed with horror, he lost control of the wheel, and the stricken bus veered into a field before it overturned onto its side.

The cause of the collision was hotly disputed. The student claimed that the jib of the crane had broken loose before it ripped through the bus. The Yugoslav authorities alleged the student had fallen asleep at the wheel and that the bus had swerved into the crane. Whatever the cause, the Edinburgh bus was the first from the expedition to arrive on the scene, only an hour after the crash. Ian was driving, and I was chatting in the back row, and, as we joined a snaking queue of slow-moving vehicles, I can still distinctly recall wondering why there was such a traffic jam, until we inched past the accident. I will never forget the gruesome sight of fourteen black body bags that the emergency services had laid out on the right-hand side of the road, and, to the left, the wrecked bus on its side in the field.

If the crash was bad enough for my sister and me, it was worse for my parents. Each bus had the words 'Comex Expedition to India, Patron HRH the Duke of Edinburgh' painted prominently in gold colours on both sides. When journalists from news agencies reached the scene, the only word recognisable on the side of the mangled bus was 'Edinburgh'. Moreover, all the buses, which were brand new, had been registered consecutively, and the twisted number plates of the bus were identical to our own, but for one letter. In the ensuing confusion, Reuters telexed back to Britain that it was the bus from Edinburgh, and not Durham, which had been in the accident.

That weekend, my parents were in a holiday cottage they rented in the Pentland Hills, ten miles outside Edinburgh. A mile up a rough track off a desolate country road, it had no electricity or telephone. My father was up a ladder, painting the walls and listening to his portable radio when the programme was abruptly interrupted by a BBC newsflash, which reported that fourteen students from the Edinburgh contingent of the Comex Expedition to India had been killed and seventeen others injured in a bus crash in Yugoslavia. Distraught at the possibility that both of their children were either dead or injured, my parents jumped in their Mini to rush back to Edinburgh.

As ill luck would have it, there had just been a downpour, and as the car crossed a swollen burn it became bogged down in mire. After they struggled for thirty minutes to extricate it, they gave up and ran up the track to the road. An hour elapsed before they succeeded in flagging down a car driven by two nuns, who drove my parents to the head office of the *Scotsman*. There my parents spent the night, pacing up and down, awaiting information. When none came my mother contacted one of her female friends, the secretary of a well-known member of parliament who had friends in high places. He proceeded to pull strings at the Foreign Office to try to ascertain the names of the dead. Even so, another eight harrowing hours elapsed until my parents learned the truth and that we were unhurt. My mother later told me that from that night on, her hair started to turn grey, and she felt life would never be the same again.

Predictably, when the expedition disembarked in dribs and drabs from ferries at Dover, packs of journalists, photographers and camera crews were lying in wait for them. If they were hoping for a lurid story, they weren't disappointed. Many of the buses were damaged, either because they had collided with stray animals or hostile villagers had stoned them. One even had only half of the front windscreen and none at the back, and the students had had to huddle in their sleeping bags for the entire return journey from Afghanistan.

In fact virtually the only completely intact bus was from Edinburgh, whose students were more abstemious than those on many of the other buses – the 1960s counterculture had still to reach Protestant Scotland, and, under Ian's eagle eye, Gerry and I had had to drive extremely carefully.

As was to be expected, there was a public outcry about why students with only two weeks' driving tuition had been allowed to drive buses with thirty students each 18,000 miles to India and back. Accordingly, the expedition that departed the following year was thoroughly reorganised. The crash nearly caused an international incident between the British and the Yugoslav authorities, as the student driving the Durham bus was arrested and detained in prison by the Yugoslavian authorities, pending trial. But before it was held, a professor of mechanical engineering from Birmingham University was flown out to Yugoslavia. He certified that, judging by the tire marks, the bus couldn't have driven into the crane. All the same, the student was found guilty, and it was only the influence of the British foreign secretary, along with the student's decision to accept President Tito's offer of a pardon instead of appealing, that he escaped a six-year prison sentence.

Then came the startling events at Edinburgh University. Geographically isolated on the fringes of Western Europe, it had been a deeply conservative institution ever since the eighteenth-century Scottish Enlightenment. Even so, it couldn't remain indifferent to what was happening in the United States and on the continent, where, during the dying days of 1967, students far and wide were occupying colleges and universities. One of the demands of those in France, who viewed sexual oppression as a symbol for political and social injustice, was the right to have sex in their halls of residence. Shortly, the Student Representative Council (SRC) in Edinburgh recommended that, as abortions were still illegal and students could only get contraceptive pills by dubious means, the latter be made 'freely available' at the university's medical centre. This was one step too far for the rector, the notoriously conservative writer and broadcaster Malcolm Muggeridge, who resigned in protest. A new election, to take place later in the year, was called.

In the meantime, owing to these upheavals, as well as my studies and the war in Vietnam, I had become even more politicised. In addition, I had got to know Mike, who, like myself, was in his third year studying politics. From Dundee, and slightly built, with prematurely thinning hair and thick spectacles, he had been making a name for himself as a charismatic, left-wing firebrand, not least in the orchestrated campaign run by *Student*, the university's student newspaper, to paint Muggeridge into a corner and force his hand over the SRC's recommendation, by encouraging him to either accept it or resign.

Some weeks later, in another furore, the editor of *Student* was suspended for writing an article that some saw as glamorising the taking of LSD. This action was taken by the executive of the SRC, which published the newspaper. However, the principal and vice-chancellor, who was a derided establishment figure to numerous students, and who had made numerous enemies by presiding over the destruction of one of Edinburgh's finest Georgian squares to build two huge skyscrapers to house the ever-expanding university, reassured the police, to whom the article had been referred, that the SRC would 'act responsibly on the matter'. Shortly afterwards, the hurriedly convened SRC tabled a motion that an emergency general meeting be held to condemn the suspension. The meeting was held on the ground floor of one of the skyscrapers, where more than 1,000 animated undergraduates convened to hear a series of ineffectual, albeit impassioned speakers. After an hour, Mike rose. 'Look,' he thundered, 'this is a patent attack on the freedom of expression ...'

'Why?' a sceptical voice cut in from the floor.

'I could give any number of reasons.'

'How many?'

'At least nine.'

'Go on then,' persevered the voice drily.

'Right. One ...' he began. 'Two ...'

Ten minutes later, after listing nine compelling reasons, he sat down to deafening applause. Thereafter, once the editor of *Student* was reinstated, Mike's fame within the university reached undreamed-of heights; everyone was talking about him, a substantial part of *Student* was dedicated to him, and many left-wing students believed that the university had produced a brilliant student leader comparable to any on the continent or in the United States.

They were extraordinarily stimulating times, and that February, caught up in what was happening in Czechoslovakia, where Alexander Dubček, the head of the Communist Party, was trying to create 'socialism with a human face', I entered a politics department competition for a student exchange to Charles University in Prague. To my amazement, I was awarded one of the places and, not long afterwards, I found myself on the train to

Czechoslovakia, together with Mike, who had also won a place, and five other prominent student leaders. It was the height of the 'Prague Spring' and the atmosphere in the Czech capital was at fever pitch, with rumours circulating that the Soviet Union, alarmed that Czechoslovakia was about to fall to 'bourgeois capitalism', was planning to invade. Every morning vast crowds massed on street corners waiting the arrival of newspapers and discussing the latest political developments. In the meantime, we spent our days in a giddy whirl of lectures in English, especially those of the economist regarded as the brains behind the Czech reforms, while at night we went to the Theatre on the Balustrade or other experimental backstreet theatres.

One evening, Mike and I attended a lecture being given by Rudi Dutschke, Europe's most famous revolutionary student leader, in a lecture room in the philosophy faculty. It was packed, and everyone listened attentively as he spoke in German for an hour. Many of the audience, however, palpably didn't share his analysis of the situation in Czechoslovakia, which was hardly surprising, considering that they were bent on building up the institutions he and the majority of Western European Marxists were committed to destroying.

Afterwards, Mike asked if I would join him in approaching Dutschke for an interview for *Student*. I readily agreed, as did Dutschke, and at 11 p.m. the three of us met in the cellar of a stuffy, smoke-filled bar. Dutschke, a scrawny man in his late twenties with an unsmiling face and an earnest manner, had hunched shoulders and lanky brown hair, and spoke English with a heavy German accent.

In the four-hour interview, during which I took copious notes, he addressed us with a quiet but firm voice and fixed us with a penetrating gaze. A few days later, after the exchange to Prague was over, I boarded the train to Berlin, along with Paris an epicentre of the student insurgency in Europe. I was relaxing in my compartment when I glimpsed a banner headline in a newspaper reporting that Dutschke had been shot in the head by a mentally unbalanced right-wing youth, and was gravely ill in hospital. By the time I arrived in Berlin, clouds of choking tear gas were already drifting across streets near the Frei University, where I was staying, as students demonstrating against the attempt on his life fought pitched battles with riot police.

When I got back to Edinburgh, Mike asked me to lend him my interview notes. Naturally, I gave them to him, assuming that he was going to use them to write a piece for *Student*. Three days later, I opened the *Guardian*. In it, spread over four columns, I was astonished to read an article written by Mike, which reported how, without mentioning me, he had interviewed Dutschke for four hours in a hotel in Prague. However, I hardly gave it a second thought; Mike was so charismatic that I, like scores of other students, was in thrall to him and, anyway, wasn't it he who had put forward the idea that we interview Dutschke, and then had the initiative to approach the newspaper?

It wasn't long until the tumultuous happenings at university were forgotten as everyone broke up for the summer. Spurred on by our passion for travelling that the journey to India had awakened, my sister, who had just met her future husband, and I had decided to spend the vacation in North America. She had a job as an au pair for a rich family who lived near the Kennedys in Hyannis Port on Cape Cod: I planned to travel around the USA on a $99-for-99 days Greyhound bus ticket, before I travelled to Canada to work on a tobacco farm on a scheme organised by BUNAC (British Universities North America Club).

The journey was marked by a series of shocking events. We had no sooner arrived at our hostel in New York than a youth plunged a knife into the chest of the man standing in one of the elevators. From there, I took a bus to Washington DC, where fires were still smouldering after police had quelled devastating riots in the black ghetto. Next, I travelled down to New Orleans and San Antonio, but already I so detested the States, as it was the culmination of the Vietnam War and Martin Luther King and Robert Kennedy had just been assassinated, that instead I decided to go to Mexico. I was in the queue for visas in Laredo in Texas, when I found myself behind a German engineer who was employed by Volkswagen in Mexico City. He had had to go to the nearest border to obtain an extension to his visa, which had expired; now he was returning to the Mexican capital and he offered me a lift. At more than 1,000 miles, it was the longest car journey I had ever had, and when we parked outside his house in the capital, I accepted his offer to put me up for a few days.

I didn't stay long. The atmosphere in Mexico City was febrile, as twenty-five students demonstrating about the Olympic Games it was due to host had recently been killed in a gun battle with security forces. Undecided what to do next, I was in the main square when I spotted a bus with the destination 'GUATEMALA CITY' in bold letters above the driver's cab. It sounded so exotic that I hurried to the bus station, immediately bought a ticket and, twenty-eight hours after arriving in Mexico City, I was in Guatemala City.

It was like going from the frying pan into the fire; it was midnight and, after Marxist guerrillas had assassinated the United States ambassador, the right-wing junta had ordered tanks into the streets.

For the second time in as many days, I didn't delay. The following morning I travelled to the historic colonial town of Antigua, directly in the shadow of Volcan de Agua, a 12,340-foot-high volcano. Three days later, I hitched a lift to Lake Atitlán. The driver was a doctor from Guatemala City going to his weekend retreat and, as we drew up by the lakeside, he invited me in. Halfway up a forested hillside, it had panoramic views down to the volcanoes that surround the lake. There he introduced me to his mistress, a gorgeous, ebony-skinned young woman with waist-length black hair, and an hour later he took us out in his speedboat. As it curved across the lake, I was green with envy of him and his lifestyle.

In early October, I returned to the United States and, on my way to Canada, travelled up the West Coast to Los Angeles. It was the shortest visit to a city I ever made; I got off the bus at 6 a.m., took one look at the concrete canyons, flyovers, six-lane highways and skyscrapers and, at 8 a.m., fled to San Francisco. With its small-scale, attractive wooden houses, I was as enchanted with it as much as I hated Los Angeles. But although I was well travelled by now, I was still remarkably naïve: it was the year after the Summer of Love and Flower Power, and I can still see the advertisements for the Grateful Dead and Jefferson Airplane in Haight Ashbury, where the hippies congregated, and picture myself wondering who they were.

When I got to Canada, the contrast between the rioting cities in the United States and the tobacco farm couldn't have been starker. Situated in the sleepy countryside of southern Ontario and enclosed by forest, it consisted of a farmhouse, a bunkhouse and a cluster of green, red and white wooden kilns.

The farm was owned by Roy, a, gaunt, fair-haired man who had fled communist East Germany after the Second World War. Every morning, at 5 a.m. we had to empty the kiln of the previous day's cured tobacco. It was exceedingly hazardous, as we had to balance on thirty-foot-high rafters under the roof and then work our way down. Then, after breakfast at 7 a.m., we started work in the fields. It was absolutely back-breaking. Bent double, and drenched to the skin by 8 a.m. as we toiled along the still-moist, six-foot-tall rows of tobacco, we were supposed to take three ripe yellow leaves from the bottom of each plant. Nonetheless, if there weren't any, we took green ones instead, seeing that the kiln had to be filled each day.

As might be expected, Roy was forever prowling about, and if he found out he was so incandescent that he threatened to fire everybody on the spot. Before the huge bundle of leaves we tucked under our arm became unmanageable, we carried it to a sled hauled by an amiable bay nag. When the sled was full, she hauled it to a conveyor belt near the kilns, where women sorted the leaves and sewed them onto wooden sticks, ready to be cured in the kiln. It was baking hot, so everyone wore a hat, a long-sleeved shirt and long trousers to protect themselves from tar in the leaves. It made no difference; by the end of the day, your hands and arms were so black with the thick glutinous substance that you could scrape it off with a knife.

For the first week, my body ached so badly I doubted if I and the only other novice, an Asian undergraduate from Bradford who had also come out with BUNAC, would last until lunchtime, let alone the afternoon. Nor could we keep pace with experienced pickers, who had to hang around impatiently for us at the end of each row. It quickly became obvious, though, that we weren't the only ones who couldn't keep up, because the crew chiefly consisted of down-and-outs, itinerants and alcoholics who not infrequently dropped out after only a day.

After a short time, we grew used to the pain, and on an average day we finished work by 3 or 4 p.m. But if there were seasoned pickers in the crew, it could be as early as 2 p.m.; once, twin brothers who joined our crew were so fast that we even finished by 1 p.m. To earn as much as possible, the novice, with whom I had become friends, and I nearly always volunteered to do overtime in the evenings. This consisted of 'suckering', that is, removing from the top of the tobacco plant flowers that drain its strength. It was easy money, as you weren't bent double. All the same, we occasionally placed our hats on top of a couple of plants, then, to give the impression we were continually on the move, we gave them a waggle before we squatted between rows for a chat. This continued until one evening when we looked up to see Roy towering above us. He was livid, understandably, but after he reprimanded us severely, he forgot about it.

On other evenings, after we had eaten, I went for a ride. I had never mastered how to ride a horse, although, when I was a child, my mother had sent me for lessons on Saturday to a riding school in countryside close to Edinburgh. I had loathed the whole experience, most of all waiting for the bus to the stables, when I had been scared that my local friends would think I was a sissy if they caught sight of me in the jodhpurs, riding hat and tweed jacket my mother insisted I wear. Now I was agreeably surprised to discover it hadn't been a complete waste of time, as I could not only canter around the tobacco fields, I could even do it bareback.

My aching back notwithstanding, I revelled in the experience of picking tobacco. I thrived on being in the great outdoors, with the searing sun, day in day out, high in the cloudless azure sky. The work was well paid by British standards, and I saved a huge sum of money, as we not only lived for free in the bunkhouse, but we could have unlimited helpings from plates heaped with beef, runner beans and roast potatoes that were dished out at breakfast, lunch and dinner. During the meals, I delighted in winding up Roy, a virulent anti-communist. After work, I enjoyed the camaraderie between the pickers and local women on the conveyor belt, with whom we all joked and exchanged banter as we larked about, half-naked, with the hosepipe that served as a shower. But best of all were the itinerant hobos that the harvest attracted. They were like characters out of John Steinbeck's *The Grapes of Wrath*; indeed, when they were paid at the end of the harvest, things got so out of hand in nearby Tillsonburg – where they flocked to spend their hard-earned money on gambling, drink and prostitutes in an atmosphere of lawlessness – that the Riot Act regularly had to be read out.

One dusky evening, a twenty-two-year-old Canadian who lived locally and was one of Roy's regular workers invited me to ride pillion round the farm on the new 800cc Triumph motorbike he had bought with money saved from the previous year's harvest. Within seconds, I was desperately hanging on as we hurtled at eighty miles per hour along the track that passed close to the kilns. It was only afterwards he divulged that, three years ago, the brakes of his motorbike had jammed and he had driven straight into the wall of one of the kilns. He had had to write it off, and thenceforth he had had to hitchhike home every day. One afternoon, when nobody would stop, he had lain down, partly in desperation and partly as a joke, on the quiet road outside the farm. An hour later a woman in her Chevrolet, who was engrossed in a conversation with her companion, had driven over him and he had spent three months in hospital with two broken legs.

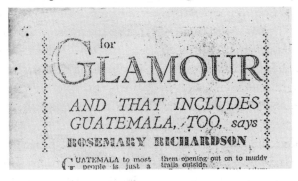

for
GLAMOUR
AND THAT INCLUDES
GUATEMALA, TOO, says
ROSEMARY RICHARDSON

GUATEMALA to most   them opening out on to muddy
people is just a   trails outside.

After I returned from Canada to Edinburgh, I told my mother that I had been to Guatemala. Before the Second World War, she had been a journalist in London, of course, where she had written a column on cooking and astrology for the *Daily Mail*, even though she knew nothing about either. Now she disappeared, coming back with a torn, yellowing article. Entitled 'G is for Glamour' it described festivals where 'skyrockets shoot up into the starlit sky, and dancing throngs in their best costumes jostle in sixteenth-century churches to light candles and place corn, slices of orange and blossoms at the altar'. It even described the wind, which had a 'hothouse smell, warm and scented'.

'I didn't know you'd been there!' I exclaimed.

'I haven't,' she countered with a straight face. 'I simply went to the library, leafed through travel guides and made it up.'

It was sometime during the beginning of my final year – if I remember correctly – that a student of English literature called Robin Cook moved briefly into my flat, although thereafter I didn't see much of him. Resembling a gnome, with his pug nose, ginger beard and ginger hair, he too was heavily engaged in radical student politics, and dedicated most of his time to the Labour Society, where, as president, he was already making a name for himself as a budding politician. Nonetheless, he sporadically rustled up an evening meal at the flat for himself and his girlfriend – his future wife – which he took on a tray into his bedroom before he shoved it underneath the bed. Ultimately, he became foreign secretary, the third I had known, in Tony Blair's Labour government. Politically, at least, I had always seen him as highly principled, and when he was in office he had tried to introduce an ethical foreign policy. Sad to relate, his career was blighted by the shocking way he was compelled to announce he was divorcing his wife, via a press statement in the VIP lounge at Heathrow airport, after he was notified Sunday tabloids were about to expose that he was having an affair with his secretary. For some time thereafter, I would bump into him at the Edinburgh Book Festival, where I couldn't resist teasing him.

'Why, it's Robin!' I would exclaim. 'You still owe me three and sixpence for the electricity bill!'

'So I do!' he would reply, laughing heartily, and we would chat for a spell, before his entourage swept him away.

Back at university, there were sensational developments afoot. In the intervening period before the election of the new rector, Mike had buried himself away in various libraries where, while poring over academic statutes, he had been astounded to discover a document stating there was nothing to prevent a student from standing. This was of tremendous significance, as the powers of the rector included not only the very important, but long-elapsed, constitutional right to draw up the agenda as well as chair meetings of the University Court, the university's governing body. Of course, the obvious person to stand was himself, so he set about establishing the student-for-rector campaign. Not long afterwards, he told me that the BBC wanted someone from the campaign to do a radio interview, and he asked me if I would like to do it. I was taken aback; I was still very shy, and after almost forgetting my lines in the school play, I had no aspirations to be put under the spotlight again. However, I was interested in going into politics, and so, after telling myself that this was the sort of thing I would have to get used to doing, I agreed.

Some days later, BBC Scotland invited me to their Edinburgh studio. When I arrived, the interviewer sat me down in front of a battery of microphones. 'OK,' he began, 'we'll do a quick trial run before we broadcast live.'

'All right,' I gulped.

'Five, four, three, two, one,' he droned into a microphone. There was a lull, before I heard what sounded like a disembodied voice hanging in the air. 'Today we'd like to welcome the representative of the first student ever to run for rector of Edinburgh University,' it announced. 'So, Patrick, can you tell us why a student should want to do that?'

For fully thirty seconds I gazed at the sound technicians until I unpinned my microphone and stood up.

'Sorry, I can't do this …' I stammered.

It was the end of my career as a budding politician, I told myself. Nevertheless, along with his other supporters, I then flung myself into the campaign. Despite his controversial reputation, it was a close-run election, and he was only narrowly defeated by Kenneth Allsop, the popular BBC commentator and journalist. Shortly afterwards, the *Times Educational Supplement* interviewed him, and the following week, in a two-page spread, their reporter described how he had gone to a 'shabby Georgian flat full of chipped crockery' to interview 'one of the country's leading revolutionaries'.

Shortly before then, in the middle of the student-for-rector campaign, came the 'dots affair'. After the editor of *Student* had been suspended for writing an article endorsing the use of LSD, another left-wing editor had replaced him before his girlfriend took over. An intimate friend of Mike's, she was a flamboyant young American from Boston who was also in her fourth year studying politics. Wearing multi-coloured feather boas and floppy hats, she was bubbling with the radical, innovative ideas that were pouring out of the United States; nor did she waste much time putting them into practice. One Monday morning, readers opened her second issue to discover that the back page was blank except for a series of dots, accompanied by an invitation to link them up. Within an hour, students all over the university could be seen doing precisely that. When they did, everybody was amazed to discover that they depicted a cartoon of the stuffy principal and vice-chancellor of the university being fellated by his secretary. He was so outraged that he called the editor, dressed as always in her skimpy miniskirt and thigh-length black leather boots, into his office, where a copy of the cartoon he himself had just completed lay on his desk. Not long afterwards she was sacked.

It was around this time that Mike also moved into my flat, although, apart from the occasional lengthy conversation in the sitting room about Marxist economics, I saw even less of him than I did of Robin, as he spent much of his final year in dingy, smoky flats, staying up until dawn discussing ideas in politics and philosophy with the cream of the undergraduate body. There was nothing he wasn't interested in: the diaries of Antonio Gramsci, the Italian Marxist who died in prison in the 1930s; the left-wing theories of Herbert Marcuse, a cult figure at the time in the United States; and the revisionist philosophy of the influential Polish political philosopher, Leszek Kolakowski. Mike's boundless energy didn't stop there – he even found time to direct the play *Marat Sade* for the Dramatic Society.

I now spent much of my time with a close-knit group of friends who revolved around the fringes of the student-for-rector campaign. There was the erect, ex-public schoolboy from Perthshire who, with his spectacles, jolly laugh and trench coat slung permanently around his shoulders, was in his second year, studying English and philosophy. There was his girlfriend, who had an aureole of tight, frizzy black hair, an equally hearty laugh and had studied theatre design at art college in London. There were the three girls, all friends, who were studying English: the first, an amusing, fleshy, twenty-year-old with a strong Yorkshire accent who loved sex; the second, who was so fashion conscious and had such a wardrobe of resplendent clothes that she never wore the same outfit twice; and finally Amanda, an engaging ex-debutante from Berkshire with a slight lisp and wavy fair hair, who was a member of Dramsoc (the Dramatic Society).

It wasn't long before I was having a relationship with Amanda, and it was through her I became acquainted with numerous people in Dramsoc. Indeed I again became so attracted to acting that I auditioned for, and was given a part in, Edward Bond's *Saved*. A contentious avant-garde play, it was about three hoodlums who stone a baby to death in its pram. I was one of the three, and the others were played by the two established stars of the Dramatic Society: Ian Charleson, who achieved fame subsequently for the way he portrayed the protagonist Eric Liddell in the Oscar-winning film *Chariots of Fire*; and Hilton McRae, who became an actor with the National Theatre. But once more, I was so jittery that I could barely remember my lines and, after the run ended, I resolved never to act again.

If the principal believed Mike's narrow defeat in the student-for-rector campaign would be a terminal blow for the student revolt in Edinburgh, he was profoundly mistaken. The fact was, by now the genie was out of the bottle. A year later, a geography student called Jonathan, who had been with Mike and myself on the exchange to Charles University, stood for rector. Bearded, eloquent and self-assured, he was remarkably popular thanks to his exceptionally accomplished weekly cartoons in *Student* lampooning the university's leading figures, and for the first time in its history a student was elected rector. The following year, a radical, eighteen-year-old undergraduate called Gordon, who had become editor of *Student*, was appointed as his successor. Using the long-defunct powers uncovered by Mike, for a year he waged a continuous battle with the university authorities, which included a protracted, but temporarily successful, legal wrangle to confirm the right of a student to chair meetings of the University Court. In fact the two student rectors caused such disruption that Parliament had to subsequently pass a special statute to curb the rector's power.

The careers of the three left-wing students who had stood for rector varied markedly. Mike became the chief executive of a vast business empire valued at more than half a billion pounds. Jonathan became the boatman for Muckle Flugga lighthouse, the Scotland correspondent for *The Times*, a senior producer at BBC Radio Shetland, the editor of the *Shetland News*, and the operator of one of the island's wildlife tourist businesses. Gordon became a lecturer in politics, a journalist at Scottish Television, a tutor for the Open University, a member of parliament, the chancellor of the exchequer in Tony Blair's Labour government, and, ultimately, prime minister of Great Britain and Northern Ireland.

BOOK II

Adrift at Sea

After I graduated from university, I was yet again, as had happened when I left school, all but wholly unprepared for the outside world. Most of my year had taken on lucrative posts in the trade union movement or were doing postgraduate degrees. I, though, disillusioned by the failure of the student protests to reform the structure of power, was no longer attracted to the former and my second-class degree wasn't adequate for the latter. All I knew was that I was going in the summer to Italy, where Amanda had promised to join me. I had no sooner arrived at our rendezvous in Sicily than I received a telegram from her apologising for being unable to come, as her brother had spontaneously decided to get married.

At sixes and sevens about what to do, I was reading a newspaper in a café in Palermo when I heard a loud, assertive male voice say, 'Jesus, someone in Palermo reading *The Times*!'

I glanced up. I thought that what I was doing was fairly commonplace, although the newcomer manifestly didn't. Heavily built, he had a bushy black beard and was virtually bald, although he was as likely as not only in his mid-twenties. Barefoot and wearing a dirty neckerchief and waistcoat, a tattered collarless shirt and torn jeans, he looked like a gypsy, although I couldn't help thinking that his appearance appeared somewhat contrived.

'Got a smoke?' he began as he lowered himself down to my table.

'No!' I snapped back, and continued reading; at the time, Europe was overrun with such hippies and I didn't want to encourage him.

'You're not much use, are you?' he persisted. Then, amiably, 'So what's in the news?'

'Nothing!'

'OK, keep cool!'

He hauled himself to his feet and lumbered across to the counter.

Observed warily by the waiter, he pulled a face, emptied his pockets and made a joke in what sounded to me like fluent Italian. The waiter gave him a winning smile, dipped behind the counter for a packet of cigarettes, offered him one, and within seconds they were chatting away.

Five minutes afterwards, another hippy entered. He was six foot tall and looked imposing, with an aquiline nose, long legs, broad shoulders and shoulder-length fair hair. He had an easy-going, nonchalant manner, and he wore ragged bellbottoms, a bleached T-shirt, a piece of worn string around his wrist and a leather cord around his neck.

'Hey, Michel, where've you been?' the first hippy said.

'Getting cigarettes,' came the reply.

Satisfied with the answer, the heavily built young man resumed his conversation with the waiter. Intrigued, I asked the newcomer who his friend was.

'Jacob?' he answered. 'Oh, he's a genius.'

Michel, who, it transpired, was Belgian, told me to my amazement that Jacob was barely nineteen, spoke seven languages and had won a scholarship from Eton to Oxford, where he had just completed his first year. His parents, who were fabulously wealthy, owned a flat in Mayfair, a picture-postcard 'cottage' in a quintessential English village outside Windsor, and a villa on Marbella on the Costa del Sol. Michel and Jacob had been friends since they were children, when Michel's parents had owned an adjacent villa in Marbella. Elias, Jacob's father, was one of Europe's top business executives, and Yvonne, his mother, was from Paris, where Jacob had been brought up. In addition, he had a gauche, seventeen-year-old brother who was at a cramming college after being expelled from public school for smoking marijuana.

I was mulling this over when Jacob wandered back. 'Let's go,' he announced to Michel.

'Where?'

'To the boat, of course.'

'Oh, all right.'

I scrutinised them. 'You're going back to the mainland?'

'No,' Jacob replied. 'Didn't Michel tell you? We're hitchhiking across North Africa to Spain, where my parents have a place.'

They stood up to leave. As they sauntered to the door, Michel murmured something under his breath to Jacob in a language I couldn't identify, but was probably Dutch. Jacob stubbed out his cigarette and turned towards me.

'Come with us to Tangiers, if you like,' he said with alacrity.

Momentarily, I was thrown off balance. I had nothing to do, although I wasn't sure I wanted to head off into the unknown with two hippies I had happened upon only ten minutes previously.

'Well, I don't know,' I replied.

'Suit yourself. We're off.'

I observed them go out of the door and cross the square. Then I seized my rucksack impulsively and – little suspecting what a watershed this was in my life – hurried after them.

'Hold on!' I yelled. 'I'm coming, too.'

When we got to Tunisia, we contrived, by one of us hiding behind a bush, to hitchhike together, but as that proved impossible, we arranged to meet in a week's time in Tangiers. Thereafter, I caught sight of them only twice. The first time was when, from a speeding car in a small town in western Tunisia, I glimpsed Michel strumming a guitar in a crowd of Arabs while Jacob held out a hat for donations. The second time was when I arrived at a youth hostel in Algiers, just in time to spot them speeding off in a blue Alfa Romeo. Later, I learned that the driver, a Moroccan butcher, found Jacob's stream of humorous anecdotes so entertaining that he took them the whole way to Tangiers. Nor did I see a great deal of Tunisia or Algeria, as I was travelling equally fast, and the only memory I retain of North Africa is a whirr of white, nameless towns and sun-baked brown plateaux.

Six days after I departed from Sicily I met up with them in Tangiers. From there, we caught a bus down to Marrakech, where Jacob intended to wait for Dan, a Welsh friend who was also studying at Oxford. At the end of every day, together with a motley troupe of hippies he always seemed to gather, Jacob wound through a warren of backstreets to cafés in the medina, where everybody got out chillums and spent the evening enveloped in clouds of smoke. Initially I wondered what on earth I was doing with them; I had never smoked hashish, which my radical friends at university had regarded as a bourgeois activity that did nothing to advance 'the revolution'. But where were they all, except earning bloated salaries in trade unions or tucked away in comfortable ivory towers? Of course, Jacob was at university, too, although he was already thoroughly disenchanted with both it and society. And, apart from being so precocious, he was so mesmerising …

Wherever he went something was happening – he would be telling stories or demonstrating tricks with matchboxes or making some zany suggestion or other. And unbelievably, after two weeks in North Africa, he had even picked up sufficient Arabic to hold a basic conversation with the Moroccans.

For the first few days, I had hardly any contact with him, as he was constantly discussing things with his friends, watching acrobats, snake charmers and dancers and musicians in the main square, or smoking hookahs with wheezing hoary men in cafés in the medina. Nevertheless, before long I found myself sitting next to him. As he hadn't read any of the fashionable political theorists I had studied at university, he obviously enjoyed listening to me talk about them and – as he hadn't travelled widely – my journeys to Israel, India, and North and Central America.

One evening, after I had my first smoke of marijuana in the medina, he came into my room in the rundown hotel where the three of us were staying.

'I'm leaving tomorrow with Michel for my parents' place in Marbella,' he began. 'I was going to invite everyone there for a bit before they arrive, but I've just got a letter from my mother saying they're arriving a week ahead of schedule. Still, I'm sure she wouldn't mind if I bring a friend along. Fancy coming?'

'Love to,' I responded, flattered.

The next day we took the ferry to Spain and hitchhiked up to the Costa del Sol. At last, two miles before Marbella, a side road branched off the main road and veered down to the glistening Mediterranean. Through flowering acacia, I could see ochre-tiled roofs of exclusive-looking villas, where sprinklers sent jets of water over impeccably maintained gardens. Four hundred yards further on, Jacob stopped in front of imposing iron gates. He swung them open and set off across a seemingly endless lawn towards the patio of a palatial villa, where people in wickerwork chairs were sipping cocktails at a large table.

'Ah, c'est toi, enfin!' a lively female voice chimed. Then, unenthusiastically, 'et Michel aussi.' An olive-skinned, petite woman with hazel eyes and an immaculately groomed figure had risen from the table and was hurrying across the lawn to greet us. 'And who is this?' she enquired in an unmistakable French accent, smiling coquettishly and extending her hand to me.

'Patrick, this is Yvonne, my mother,' mumbled Jacob, as if embarrassed by her.

'Enchanté!' she gushed effusively, before she clapped her hands. 'Manuel, vite!'

A servant in a pristine white tunic emerged from the villa with a silver salver of drinks. I had no sooner accepted one than Yvonne grasped Jacob by the arm and propelled him towards her guests. The men wore cream flannels, white brogue shoes and panama hats. The women wore fashionable dresses and smoked cigarettes in long silver holders.

'Who're these ghastly people?' Jacob muttered.

'Friends of mine who I met last year when you weren't here.'

'And where's Elias?'

'Mais tu sais! Your father isn't coming until next week …'

Jacob sighed with exasperation. 'You didn't tell me!'

'Et bien, I forgot,' she continued dreamily. 'Ça fait rien. Come and let me introduce you to my friends, who I have invited to dinner tonight, along with Sean and Diane.'

As he reluctantly trailed after her, I took stock of my surroundings. The villa was of classical Andalucian design, two floors high and built of white marble. Through polished glass doors, a valuable-looking Persian carpet hung on the walls of a colossal sitting room. A plush settee and a suite of armchairs were grouped around a fireplace, and above it was a large modernist painting. Outside, the lawn, which, I later learned, two full-time gardeners maintained all year round for the bi-annual visits of his parents, stretched away to beds of rosemary, lavender and asphodel, and sumptuous wine-red roses.

Next, I took in Jacob's mother. She was a demure, forty-year-old woman with a pert nose, smooth tanned skin, short black hair curled around her ears, and manicured fingernails. She wore a classic black dress, pearl earrings and a pearl necklace. She had expressive features and habitually gestured with her hands. She also laughed at the end of every sentence. But it was obvious that she riled Jacob, who shrugged her off whenever she tried to take him by the arm. Nor could he disguise his dislike for her guests; every time she introduced him to one of them, the curt way he shook the proffered hand was bordering on downright rude.

Yvonne played it down. 'The poor boy's a little fatigué,' she trilled to no one in particular. She turned to me.

'Mais dites-moi, Patrick, what do you do?' she enquired, beaming.

'I've just graduated from university,' I answered. I had taken to her straight away, and I felt sorry for the way Jacob treated her.

'Et qu'est-ce que … what did you study?'

'Politics.'

She clapped her hands. 'Mais, c'est fantastique! J'adore politics! In France we have a long tradition of socialisme! Now, pardonnez-moi, I must supervise the dinner.'

Presently, a servant beckoned me to accompany him. I trudged after him along the first-floor terrace to one of several doors with aquamarine shutters. 'Monsieur, votre chambre,' he announced, depositing my rucksack on a plush sapphire-blue carpet and opening the shutters. The room was light and spacious. Between twin beds with matching silk duvets there was a small ornamental table with an antique Chinese vase, a bouquet of lilies and monogrammed towels. I had scarcely had time for a rest when another servant summoned me to dinner. Attended by nine other guests, it was an embarrassing affair. As I entered the dining room, I could hear Jacob, who was irate.

'Mother, I am *not* dressing for dinner!' he blustered, until he emerged, barefoot and wearing his usual dirty jeans.

The table had been laid with Royal Worcester dining plates, engraved cutlery and crystal wine glasses. By and by, a third servant entered the room bearing a salver of succulent beef. Jacob shovelled some slices onto his plate and listened with indifference as his mother chatted to her guests. I was seated at the far end of the table, next to a retired banker and his wife who lived nearby. The conversation was banal – trite pleasantries about the weather and the 'benefits' of playing golf, if I remember rightly – and I was highly relieved when the meal was over. It wasn't until afterwards that I discovered that the 'Sean' and 'Diane' his mother had invited were Sean Connery and his first wife, who owned a nearby villa but had had to call off without warning.

The next morning, Yvonne and I sat discussing politics while Jacob and Michel lounged about, browsing through magazines. She considered herself a socialist, in a fashionable, Left Bank sort of way. She was also scatterbrained, and no sooner alighted on one topic than she flitted like a butterfly off to another. After Jacob and Michel had wandered inside, she leaned across to me. 'Jacob is changing all the time and doesn't know who he is,' she whispered conspiratorially. 'Still, I hope he will grow out of it.'

Uncomfortable at her confiding so speedily in someone she had just met, I said nothing. But I knew what she meant; I was more than five years older than him and I also, at times, found him somewhat immature.

At lunchtime, however, Jacob visited me in my room and was similarly forthright about his mother. 'I love her, of course, but she's so French!' he burst out. 'Everything has to be sophistiqué, sophistiqué!'

At lunchtime, he drove Michel and me in the family's open-top convertible into Marbella. At that time, although it was already becoming fashionable, it was still a compact, whitewashed town of Andalucian haciendas with black iron grilles and window boxes spilling over with geraniums. The harbour was clogged with fishing boats and yachts, and lined with palm trees. Behind, at the foot of an arid, craggy mountain, was the old town, where swarthy fishermen with leathery hands and faces quaffed beer in smoky bars in the back streets, and shrivelled widows in black leaned out of windows, gossiping or watching their grandchildren romp around.

For an hour, we lounged outside a stylish café on the main street, watching smartly dressed women parade up and down, or slide in or out of sleek sports cars. When we got bored, Jacob suggested that he show me Marbella's most exclusive hotel.

'It's owned by the son of some South American dictator, and it's teeming with fascists,' he explained with a look of distaste. 'I can't stand it, but I go there when I've nothing better to do.'

We drove back to the house of Jacob's parents, after which we tramped down a footpath that ran parallel to a golf course until it terminated in front of a grandiose archway. Inside, a 500 SE Mercedes, an Alfa Romeo coupé and a Bentley convertible were parked on gravel. Beyond was a courtyard, where a statue of a naked nymph sprayed water into a fountain. As we neared reception, golfers attired in pastel shorts and shirts goggled at Jacob's dirty bare feet and Michel's long hair.

'Any mail for me?' Jacob said in English to a clerk behind a desk.

The clerk looked up. 'No, sir,' he answered respectfully. 'But very nice to see you back.'

We trooped through the lounge and into the open air at the back. By a swimming pool, bronzed women in bikinis sunned themselves, and, at the cocktail bar, a flag drooped limply from a pole.

On the other side of a low wall, a speedboat sliced through the shimmering Mediterranean. Jacob paused by a buxom young girl lying under a sun umbrella. Absorbed in a book, she had oily, swarthy skin, and sunglasses propped in her shoulder-length hair. 'Hi, Patricia!' Jacob began, eying her bulging breasts.

She glanced up. 'Ah, Jacob!' she enthused in a strong French accent. 'Here again?'

'Yes, here again.' He hesitated. 'Come without your parents?' he enquired hopefully.

'Oh, non, elles sont là!' she replied, gesticulating to a middle-aged couple perched on stools at the cocktail bar.

'Pity,' he murmured almost inaudibly, before we drifted off. Then, to me, 'Not bad for fifteen, eh? Shame her father, who's a millionaire, keeps such an eye on her. Come on, let's get out of this fucking place.'

That night we drove along the highway to Pepe Moreno, Marbella's most fashionable discotheque. On the outskirts of town, it wasn't far from the beach, and a half-moon glimmered on the silken sea. In the discotheque, which was in the open air, couples lounged around candlelit tables under straw awnings, holding hands and kissing. In the middle, bodies on a dance floor gyrated to thumping music. The men were tall and muscular, and the women were tanned blondes with heavily made-up eyes and fixed smiles. Jacob eyed them hungrily, and spent the next hour buying drinks for a stunning Swedish girl before, to his disgust, a young man in tight trousers and with a gold medallion dangling down his chest swept her off to dance.

I swiftly settled into a rhythm in Marbella. After breakfast, Yvonne and I would discuss politics on the patio, while Jacob and Michel lounged about, as usual, flicking through magazines. I was flattered by her interest in me, and found her kind-hearted and hospitable. She obviously thought that I was going be a beneficial influence on her rebellious son, as I had a university degree and appeared to be mature, sensible and intelligent. On the other hand, she patently had little time for Michel, whom she considered to be a feckless wastrel. Not that he cared. One morning, as he and I were drinking a cup of coffee, she cast her eyes across the table at me.

'So, Patrick, what do you intend to do in life?'

'I haven't made up my mind. I used to want to go into politics or the trade unions, but I'm not so sure any more.'

'And you, Michel? What do you want to become?'

'A Coca-Cola bottle,' he answered with a cryptic grin.

Most afternoons, Jacob, Michel and I drove into Marbella, where we lounged about in chairs outside cafés on the main street, ogling women. At night, we drove to Pepe Moreno's. Michel – who, with his broad shoulders, long legs and insouciant manner, clearly appealed to the opposite sex – picked up a Finnish girl and I picked up an empty-headed but sexy, blonde-haired, twenty-year-old Swede. Jacob, on the other hand, had, as it quickly transpired, his customary lack of success. At first I found this baffling; although he was rather solidly built and prematurely balding, he was exceptionally open and friendly. Nor, as Michel was equally scruffy, could it have been because of his hippy appearance. It wasn't until much later that I realised it was probably his over-friendliness and bluntness, combined with his palpable need to impress, that the female sex found rather unappealing.

After a short time, Elias, Jacob's father, and his younger brother, a spotty youth with spectacles who was unquestionably in Jacob's shadow, arrived at the villa. Elias, like Jacob, was thickset and without a hair on his head, although his barrel chest was as hairy as a doormat. He made it patently clear that he wasn't accustomed to being disobeyed; nor did he conceal that, like Jacob, he found Yvonne exasperating. But mostly he kept himself aloof from the family, as if he had better things to do; on the few occasions he graced us with his presence, she treated them as though they were noteworthy events, and cheerfully brushed aside his slights.

One afternoon we were having drinks at our favourite café in Marbella, when Michel got chatting to Sally, a young girl at an adjoining table. Despite looking not more than sixteen, she was clearly attracted to him and, before she left, she invited the three of us to her mother's house in Ronda. The following afternoon we drove up the road that winds into the alabaster-coloured mountains behind Marbella. Ronda was a dazzling white town, and the house, which was on the main street, and just before a bridge over the precipitous gorge that divides the town in two, was strewn with books and crumpled clothes.

Sally introduced us to her mother, Hilly, a middle-aged, bohemian-looking woman still in her nightdress. While she sloped about the house, smoking continuously, Sally chatted to Michel. After two hours, Jacob, Michel and I drove back to Marbella, where Michel told us that he felt Sally was too immature for him. Years later, I read the writer Martin Amis's account of how his younger sister, who was only in her thirties, drank herself to death. It was only then it dawned on me that she was the young girl we had happened upon in Marbella, and the older woman in Ronda was Hilly, Martin Amis's mother and the first wife of Kingsley Amis.

After I got back from Spain, unwilling to acknowledge that my student days were finished but not knowing what to do with myself, I hung about the Meadow Bar in Edinburgh for a few months. A dingy pub close to the university that was patronised by left-wing lecturers, it had been one of my haunts when I was studying there. One afternoon, I was introduced to Annabelle. A long-limbed, willowy, seventeen-year-old with olive skin, cascading luxuriant black hair, an elongated, graceful neck and a sweeping velvet, laurel-coloured skirt, she was the image of Jane Burden, Rossetti's pre-Raphaelite model and muse. One of two sisters whose father was a successful inventor in Yorkshire, she was now preparing a portfolio to try to get into art college in London.

At the time, I was living in a spartan attic whose only furniture consisted of a mattress on the floor and dozens of discarded orange boxes. In a neglected cul-de-sac of the New Town, it was owned by a manic-looking, thirty-five-year-old hippy with a demented grin and long, flowing hair, who had taken too much LSD and looked the image of Charles Manson, the psychopath who had just butchered Sharon Tate, the film star and wife of Roman Polanski. Even though I was seven years older than Annabelle, before I knew it I was swept off my feet by her languid beauty and girlish giggle, so I courted her relentlessly until she started coming round to the attic.

Soon I was chopping up the boxes with an axe and we were making passionate love as I had never made love before on the mattress in front of the fire. But our romance was short-lived. Two months later, we strolled to the Dean Village, a picturesque hamlet with steep red-tiled roofs tucked away in a dell by the Water of Leith. We were leaning on the wall of the tiny, hump-backed bridge that overlooks a neighbouring weir, when she announced that she had been accepted by Central St Martin's College of Art, and was leaving at the end of the summer.

I was stricken with grief, but worse was to come. Before she departed for the south, I could only look on impotently as a seventeen-year-old Rudolf Steiner schoolboy with hair down to his waist lured her away from me in the Meadow Bar, where we met every afternoon. Plagued by the memories of our unforgettable lovemaking in front of the fire, I made up my mind to move out of the attic. However, when I went to pay the rent to the landlord, who lived in a top-floor flat in a backstreet, he demanded double what we had settled on. So I handed him the money, returned to the attic and, beside myself over losing Annabelle, chopped up the furniture with the axe before I stormed out.

After Annabelle left for London, I succeeded in landing my first professional job as a supply teacher of English at a secondary school near the King's Theatre. In those days, such posts were astonishingly easy to obtain, as only a university degree was required. I was aware beforehand that the school had a reputation as a dumping-ground for teenagers from one of Edinburgh's most deprived, working-class estates. All the same, I was horrified at how the majority of the teachers resorted daily to corporal punishment; indeed some of them had been using it for so long that they had become almost as brutalised as their pupils. One morning, driven to distraction by a particularly obstreperous boy, I hauled him out to the front of the class and beat him. Mortified by what I had done, I couldn't wait until my contract expired, when I resolved never to teach again, but to return to Canada to pick tobacco.

There, work on the tobacco farms had been transformed. To make harvesting the crop more efficient and life easier for pickers, farmers had introduced giant new machines; each had three seats to the left and three seats to the right, with the driver perched high up in the middle. Initially they had encountered stiff resistance, as experienced pickers considered them to be for weaklings, but once it had became clear that the old, back-breaking days were over, they had been quickly accepted. Now, once again, I did as much overtime as possible in the evenings, while, on my days off, I again worked on neighbouring farms. At the end of the harvest, however, instead of returning straight away to Britain, I decided to work on nearby apple orchards, some of which were so enormous that they all but stretched from one horizon to the other. The pickers were paid depending on how many baskets they filled, but soon I didn't care what I earned, and I merely stood at the top of my ladder, picking an occasional apple and chatting through branches to other workers.

After I got back from Canada, flush with money, I felt I needed a change, so I determined to go and live in London. There, I successfully answered an advertisement by three people in Queensgate, in fashionable South Kensington, who were looking for a flatmate. Unable to think of anything else to do, and feeling decidedly sheepish at so speedily reversing my decision never to teach again, I found a job as a supply teacher of English in an inner-city secondary school in Kennington, a godforsaken part of south London.

It was, if anything, even worse than the school in Edinburgh; if teachers completed a lesson without disruptive pupils setting fire to newspapers at the back of classrooms or smashing windows, it was viewed as a triumph. At least I now knew what to expect, and the headmaster, in contrast to schools in Scotland, was the only person allowed to administer corporal punishment. In addition, with my bell-bottom trousers and fashionable, shoulder-length hair, I related much better to the pupils than the older, more conventional staff. In fact the deputy headmaster was so impressed that he soon proposed I take the worst-behaved class in the school. Flattered, and heavily influenced by the ideas of A.S. Neill, who had founded Summerhill, the unorthodox 'free' school that was, at the time, an influential model for progressive education, I accepted.

At the same time, I was getting to know Jacob's friends. Like him, 'Spin Dry Dan', to whom Jacob had introduced me in Tangiers, was studying at Oxford. A small twenty-year-old from Bristol with a Mick Jagger-like mouth, he had earned his nickname by once, while on LSD, wriggling into the spin drier of a launderette. William, who had been at Eton with Jacob, had a mop of tight black curls framing his high forehead, a hawk-like nose, a cut-glass accent – his mother was a wealthy dowager – and was at film school. Bashir, an articulate Lebanese art student, was smooth-mannered and ingratiating.

But Jacob's best friend was Michel, who lived in Antwerp but kept turning up unannounced in London. Here he had a cult reputation as an enigmatic, Zen-like figure on account of his imperturbable nature, gnomic utterances and success in seducing attractive but brainless debutantes. He was also the black sheep of his family, as he hardly ever appeared to have any money or a job, although he now and again claimed that he sold 'pullovers'.

Often we took the bus or tube to greasy, working-class cafés in Soho or Notting Hill Gate, where we lingered over bacon sandwiches and cups of coffee, and Jacob took every opportunity to try and impress us by chatting to foreigners and practising his awe-inspiring command of languages. Like Michel, he gave the impression of never having any money, and he was forever cadging roll-ups. I found this irritating, as I had a suspicion that, unlike Michel, his lack of cash was an affectation. Nevertheless, I tried to ignore it, because, whenever you were around him and his friends, you had the feeling that life was bursting with limitless possibilities and new avenues to explore. For instance, one weekend he invited me to Paris, where he introduced me to his friend Pierre, who, when a child, had starred in a critically acclaimed film by his father, an iconic French film director. On another occasion, he took me to the estate of William's parents in Hampshire, where William was making a film. Jacob played the main protagonist, of course, while Michel was supposed to play an angst-ridden existentialist marooned on a tiny island. For some obscure reason, he was unavailable, so William suggested that I take his place. Thinking it was too good an opportunity to miss, I readily agreed, but once more I felt my portrayal of the character was wooden and simply confirmed I had no talent as an actor.

Jacob, like his mother, was hospitable to a fault and often invited me to stay in his parents' flat in Mayfair. All white, it was massive, with cream-coloured chesterfields and lampshades, priceless-looking blue-and-white oriental vases, and other costly objets d'art. Jacob made no attempt to hide his contempt for his parents' luxurious world, especially at mealtimes, when two live-in Spanish servants collected food from a kitchen hatch and served it up in the dining room.

'For God's sake, can't we even help ourselves?' he would burst out in-dignantly.

Still, although he regarded himself as a rebel, and I continued to consider myself a Marxist, this didn't prevent us availing ourselves of the benefits of their wealth. Intermittently, he invited me to their half-timbered thatched 'cottage' – it had four bedrooms – outside Windsor. Once or twice, I also visited him in Oxford, where I slept on the floor of his room in Christ Church College. The second time, we dropped in on his friends who lived in a row of cottages in Jerusalem, Oxford's run-down, bohemian suburb. Here I took LSD for the first time. I was soon disappointed to discover the world didn't dissolve into a kaleidoscope of psychedelic colours, as I had visualised. In spite of that, it was an intense experience; the walls seemed to be moving and, as everybody in the room had shrunk so much that they looked like dwarves, it was like looking at everything through the reverse end of a telescope.

One day, when I was in London during the school summer holidays, I saw an advertisement in the Tube for Undergraduate Tours, an exclusive company near Regent Street that offered private tours to tourists staying in de luxe London hotels. It claimed that the drivers were extraordinarily well paid, so I resolved to try to get a job with them. To be taken on, however, you had to fulfil four conditions: you had to be an undergraduate at Oxford or Cambridge; have a luxury car; possess a solid grasp of British history; and be able to navigate round London. Along with half- or whole-day tours of the capital, it also offered whole-day tours of south-east England and even tailor-made, seven- and fourteen-day tours of Britain.

After my parents gave me the go-ahead to borrow the beautiful, but ageing, second-hand Jaguar which they had just bought, I swatted up my knowledge of British history and, with an *A to Z of London*, learned how to drive to the main tourist attractions. Then, in the interview – before which I swapped my navy-blue donkey jacket to show my solidarity with the working classes for a smart suit – I maintained that I was at Christ College, Oxford, and presented them with photographs of the Jaguar. Impressed, they accepted me on the spot, so I fetched the car from Edinburgh and within a week I was doing half-day tours of the capital. At the beginning, the job was nerve-racking; several times, when I was trying to get to the Tower of London and London Bridge, I found myself in alleys behind Covent Garden fruit market or Smithfield meat market. But it didn't matter, as I simply explained these were atmospheric parts of London tourists rarely had the chance to visit.

The majority of the clients were very conservative Americans, so, before I picked them up at their hotels, I tucked my shoulder-length hair underneath my collar. I also ensured that they got into the Jaguar from the left, so they wouldn't notice a gaping hole in the right-hand sill. Most of them were astonishingly gullible. Whenever we approached a historic building, they ordered me to stop.

'Say, which king built that?' they would ask.

'James the Seventh,' or 'William the Tenth,' I would say confidently, if I didn't know the answer.

'Gee!' they would exclaim, open-mouthed.

After twenty or so half- and whole-day tours of London, I was promoted to doing whole-day tours of south-east England. This took in cathedrals and stately homes that I had never been to, but I must have satisfied the tourists, as I was soon given my first fourteen-day tour of Britain. I was very nervous, though, as I drove to Heathrow airport to meet the 10.20 a.m. flight from New York. The office had instructed me to look out for a thick-set, suntanned Texan wearing a black beret and smoking a cigar, and his wife, a woman with grey hair in a bun. Apparently, he was an ex-colonel in the US army, and, because the Vietnam War, which I was vehemently opposed to, was raging, I wondered how on earth I was going to get along for two weeks with a former officer from the most reactionary state in America. Shortly, I made out a squat, dark-skinned man amongst the crush of waiting chauffeurs. Wearing a beret and chewing a cigar, he looked very relaxed, but the minute he caught sight of my sign saying 'Undergraduate Tours for Colonel Meyer', he turned to his wife.

'Goddam, grandmaw, they sent me a fuckin' hippy!' he trumpeted in a broad Southern accent. For a few seconds, I thought the tour was over before it had even begun. Then he grinned and said: 'Look, why don' yo' just git yo' goddam long hair out an' quit foolin' around?'

Within minutes we were chatting away about Texas, through which of course I had travelled to Mexico three years earlier. All the same, to make certain that we were compatible before we set out on such a lengthy trip (so he confessed afterwards), he instructed me to spend the first day driving round destinations within striking distance of London. To my astonishment, I took to the Meyers at once, as, for a colonel, he was astonishingly open-minded and unaffected, and she was homely and motherly. Nor did they want to visit the normal sights, and on the second day he asked to visit Colchester Cathedral. I was driving along the motorway to Essex, when I heard his deep, husky voice call out from the back seat.

'Look, ah ain't inerested in motorways, ah wanna see fuckin cows!' he drawled.

For the next fortnight, as we travelled north we didn't come across another motorway. I had never been to many of the places on our itinerary, so every night in my bed and breakfast I swatted up about them in the *AA Illustrated Guide to Britain*, and the following day, trying to sound as knowledgable as possible, regurgitated what I had learned. Nor was I familiar with the roads, so, whenever I thought neither of them was looking, I peeked at a map I had concealed underneath the driver's seat. In spite of that, from time to time I lost my bearings until, on the fifth day, he removed the cigar clamped semi-permanently between his teeth.

'For Chris' sake, put that fuckin' map away an' quit pretendin' yo' know where yo' goin'!' he declared. 'We know yo' ain't been none of these places before, but we don' give a shit.'

By the time we reached Edinburgh, we were enjoying each other's company so much that I introduced them to my parents, and the five of us had dinner in Prestonfield House, a sumptuous baronial hotel near Arthur's Seat. Then, after we left Edinburgh and drove to the Highlands, we returned south via the Lake District and the Cotswolds. The Meyers were remarkably generous and every night they invited me to dinner in the exclusive, five-star country hotels Undergraduate Tours had pre-booked for them — a somewhat disorienting experience because, afterwards, to save as much money as possible, I slept in the back seat of the car.

There was only one awkward moment, in Oxford, when they expressed a desire to visit my college. As it was too late to admit I wasn't even a student, far less one at Oxford or Cambridge, I took them to the quadrangle of Christ Church. I was familiar with it, of course, from visiting Jacob, so I pointed out his room on the first floor, which I maintained had been my own. Somehow, I sensed they didn't believe me, but it wasn't important. When we arrived back in London, the three of us embraced and he gave me a $100 tip, an unheard-of sum in those days, and we vowed to keep in contact. They must have given me a flattering report because Undergraduate Tours promptly gave me my second fourteen-day tour. This time it was with a wealthy Brazilian industrialist, his wife and their fifteen-year-old daughter, but, to my dismay, the parents were autocratic and pretentious, and she was a capricious, overbearing brat with braces. Not only that; in addition to being a tourist guide, they expected me to be a chauffeur and they wouldn't even get out of the car until I opened their doors. The trip, the last of the summer, wasn't a success, and I couldn't wait for it to end.

In September, I returned to teaching at the school in Kennington. By now the challenge of trying to control its rowdiest class had palled, although teaching continued to have its moments. One afternoon, a singularly troublesome teenager bolted out of my classroom, so, without thinking, I sprinted after him along the corridor, through the gym – to the stupefaction of the class in progress – out into the playground and the street, before I finally caught him and frogmarched him back to the school.

Casting about for something else to do, I toyed with becoming a barrister at the Inns of Court. It was very expensive, but, to my mother's annoyance, Yvonne, who had become very supportive of me, offered to finance me though it, until I concluded I couldn't face the prospect of another lengthy period of study. Furthermore, while her husband was away on business and Jacob was studying in Oxford, she occasionally took me in the family's chauffeur-driven Rolls-Royce to dine in London's most exclusive fish restaurants. Of course, it crossed my mind this might be her way of gaining revenge on her husband for his reputed predilection for young women; nonetheless, as she never made any advances towards me, I disregarded it.

But my friendship with Jacob was diminishing somewhat. Once, he had come to stay with me and my parents in Edinburgh where, during a meal with them, he hadn't bothered to hide his disdain for 'the bourgeoisie'. Unusually for her, my mother had held her tongue, but I could sense her disapproval, and, after he had gone, she remarked how impressionable I was to be taken in by someone so 'immature'. Of course, I shared his dislike of 'the bourgeoisie', but her sentiments struck a chord in me; I thought his comments in front of my parents – his hosts – unduly provocative and disrespectful, and only confirmed my growing feeling that he was too young for me.

Instead, I was becoming much more friendly with Michel, who was the same age as myself. For some time, intrigued by his reputation, I had periodically taken the ferry across the Channel to stay with him in Antwerp, where he lived in an attic flat that had hardly a stick of furniture, and was so close to the cathedral you could almost lean out of the window and touch its clock. It was the first time I really got to know him and it didn't take me long to discover that although in some respects he did indeed live up to his cult reputation as a Zen-like figure, this wasn't because he had spent long periods studying spiritual texts but because he was merely an exceptionally uncomplicated, free and easy, laid-back hippy whose sole interest in life was chasing women. In fact, because he had never been to university, he had no skills or talent whatsoever, although he would have loved to be a rock star; strutting around with his imaginary guitar, he was very adept at imitating one.

The result was that we got on remarkably well, and at intervals, when I was visiting him, he took me with him when he went to see his parents. His father had made his fortune exporting coal to South America and, after they sold their villa in Marbella, they had bought a French-style manor house in a dense forest outside Antwerp. It was exquisite, with countless rooms, light-green shutters on the windows and, behind, an apple orchard. His father was a red-faced man with a protruding belly, spectacles and receding hair, who was constantly attired in an impeccable navy-blue blazer, white shirt and tie regardless of the weather. His mother was a likable woman who had obviously been a real beauty in her youth. Now, they spent a great deal of time touring the world, but when they were at home, they made it clear, as had Jacob's parents, how much they approved of me, as they assumed that, because I had a degree and a job as a teacher, I would have a stabilising, beneficial impact on their wayward son.

I had been teaching for three months when I received an unexpected telephone call from him.

'Hi, Patrick, you want to go to Sweden?' he proposed.

'Why not?' I replied, thirsting for a change from teaching, and that December we hitchhiked through three-foot-high snowdrifts to Hamburg, from where we took a ferry to Gothenburg. There, we hitched a lift to the town of Örebro, where I hoped to visit the sexy, blonde, twenty-year-old Swede with whom I had slept in Marbella. The address she had given me was in a block of flats, and when we knocked at the door, her father, who she had warned me was a pompous general in his early fifties, opened it. He had closely cropped hair and a clipped, military moustache and, for a moment, he stood open-mouthed as he took in our dishevelled appearance. Then he erupted like a volcano.

'She's not here!' he bawled, whereupon he slammed the door in our faces.

That evening we encountered a gang of pale-faced, weedy-looking youths in a café, where they invited us to sleep on the floor of their 'apartment'. It was littered with unwashed clothes, dirty dishes and empty bottles of beer, and they whiled away the night swallowing an apparently bottomless supply of amphetamines and other unidentifiable pills. Suddenly, at midnight, three of them announced that they were going to get 'some cigarettes'. When they returned an hour afterwards, they were laden with dozens of cartons of Marlboros.

'Want some?' one of them said to Michel generously.

'No thanks,' he answered, 'we smoke only roll-ups.'

The following morning, we were standing at a roundabout on the outskirts of Örebro when a police car drew up alongside us.

'Where are you from?' one of the officers enquired suspiciously in a sing-song English accent.

I told him.

'What are you doing here?'

'Trying to get a lift to Stockholm.'

'Let us see inside your bags.'

'What's this all about?' I remarked testily, as they rifled through our possessions.

'Last night some young men broke into a tobacco shop and stole 5,000 cigarettes,' he explained.

We spent a few days in the Swedish capital before we took the ferry to Turku in Finland, where Michel wanted to look up the Finnish girlfriend he had met in Marbella. The ship, swarming with drunks lured by the tax-free liquor in the bar, threaded through a series of wooded archipelagos. After it docked in Turku, we slogged through snow to the end of the main street, but the temperature was so arctic – it was minus thirty-four – that we turned round and took the same ship back to Stockholm. From there, we hitchhiked back down through southern Sweden, where the countryside was blanketed by waist-high snowdrifts and, outside scarlet wooden houses, Christmas trees were decorated with twinkling white lights. Once, we hitched a lift with Sicilians who had a touring puppet theatre, and Michel and I sat squashed into the back of their van, together with life-size wooden figures of men with painted moustaches and women with provocative scarlet lips.

After I got back to Britain I couldn't face the thought of teaching again, so I applied for the recently introduced course in creative writing at Essex University. My interest in writing wasn't new. In my late teens, I hadn't been overly interested in literature, although I had written a smattering of embarrassing adolescent verse full of spiritual longing. Then, after graduating from university, I had started keeping journals and reading voraciously, principally Dylan Thomas, Hemingway, Steinbeck, Proust and Kafka. They had greatly influenced me, and I had begun a Proustian-style autobiography awash with convoluted sentences, which I had shelved to try to write a dystopian, Kafka-inspired novel. Set in an unidentified, sepulchral town with a forbidding fortress, it was based on Edinburgh, and its chief character, a troubled man called H, was loosely based on myself. At the time, neither of these attempts at writing had been successful, and I had concluded I had neither the imagination nor the staying power to be a writer. Now I hoped that the course at Essex might enable me to tap into a muse I had so far failed to find.

To my disappointment, my application was turned down, so to play for time before I made up my mind what to do next, I applied to Edinburgh University to do a two-year, postgraduate law degree, a remarkably easy option, as the sole qualification was to have an honours degree. To my relief, I was accepted, so as soon as I arrived I set about trying to find somewhere to live. It wasn't long before I ran into Jack, a small, thin student at the College of Art, where his nickname was 'Rasputin', on account of his long, thin face, waist-length black hair, straggling black beard, black waistcoat, black coat and black hat. One day he mentioned that he was friends with a couple who had squatted – a popular thing to do at the time – a flat on the top floor of a derelict tenement near the law faculty, and the flat on the other side of their landing was abandoned.

When I investigated it, I found that, by some anomaly, the electricity was still connected, there was running water, and even the toilet flushed. So I moved in. I painted the walls purple and the woodwork lilac, and bought a mattress, which I laid on the floor in the sitting room, which overlooked a communal back garden choked with weeds. When I was finished, I asked a South African friend of Jack if he would like to move in. He jumped at the chance, and took the room at the front, opposite another blackened tenement that was uninhabited apart from a gruff drop-out called Boris, who lived on the first floor with his pet hawk.

Like Jack, the South African was at the College of Art, although he was studying design and Jack was studying sculpture. Unfortunately, he proved to be very moody, and after he moaned that I used his matches without asking him, he moved out. As luck would have it, Jack was now seeking somewhere to live, and it wasn't long before he was drifting in and out of his room, which, apart from a pile of unlaundered washing, paint pots and a mattress, was totally bare.

His friends on the opposite side of the landing were a tall, taciturn, humourless ex-student and his girlfriend. He had dropped out of the law faculty to study the tarot and the Kabbalah, and belonged to an esoteric group who claimed they could use psychic power to activate the San Andreas Fault in California and destroy the United States. She was an attractive woman with blonde hair who had transformed their tiny, two-room flat into a cosy home, replete with plants, rugs and books. For some reason that I never fathomed – possibly because I was studying the very subject in the institution that he now held in such contempt – he was very suspicious of me, and hardly ever invited me in. The rest of the tenement was empty, apart from the snug, antiquated pub on the ground floor. It had sawdust on the wooden floor, and every night a handful of toothless old men in cloth caps – the last survivors of the community before the area was cleared for redevelopment – crowded around a glowing coal fire.

After a while, Richard and Susan, both students at Edinburgh College of Art, moved into the floor below. He had a wispy goatee beard and wide-eyed, innocent-looking features. She was small, with a squeaky voice, and wore ankle-length dresses and National Health Service spectacles. A few weeks later, they were followed by Bill and Paul, two drop-outs who moved into the top landing, along with Bill's affectionate black Labrador puppy, who a stall-holder in Doncaster market had asked him to look after temporarily before he had disappeared. Their new 'home' had been used to store coal, but everyone helped them empty it out and, although it was a filthy job, after a week it was habitable – just.

Both Bill and Paul were, like Richard and Susan, from Doncaster. Paul, who was slightly built, quietly spoken and reflective, had studied to be an actor at the Central School for Speech and Drama, but was now attracted to Buddhism. Bill, who had an open, friendly personality, had never been to university, but he had been a reporter for the *Doncaster Free Press* and was an accomplished jazz pianist. Then his father had died in his arms, he had been summarily sacked, and he had been admitted to hospital with such severe depression that he had had electric shock treatment, which he found so traumatic that he begged his friends never to allow it to happen again. Since then he had been drifting around, and now he, like his friend Paul, had washed up in Edinburgh.

Initially I relished being back at university. I found criminology interesting and I joined a new radical group called RAP (Radical Alternatives to Prison) that had converted a disused café in the city centre into a space for evening poetry readings, live music and topical debates. I joined a newly founded experimental club that sat round in pubs discussing Nietzsche and cult writers such as William Burroughs and Allen Ginsberg. In a second attempt to resurrect my career as a budding politician, I also became involved in the students' campaign against apartheid, and once I even addressed the Union in a debate about the university's controversial investments in South Africa, but I was very nervous and I realised yet again that public speaking wasn't for me.

At the same time, when I wasn't at university, I still hitchhiked down to visit Jacob and his friends in London. It was the tail end of the Swinging Sixties, and they were heady times. Despite my continuing reservations about what I perceived to be Jacob's immaturity, he and I would wander along the King's Road, eying the girls in their miniskirts and Afghan jackets. On Sunday evenings, he, Dan and myself gathered in William's mews flat off chic Fulham Road, to watch *Monty Python*, a cult television programme at the time. Once or twice, I took the bus to South Kensington to buy marijuana from a tall, lanky, good-looking friend of a friend of mine. He had been at school with me, but rather than join the conveyor belt of lawyers, academics or captains of industry that the school produced, he had become a marijuana dealer instead. He was paranoid about the police, as he buried his drugs in his front garden and invariably took taxis to his clients. It paid off; it wasn't long before he was importing shipments of marijuana from Afghanistan. Nor, so a mutual friend told me subsequently, was he intimidated by the ruthless international drugs barons with whom he had to deal. In fact he was so attracted to flirting with danger that apparently, before becoming a dealer, he had contemplated robbing a bank; years later, I wasn't surprised to hear he had died of a drugs overdose.

One evening, I went with a poet friend to a pub in Portobello Road. There, she picked up a man and I picked up a sexy-looking, reddish-haired young woman. After an hour we took them back to a friend's flat in World's End, but I had no sooner begun to undress the woman I had picked up than I was mortified to discover 'she' was a Glaswegian shipyard welder in drag.

Then there were the incidents with Amanda, my former girlfriend, with whom I had stayed in touch. Once, she invited me to stay with her on her mother's country estate a few miles from Runnymede. There her parents had lived in a large country house, until, shortly after her father died, her brother had inadvertently set fire to the curtains and burned the house to the ground. Unluckily for them, they had forgotten to take out insurance, and now Amanda's mother lived in the servants' cottage at the entrance to the estate. One afternoon, Amanda and I went for a spin in the grounds in her mother's Mini. While I was driving, I started larking around with her before I lost control at the wheel and drove into a ditch. Luckily, the car suffered virtually no damage, but when we informed her mother what had happened, she was so angry that she flung a pan of scrambled eggs at me. It missed, and slithered down the kitchen wall instead.

It wasn't the only time I encountered Amanda's relatives. One Saturday, when I had nowhere to stay in London, I telephoned her to ask if she could put me up. She explained she couldn't, although she was sure that her uncle, a stiff-upper-lip ex-colonel in the Household Cavalry who was away on business, wouldn't object if she gave me her keys to his flat for a couple of days. It was a white basement in an exclusive part of NW1, but to my dismay he returned prematurely at midday, and found me in bed.

'You bloody indolent, good-for-nothing blighter!' he spluttered, his bristle moustache quivering with rage, until he threw my clothes and me – still half-naked – unceremoniously out onto the pavement.

Changing Tack

At the end of the third term, I concluded that I'd committed another major blunder by returning to university, where I had found Scots Law I and II so tedious that I had almost never attended any lectures or read any of the textbooks. As a consequence, I had dismally failed both exams and, faced with having to resit them or the well-nigh impossible task of doing five subjects the following year, I resolved to drop out. Now, heavily influenced by the tiny, tightly knit community in West Adam Street, as well as by Jacob, who had also dropped out of university and was working as a gardener, I wanted to do something creative. So, given that I had made an effort at writing, I made up my mind – preposterous though it sounds – to become a classical guitarist instead.

The decision didn't come entirely out of the blue. When I was thirteen my mother had insisted that I take violin lessons at school, and I had even got as far as playing 'Twinkle, Twinkle Little Star'. In spite of that, I had soon given up, because playing the violin was regarded, along with learning French, as a hopelessly effeminate thing to do by my friends. Regardless, from the age of sixteen onwards, I had become drawn to classical music. But first and foremost, I had fallen in love with the Spanish guitar. This had indubitably begun during my holidays in Spain, where hearing Segovia, the world's most famous classical guitarist, play on the radio had struck a chord in me. Moreover, although neither of my parents was particularly interested in music, Eva, my mother's mother, had been, like each of her four sisters, remarkably musical. Each of them had begun to learn an instrument when they were barely five years old, and in their teens they had formed their own string quintet.

Indeed by their twenties they were so professional they had given a benefit concert in Edinburgh's Central Hall for the families of the victims of the *Lusitania*, the ill-fated liner torpedoed with the loss of close upon 1,200 lives by a German submarine in the First World War.

I was very ambitious about the guitar. Of course, I was aware that the overwhelming majority of first-rate musicians start learning their instrument in childhood, but I genuinely believed that if I put in sufficient hours practising, I could make up for lost time and reach a high, conceivably even concert, level within a decade. First I went to the best music shop in town, where I bought the most expensive Spanish guitar, along with *How to Play the Classical Guitar Manual* and *A Beginner's Guide: How to Read Music*. Simultaneously, on its noticeboard, I found an advertisement for Edinburgh's best private teacher, a stooped, middle-aged man with nicotine-stained fingers who loved Spain and whose wife taught flamenco dancing. Living off the money I had saved from Canada, I started practising scales for six hours a day, along with the piece he gave me to practise at home. It wasn't long until I made such rapid progress that I got a part-time job teaching the guitar at an exclusive private school for girls in the select district of Merchiston. It was just for three hours a week, and I had learned only five or six chords, but teaching them to doe-eyed teenagers in their smart dark-green uniforms made me feel like a pop star.

Naturally, I also had a life outside the guitar. I spent most evenings smoking marijuana with Jack, even if his obsession with it irked me, because, if he wasn't smoking it, he spent much of his time talking about where to buy it,

how much it cost a gramme and which was the best 'gear' in town. In addition, he did a bit of dealing, although only to make a little money and have enough for himself and his friends. They were a dubious-looking bunch. Despite his parents being worthy, upstanding librarians from near Canterbury, his obsession with marijuana meant that he fraternised with petty criminals on the edge of the underworld. One was a black hustler who two years earlier had tried to rape the sister of one of my ex-girlfriends. Another was a puny, shifty addict who burgled chemists at night to obtain his weekly supply of methadone. Yet another was a working-class junkie who lived on a council estate in west Edinburgh and ended up serving ten years in prison after he murdered his brother while on LSD.

Fortunately, Jack took care to keep his friends away from West Adam Street, as he knew how much I disapproved of them; he also wanted to avoid providing the drug squad with an excuse to raid us. At the outset, because he was highly intelligent, and as at home talking about Yeats, Baudelaire and Rimbaud as the price of marijuana, I couldn't figure out what he saw in them. But it didn't take long for me to realise that it was their mutual interest in drugs, along with their paranoia about being arrested by the drug squad. It was never far off his tail and whenever it carried out a raid there he was, skulking in a corner, although when they frisked him, he invariably managed to be 'clean'.

A month after I moved into West Adam Street, I found myself a new girlfriend. Sarah was a twenty-year-old with lanky, straight hair and round shoulders. But she was unusually loving and deeply spiritual, and because she was a Sufi I started going with her to the Salisbury Centre, where a small group of Sufis convened every Friday evening. An innovative, holistic meeting place founded by Dr Winifred Rushforth, the eminent Jungian psychoanalyst who subsequently became a mentor to Prince Charles, it was a large, detached Georgian house near Arthur's Seat. At the back was a flourishing organic garden, and upstairs was a recently converted hexagonal hall for workshops, where we held hands and whirled round in a circle like dervishes. Every once in a while, Reshad Feild, the leader of the British Sufis, visited us. An upper-class Englishman educated at Eton who had served in the Royal Navy, he had been influenced by G.I. Gurdjieff and P.D. Ouspensky and, with his beads, mane of snowy hair and white robes, he looked every inch the part. Few were aware that his original name was Tim Feild, who, together with Dusty Springfield and her brother Tom, had formed the Springfields, one of

Britain's best known pop-folk groups.

It was through Sarah that I first became attracted to spirituality. Disillusioned with communism after the Soviet Union crushed the movement to create 'socialism with a human face' in Czechoslovakia, and dismayed by the abject failure of the student insurrections in 1968 to reform capitalism, I had begun casting about for a different set of values. Having been brought up as a Quaker, I repudiated Christianity on account of what I regarded as its bloodthirsty history and support for a discredited society. Now, believing that the only way to transform the world was to start with the individual, I had begun reading Krishnamurti, Alan Watts and other writers on Buddhism.

One day, Richard, Susan, Sarah and I travelled down to a Sufi gathering at Attingham Hall, the stately home owned by Sir George Trevelyan in the north-west of England. A courtly visionary with a crop of silver well-groomed hair and sparkling china-blue eyes, he was generally regarded as the grandfather of the New Age movement in Britain. After hearing a lecture by a pupil of Rudolf Steiner, for years he had been fascinated by angels, crystals, ley lines, herbal remedies and organic farming, and he had founded the Wrekin Trust, an adult education college based in Attingham Hall, which organised courses in spiritual reawakening. Here I ran into Roc. An eminent ex-scientist whose real name was Richard Ogilvie-Cromby, he wore greenish-blue tweeds, a V-neck pullover and a white shirt and tie, and looked decidedly conventional. He was, however, anything but. One evening, when he and I were strolling through adjacent woods, he explained about devas (elemental beings or nature spirits) whom he was convinced dwelled in trees. Then, when we were back in Edinburgh, as he and I ambled down the Mound, he started talking to someone. I was stumped, as there was no one there except myself.

'Who are you talking to?' I said.

'Pan, of course!'

'Who?'

'Pan. You know, the Greek god of music. Can't you see him? He's perched on my left shoulder.'

I wasn't the only one to see this side of him; another Sufi heard him talking about how he had met the notorious occultist, mystic and ceremonial magician 'Aleister Crowley, my arch-rival', who had in fact died more than twenty years previously. It was only afterwards I found out that Roc had been instrumental in the foundation and development of Findhorn, the world-celebrated spiritual community in north-east Scotland that was already beginning to make a name for itself owing to the king-sized vegetables being produced in its gardens.

At the same time, Sarah and I attended meetings of Gandalf's Garden. Belonging to a nationwide group of ecologically committed bohemians, the close-knit Edinburgh group convened in a backstreet flat in Stockbridge. In contrast to the Baader-Meinhof gang in West Germany and the Red Brigades in Italy, who were terrorising Europe at the time, they published a local news sheet advocating the need for the non-violent transformation of the individual. In addition, they had a programme of guest speakers, including a dignified white-haired woman who talked of a pyramid of divine light in the ether that you could tune into if you developed your consciousness sufficiently.

After eighteen months, I ended my relationship with Sarah, with whom I had found myself sexually incompatible. I had no sooner done so than, yet again, as with Julia and Vanessa, I was plagued with doubts about my decision, especially after I discovered she was seeing somebody else. It was the start of my first real crisis. I was squatting in a crumbling tenement. I had dropped out of a postgraduate course to try to become a classical guitarist, a herculean undertaking given that I had never played the instrument in my life before. I had no income or the likelihood of having one for a long time, and I was smoking marijuana every day, which invariably made me deeply introspective. For four full days, like a drowning man trying to clutch a lifebelt, I contemplated asking her to marry me. Unable to decide what to do, I sought the advice of the university chaplain. A small, radical Dominican padre with a black beard and spectacles, he was unusually warm and sympathetic. After I broke down and wept he cradled me in his arms.

'You know, Patrick,' he said gently, 'you're too sensitive. You need to learn that failed relationships are part of life.'

Wary of his motives – he was rumoured, incorrectly, to be gay – I then consulted a psychiatrist at the university health centre. He was as unfeeling and clinical as the chaplain had been caring and understanding, although, like him, he was of the opinion that I was only suffering from the break-up of an unhappy love affair. Both of them were profoundly wrong; what I didn't know was that my trying to find happiness through a woman was the onset of a pattern that, twenty years later, was to bring me to the brink of self-destruction.

That Christmas, needing time to take stock, I packed my guitar in its case and flew to Vienna. From there, I travelled to Salzburg, where I caught a local train to Lake Hallstatt. The train tracked a rushing river through bottle-green forested mountains and trundled through minute railway stations where people in fur coats stood on platforms, their breath billowing in the Alpine air. After two hours, the train trundled into Hallstatt 'station'. It was only a shed, but the public ferry – a wooden rowing boat – was already waiting. Within minutes, we were gliding past a flock of swans across a mirror-flat lake to Tyrolean-style houses and a miniature church clustered at the foot of a vertiginous mountain.

I found a room in an almost vacant hotel on the lakefront, where I remained for a week in my room, practising scales. Then I took the train back to the Austrian capital where, at sea about what to do with my life, I sat in a pew at the back of St Stephen's Cathedral and wept.

The end to our tightly knit little community in West Adam Street was shockingly abrupt. For months, we had ignored official notices that the council had slid under our doors, warning us to vacate the tenement. Then, one Wednesday, after I had gone to London for a week, workmen from the council materialised and started to brick up the entrance. I don't know how my mother found out what was happening – presumably Jack telephoned her – but she tore round to West Adam Street.

'You can't do this!' she shouted at them. 'There're people and pets in here!'

Taken aback, the foreman phoned the council. After a lengthy discussion, he notified my mother that we had been granted an extra twenty-four hours to leave. While Jack and the others hastily evacuated the building, my mother flung my meagre belongings into plastic bags and the following day the door was bricked up.

When I got back from Vienna, as I had nowhere to live, I went to stay with my parents. Then, six weeks later, my father came up with a novel proposal. Years earlier he had bought a small flat in Stockbridge, an atmospheric village in the heart of the city that, with its diminutive clock tower, police box, butcher and baker shops, looked like a toy town. The flat, which he rented to a slim, blond-haired architect who had been on the Edinburgh Comex bus to India, was on the top floor of a tenement overlooking the Water of Leith. He was urbane, witty and debonair, and after he had had a relationship with my sister for two years, he had become a friend of the family. Now, whenever I dropped in on him, I noticed a padlocked door on the other side of a dim internal corridor linking his flat to the landing.

After some time, I asked my father if he knew what lay behind it.

'I've no idea, but why not break it down and have a look?' he answered. 'Nobody would be any the wiser, because as far as I know it's been uninhabited for quite a while.'

One day I put my shoulder to the door. Inside was a minuscule living room covered with cobwebs, along with a box room chock-a-block with rusty spades and shovels, and a recess containing a grease-caked cooker. So I moved in. I bought a creaking, second-hand pine bed, which I put in the box room, and a few pieces of shoddy furniture, crockery and cutlery. When I was ready, I again asked Jack, who had also been homeless since our eviction, if he would join me. He again leaped at the opportunity and, after he deposited his mattress and paintbrushes in a corner of the living room, it was just like being back in West Adam Street.

Practising scales alone for up to six hours a day was a hermit-like existence, and I invariably looked forward to seeing him in the evenings, when, to evade the drug squad, he slipped furtively via back alleys across town down to the flat. I would light the coal fire and, over countless pots of tea, we would play backgammon and smoke marijuana until after midnight. By now, the latter so intensified my senses that I only wanted to be alone and once, at 5 a.m., after we had been smoking for hours, I went for a walk by myself along the Water of Leith. The path runs through a sylvan dell to the terracotta-coloured, tiled roofs of the Dean Village. A hundred yards before it, I stopped under the bridge that soars over the river to listen to the echo of the rapids. It was a hushed dawn in late spring, and lime-green trees appeared to be holding their breath, as if they, too, were awestruck by the thunder of the water. All at once, as I watched the new day grow unhurriedly from the east, I became conscious of the dawn chorus, and for a second it sounded as though all the birds were singing in unison, and the universe was one cosmic, breathing organism.

In spite of the flat being so cramped, Jack and I again got on well together. The biggest problem there was mice that congregated in the oven. We tried everything to get rid of them. We set traps laden with tempting pieces of cheese. We laid out plates brimming with poisoned bait. We plugged holes in the skirting board with concrete mixed with ground glass. It was to no avail. They figured out how to eat the cheese without setting the traps off. They devoured the poison, as if we were providing them with their supper. They gnawed through the concrete, although at a cost, as they then died behind the skirting board, leaving a nauseating stench. Nonetheless, eventually we found the solution. Some time beforehand I had purchased a king-size bible in an antiquarian bookshop. One evening I opened it – at St John, chapter eight, I recollect – and placed it at the corner of the recess, before Jack lit the oven. When the mice jumped out and scurried round the corner, they ran straight into the bible, which I snapped shut and squashed them to death. Several nights later, after I had caught a dozen of them, they never ventured back.

Two months after I moved in, I took the overnight bus to London to stay with friends for a week. This suited Jack, who wished to be alone in the flat because he planned to take LSD. Furthermore, for the first time since I had got to know him, he was chasing a woman, who, apparently as usual, wasn't responding, and he looked depressed.

'Have a good time!' I said facetiously as I closed the door.

'I'll try,' he rejoined tersely, stroking his long black beard.

Half an hour after he had swallowed some Strawberry Sunshine, he heard a ringing in his ears, followed by the sound of splintering wood. Puzzled, he poked his head into the outside passageway, just in time to see an axe come crashing through the communal front door. Thinking he was hallucinating, he closed his front door, whereupon two men burst in and started to wreck the sitting room with the axe. Simultaneously, the neighbour on the landing opposite, who had been startled by the commotion and observed everything through his peephole, called the police. By the time they arrived, Jack was slumped in a corner and the men had chopped most of the furniture into pieces. After three policemen managed to restrain them, the sergeant in command bawled, 'What the hell d'you think you're doing?'

'Ask that focker!' one of the two men barked in a broad Irish accent. 'Then we'll find out what the fock he's doing in our flat!'

When I got back on Monday afternoon, the police clarified what had happened. The men were part of an extended family of semi-itinerant Irish potato pickers who lived in a council estate to the west of Edinburgh. They had been driving home in the evening when they had detected a light in the flat they used to store their tools. They had rung the bell, and when no one had responded, they had fetched an axe from their van and smashed down the door to the communal passageway, before they put their shoulders to our front door. Jack was so traumatised that the police had to take him to the neighbourhood police station, ironically the headquarters of the very drug squad that had been trying to arrest him for months, where he remained slumped in disbelief until friends came and collected him.

The potato pickers also deposited a scribbled note on the mantelpiece. Addressed to 'The fuckers who broke into our flat' it gave us seventy-two hours to go to an address on the envelope to discuss the weekend's events. The note gave us two options – pay for the damage to their front door or buy the flat. If we refused, the note concluded, they would prosecute us for breaking and entering.

That night I discussed what to do with my parents. I still had money set aside from Canada, and if I bought the flat, providing they didn't ask too much for it, I could live in it or rent it out. The next day my mother drove my father and me to a small industrial town halfway between Edinburgh and Glasgow. Before we went to see them, she drove to the local police station where she spelled out to the sergeant on duty what had taken place at the flat. Then she scribbled the address of the potato pickers on a piece of paper and requested that he come and look for us if we weren't back in two hours.

Following his directions, we drove to a grim housing estate until we braked at a sign on a fence that said 'SCRAP METAL DEALERS'. We crunched up a path through an overgrown garden blighted by antediluvian baths and dis-integrating armchairs to a pebble-dash council house. I knocked at the door, and two slovenly women with curlers in their hair squinted through windows before they opened the door. I informed them who I was, and they ushered us into a lounge where they asked us to wait on a sofa next to a pile of unlaun-dered clothes. Several minutes elapsed, then they came back with two burly unshaven men in grimy overalls and trainers caked with mud.

The meeting, where the men sat flanked by their wives on the sofas, was short and to the point.

'Sorry about your flat,' I began, trying to sound contrite. 'I thought it was abandoned …'

'Right, right!' one of the men interrupted. 'Let's get down to business. What're you going to do about it?'

'Well, I'd like to buy it, although that depends how much you want for it.'

The man deliberated. 'Three hundred pounds?' he mooted uncertainly. The others nodded in approval.

'What?' I exclaimed, trying to conceal my incredulity; I had been expecting him to demand at least a thousand.

'That's right. Take it or leave it.'

'OK, OK!' I uttered. Feigning reluctance, I scribbled a cheque for £300, and my father asked them to sign a piece of paper, before we left as quickly as possible. It had taken me five minutes to buy my first home.

After a while, life resumed its regular course. In those days, there were many more characters and unusual places in Edinburgh than there are now. There was Madame Doubtfire, who owned the junk shop at the top of the street and who later became the leading protagonist in the wildly successful eponymous film starring Dustin Hoffman. There was the contented-looking tramp in Wellington boots and a grimy raincoat who carried his possessions in two black plastic rubbish bags and would never take any money. There was Lindsay Kemp, the drag queen and mime artist who, after studying with Marcel Marceau, formed his own dance company and held court every Sunday night at the bar of the new Traverse Theatre in the Grassmarket.

There was the Old Chain Pier, a pub on the seafront, where, on the walls, there were stuffed parrots and exotic curios that sailors had brought back from the Far East for the much-loved landlady. There was the oil lamp shop in St Stephen Street in Stockbridge, whose owner was a little man who had scraggy legs and copper hair, and wore a captain's hat, a kilt, stockings and high-heeled shoes. There was the Ukrainian restaurant, a candlelit establishment in damp vaults opposite the Palace of Holyrood, whose owner slammed the door in your face, even if you had booked, if he disliked the look of you.

But I spent most of my time in the flat. From time to time, I went with Jack to buy marijuana from one of his friends, who lived in a room up steps next to the launderette. Inside, the curtains were drawn permanently, and it was as dark as the grave, as the only light came from a crimson bulb that illuminated Indian rugs on the walls. He had taken too much LSD, and had bulging eyes and a deranged grin. Apart from being a part-time drug dealer, he made stone garden gnomes, some of which, one evening when he was hallucinating, he placed at ten-foot intervals above every shop in St Stephen Street.

A hundred yards round the corner, it was an attractive Georgian street that, with its quirky antique and vintage clothes shops, was the hub of bohemian Edinburgh. For decades the street had fallen into decay until, in the 1960s, it had been threatened with demolition. Nonetheless, it had been reprieved, cleaned up and restored to its former glory. Here, at a flat at number thirty-two, which my father had bought as a pied-à-terre, my mother held afternoon teas every Saturday for the family and my sister's friends. My sister had been at art college before she started teaching at a secondary school, and, like our mother, the majority of her friends were teachers of art as well. Several of them were at her school. One was my sister's best friend, who, like my sister, was a promising painter. Another had snowdrop-white hair despite being only in his late twenties and looking like a vicar, although he had one of the most exhaustive collections of hard-core gay pornography in Edinburgh. A third was a camp, gangling, handsome Australian with a Clark Gable moustache, who relished telling risqué gay jokes and bawdy tales. But not all her friends taught art. The husband of my sister's best friend, who had a black beard and resembled Pan, taught librarianship and noisily gobbled half the sandwiches. Then there was one of the three girls who had been my friends at university, who never wore the same outfit twice, and who now taught English at one of Edinburgh's toughest secondary schools. Finally there was a lofty, dapper, distinguished-looking antiques dealer who was gay, too, although nobody would have suspected it.

Like the tiny flat he had owned in which the architect lived, my father, who had become very shrewd financially, had acquired number thirty-two when property in Edinburgh could be had for a song. Overlooking a Georgian archway that, in the nineteenth century, had been the scene of a thriving street market, it was cosy and intimate, and had chintz chairs and a settee drawn up round a blazing coal fire. Like all her friends, my sister's philosophy was that life was there to be savoured, and everybody sat regaling each other with side-splitting stories, exchanging jokes, and laughing uproariously as they feasted on my mother's customary spread of tantalising sandwiches and cream cakes. Now and then, to please my mother, I joined them. However, I normally smoked marijuana before I did, which made me decidedly introverted, and as I was still grappling with the fundamental questions in life – Who am I? Why am I here? Where am I going? – I rarely said anything, but simply, finding the company flippant and frivolous, sat there with an inscrutable rictus on my face.

It wasn't long until the newly found peace Jack and I had been enjoying in the flat was rudely cut short. The son of my neighbours on the other side of the landing was Brian, a brawny teenager with an intimidating, blood-thirsty-looking Alsatian. He associated with unsavoury-looking youths from a crime-ridden housing estate, and one night, when Jack was out, I heard frenzied barking. When I peered through my peephole, I caught sight of four tough-looking teenagers trying to batter down his parents' door, to the uncontrollable fury of his Alsatian inside.

'Come out, ya bastard!' they screamed. 'We ken yer in there!'

I had no idea what he had done to them, but because he had been unfailingly helpful towards me, I grabbed a sturdy four-by-four piece of wood that I had in a cupboard, opened my door and launched myself at them. Baffled, they wheeled round, whereupon Brian opened his parents' door and unleashed his Alsatian on them. Panic-stricken, the youths fled down to the street, where the two of us, along with the Alsatian, chased them across the deserted bridge over the Water of Leith. Wildly swinging the four-by-four, I hit one of them on the arm and, bellowing with pain, he sprinted off. But if I supposed it was the end of the matter I was wrong; a few days afterwards, the son of my neighbour revealed that I had fractured the youth's elbow and, swearing revenge, the gang was gunning for me. I didn't procrastinate, and left town for a week.

A month later, to Jack's delight, his efforts to woo the woman he had been interested in paid off. Her name was Sue, and he had first run into her when he was visiting his brother in York, where she had been born. She and her three-year-old daughter lived in a rented cottage at Loch Rannoch in the Highlands. Every month she drove down to York in her rusty, dark-green Mini van, where she loaded up with sacks of brown rice from a vegetarian wholesaler in Petergate before driving north to sell them to communes in the country along the way. Now she started calling in at our flat as well. The presence of a woman and a child made a huge difference; only an hour after she came through the door, there would be a cheerful coal fire blazing in the grate, and a pot of vegetables and rice simmering on the cooker, while her daughter, whose enormous liquid-brown eyes were the size of saucers and was the most adorable little girl I have ever seen, wove a trail of destruction through the flat. Jack's brother and his girlfriend dropped in on him, too. They were going to stay with Sue, with whom they had been friends in York, where they were studying English literature at university. Although I never let on, I admired them, because they were habitually talking about avant-garde writers and cult musicians such as Richard Brautigan and Lou Reed, of whom I had never heard.

Every four or five weeks, Jack and I piled into Sue's Mini van and travelled with her up to Loch Rannoch. It was a long, three-hour drive. Presently, after leaving the Lowlands, it was like being on a different planet, with sleepy country roads, rivers and dark forests, before the road ascended halfway up Schiehallion, an awe-inspiring mountain from where there were vast vistas down over the seemingly infinite Highlands. Sue's whitewashed cottage was off a single-track road at the far end of the loch. It had two-foot-thick walls, and at the front a tiny window overlooked the loch and Rannoch Lodge, a large country house ringed by lawns and rhododendrons. At the back, two more windows cringed before Rannoch Moor, arguably Europe's most forbidding wilderness.

There were other visitors, too. There was the photographer from London's East End who at intervals drove up on his motorbike with some home-made bottled beer. There were Richard and Susan, who by now were living in a cottage called Cheat the Beggars in the Borders. Then there were the less regular guests. There was the barefoot, long-haired youth from Essex who, one weekend, turned up out of nowhere on the doorstep. No one had the faintest inkling who he was or how he had found Sue's address. He didn't speak a word and the following day, carrying a bag of raw potatoes, he strode out across Rannoch Moor and we never saw him again.

There was the photographer's friend, a young classical violinist who was also from London. One December night she got intoxicated before she staggered outside to 'go for a walk'. Some time later the local shepherd found her soaked to the skin, and took her back to his cottage, where, after she tried to seduce him in front of his wife, he put her to bed and dried her clothes before he phoned Sue to come and get her. When she did and the photographer picked her up by car, she was so reluctant to put her clothes back on that the photographer had to carry her, still naked, on his shoulder to the car.

The cottage itself was full of character. Outside the back door were rabbit hutches and a vegetable patch with a fence to keep out ravenous deer in the winter. Inside, the hall passageway overflowed with spades, axes and mud-caked Wellington boots. In the sitting room, couches were covered with dog hairs, and piles of chopped firewood cluttered the fireplace. In the mornings, Jack accompanied Sue's daughter along the road to the primary school. A stone house by a burn half a mile away, it had only one classroom and one teacher, because there were only ten infants in the surrounding fifty square miles. Two hundred yards further on, another cottage housed the post office, where a red public telephone box stood in the middle of nowhere. In the evenings, when the setting sun reddened the sky and stained the loch crimson, Jack sat silently poking the log fire while Richard, who was very musical, and I attempted to play elementary classical duets on our guitars.

One autumn afternoon, when the forests on the southern shores of the loch had turned almost impossibly orange, I took some LSD before I set off up the mountain behind the cottage. It was an unseasonably clement, balmy day, so, halfway to the summit, I stripped naked and stretched out on the springy heather. It was extremely uncomfortable, but I didn't care; I felt like Adam, as if I was the only human being on earth. After an hour, I wandered across the hillside, listening to geese honking high in the cloudless sky and marvelling at what seemed to be mysterious patterns on rocks. At length, as the sun lost its heat, I decided to return to my clothes, only to discover I had forgotten where they were. Watched by shaggy sheep, I hunted frantically for them, until, just as the afternoon was turning into a nightmare, I found them near a familiar-looking rock. It was then I realised I had moved only ten yards the whole afternoon.

But it proved to be my penultimate experimentation with LSD. Two months afterwards, I took a third tab of Strawberry Sunshine when I was in Stockbridge. For some reason that escapes me, I became so paranoid that I had to cling on to a bus stop outside the laundrette in order not to throw myself in front of an approaching bus. It was a terrifying experience and I vowed never to take psychedelic drugs again.

Apart from going to Sue's cottage in the Highlands, Jack and I spent a considerable amount of time at Cheat the Beggars Cottage, where by now Richard had a new girlfriend. Its name notwithstanding, it was, in reality, one half of a two-storey house on a hillside high above peaceful Stobo valley. Behind, coniferous forests crowded the crest of a hill, and on the other side of the valley steep hillsides were dotted with circular, mystical-looking copses of Scots pine. Below, the glinting River Tweed wriggled towards a baronial castle whose turrets peeped out of wispy, purple-tinged forests. In fields, cows lowed, crows croaked, geese honked, lambs bleated, pheasants cackled and sheepdogs howled. Periodically, indistinct voices or the putter of a tractor echoed up from the odd white cottage. Richard had set up a workshop in a corner of the sitting room where, in only six months, and with only the assistance of a library book, he had taught himself how to make Renaissance instruments. The majority of them were lutes with delicately carved rosettes, which he sold at an indoor market in Edinburgh, although he surpassed himself once and made a consummate Celtic psaltery. The house had two bedrooms: one was for Richard and his girlfriend; the other was for guests such as Ruth, my latest girlfriend, who from time to time joined me at the weekend. Aged twenty-two, she was extraordinarily sylph-like and, with her flowing dresses and pleats tied behind her waist-length hair, looked the image of Guinevere, the legendary consort of King Arthur. The resemblance wasn't purely physical; she had an astral, intangible aura about her, as if she inhabited another, more preternatural, planet. This, she explained, was because she had possessed psychic powers since she was a child, and, because she was open to 'good, as well as dark forces', she had to protect herself.

One summer, to make some much-needed money, I found a job planting trees on an estate fifteen miles away from Cheat the Beggars. To get there, I bought a rusty van for £25 in a second-hand car auction in Edinburgh. Two weeks later, however, clouds of steam started to issue from the radiator, so thereafter I had to get a lift with local youths whom the estate also employed. Every morning at 6 a.m. we drove into the village of Innerleithen, where we were picked up by the estate's Land Rover before it drove deep into the hills. Planting trees, bent double on steep hillsides, is back-breaking work; all the same, I delighted in being in the open air, looking down over the treeless moors, and feeling the hot sun on my back.

Occasionally, I went to nearby Heriot to visit the Incredible String Band, a cult psychedelic folk group at the time. Renowned for their ethereal songs, they lived in two draughty cottages swarming with women with waist-length black tresses and flowing, ankle-length Indian cotton dresses. Ungovernable children played amongst guitars, lutes, flutes and penny whistles strewn higgledy-piggledy on the floor. One of the women was Vashti Bunyan, a free-spirited chanteuse who was reputed – incorrectly – to be a descendant of John Bunyan, the seventeenth-century writer of *The Pilgrim's Progress*. Long-limbed and sinuous, with waist-length brownish hair, she had worked with Mick Jagger in the 1960s and recorded an album of poignant, wistful songs. It had been widely ignored, so, jaundiced with the music world, she had given up her musical career and set out from London on a horse and cart to settle in the Outer Hebrides. Now she had interrupted her journey in Heriot, until, a year later, she continued on what proved to be an epic, eighteen-month odyssey to join a commune in the Outer Hebrides. Thirty years later, her album would acquire a huge cult following and she would give sold-out solo recitals in Carnegie Hall in New York and Sydney Opera House.

A few months after they had been going out with each other, Sue and Jack broke up, and she started having a relationship with the gamekeeper for Loch Rannoch. Six foot three tall, he had a bushy, flame-red beard and, with his plus fours, tweed jacket, deerstalker's hat and bedraggled Irish wolfhound, looked as if he had stepped straight out of *Lady Chatterley's Lover*, although, in truth, he was from Govan, a working-class district of Glasgow. Breaking up with Sue, albeit by mutual consent, was a blow for Jack. In addition, he was far behind with preparations for his diploma show, which had to be completed by the summer. Nevertheless, at last he hunkered down to work at the College of Art. Then came an even worse blow. He was smoking marijuana in the flat when the doorbell rang all of a sudden. Expecting a friend, he made the cardinal error of opening the door without looking through the peephole to see who it was. In fact it was the drug squad, who, to their delight, unearthed a gramme of marijuana and a few LSD tablets hidden above the kitchen door.

Shortly thereafter, Jack appeared in court. 'M'lud, my client, who has never been in trouble with the law, is a student, not a dealer, and the trifling quantity of drugs he possessed were for his personal use,' his lawyer began. 'I accordingly request that you grant him a conditional discharge, because the repercussions for him may well be catastrophic if he is convicted. He will be unable to graduate from art college, he will have a criminal record, and any chance of him becoming a useful member of society may be lost.'

The magistrate was a stony-faced man in his sixties with piercing eyes and a notorious reputation for passing exemplary sentences.

'The court has established beyond any doubt that the defendant has been dealing in drugs,' he pronounced sententiously. 'I thus find him guilty and sentence him to six months in prison. Take him down.'

Confounded, Jack instructed his lawyer to appeal. Three days later, it was presented in the Appeal Court. Jack's lawyer emphasised that Jack stood at a critical turning point in his life and requested that the sentence be suspended long enough to give him time to complete his diploma show. The appeal judge consented, but gave him only a month. When Jack emerged from prison he was still in a state of shock. His friends urged him on as much as they could, and every day they all went to the College of Art to help him prepare his show. But it was no use. The deadline for the show came and passed with his work nowhere near completion; a week later the College of Art failed him, and he returned to prison.

From there on, things changed at breakneck speed. Paul enrolled in a Buddhist meditation course in the south-west of England. Bill, who had started drinking heavily, gravitated to a community centre for the homeless in Stockbridge, before going to live in a spiritual centre in the south of England. The taciturn ex-student rejoined society by becoming a solicitor, and years later, before he died of cancer, wrote a book about a much-publicised murder case in Hay-on-Wye that became the hit of the book festival there in 1995. Richard, embittered with the College of Art because they hadn't offered him a postgraduate and had burned his diploma show after he missed the deadline to remove it, applied to a teacher training college.

I rented out my flat and flew back for the third time to Canada, where I intended to earn enough money picking tobacco to continue with the guitar. When I got back in the autumn, I contacted the prison authorities and Sue in Loch Rannoch to try to locate Jack. Neither of them could tell me where he was, although Sue had heard that, because he venerated Rimbaud and his quixotic lifestyle, he might have gone to the south of France to pick grapes.

I never laid eyes on him again, although years later I heard that he organised eco-tours in the jungle in Costa Rica.

My third time in Canada turned out to be entirely different from how I had expected. I was going through customs at Niagara Falls once again, when an officious Canadian immigration officer enquired what I was going to do there.

'Pick tobacco,' I responded without thinking.

'So where's your work permit?'

The previous year, the Canadian authorities had mistakenly issued me with a social security card after I had finished work on the farm. Now I gave it to the immigration officer, who scrutinised it dubiously before he handed it back.

'You don't wanna work on tobacco,' he remarked, more amenable now. 'That's for losers.'

'But it's good money!' I protested.

'Nope, it's peanuts,' he countered. 'You wanna job on a pipeline.'

When I got to Toronto I made enquiries at trade union headquarters, which revealed that a pipeline from Alaska was on the point of reaching Ontario. In a sudden change of plans, I resolved to try to find work on it, and after I speedily joined the Pipeline Workers Union, I took a bus to Oshawa, a nearby industrial town, to try to get a temporary job until it arrived. In a backstreet, I found a room in a clapboard boarding house that apparently had a reputation for drunks, hobos, drifters and vagrants.

There was the pint-sized, shrivelled alcoholic with a purple nose who spent most of his time behind his half-drawn curtains, watching a flickering television screen. There was the seventy-year-old drunk who had droopy eyes and looked like a bloodhound. There was the morose, sticklike man who was obsessed with religion and cadged money interminably from the obese, genial and lax housekeeper.

I spent the first five days lounging in the back garden. It was littered with empty bottles and beer cans, and a sweltering summer sun hung over the apple trees. In the distance, freight trains shunted, and from high in the azure sky came the drone of bi-planes. Intermittently, the overweight, sixty-year-old owner who looked like the bullfrog in *Alice in Wonderland* joined me for a chat. Squirrels nosed through overgrown grass, sending the shackled guard dog berserk as he battled to free himself from his chain. At the front of the house, the peaceful avenue resonated to the rat-a-tat-tat of a child imitating a soldier with a machine gun.

In the evenings, everyone congregated round the cigarette-strewn kitchen table, above all when the owner, who lived close at hand and seemed unable to keep away, produced a bottle of liquor. He had his own armchair, and he loved to sit puffing on his cigar and listening to his tenants' banter. Usually, the conversation followed more or less the same lines.

'Say, where'd you say you're from, Patrick?' the pint-sized alcoholic would slur as he emptied half a bottle of whisky down his throat.

'Scotland.'

'Really? I'm from my mother. I think that …'

'What line a business you say you're in, Patrick?' the seventy-year-old drunk would enquire.

'I'm studying the guitar …'

'Well, I was a general in the army once – a general nuisance.'

'You can all have your opinion, I will not condemn you …' the morose, stick-like man would mumble to nobody in particular, as he flicked through the pages of *Good Samaritan* magazine.

Midway through the second week, I found a job operating a jackhammer in the town's Ford plant, where assembly halls the size of churches were crammed with conveyor belts. After a week I could no longer cope with the noise of drilling holes in the concrete floor, so, even though it was highly paid, I handed in my notice. Then I answered a newspaper advertisement for guinea pigs in a project conducted by McMaster University. They were carrying out research into the effect of pornography, and my job – embarrassing to recall – consisted of sitting in an unlit room where photographs of naked women were projected onto a wall to measure the speed of my erection.

Meanwhile, I had made friends with Gary, a muscular, blond-haired young Canadian who lived a few streets away. Two weeks later, we heard that the oil pipeline had arrived in Ontario, and so we started driving at 5 a.m. in his battered Chevrolet to the yard of the Majestic Oil Company. Sited forty miles outside Oshawa in the depths of the countryside, it was lit by fifteen-foot-high arc lights and was crammed with mammoth yellow machinery. In every corner hard-bitten, unshaven men milled about, competing frantically for the handful of exceptionally well-paid jobs. For a month, we hung about at first light, trying to persuade one of the crews to take us on. At length, cock-a-hoop, we succeeded; my new Canadian friend was ordered to report to a man called Bill, and I was assigned to a

Yugoslavian with an unpronounceable name.

After I searched up and down the pipeline for him, I found him stuffing what appeared to be thick tan candlesticks into holes in the ground. He had an abrasive manner and promptly thrust a six-foot pole into my hands. 'Here,' he said, 'your job's to plunge this up and down in the holes.'

'Why?' I enquired. 'What are we doing?'

'Laying dynamite,' he snapped back. It was only then it dawned on me we were powder monkeys on a dynamite crew.

The work itself wasn't dangerous, as the dynamite sticks couldn't explode unless they were wired up. When they were, everybody was evacuated, of course, as passing cars could detonate sections of the pipeline if drivers accidentally tuned their car radios to the frequency reserved for it. To forestall this, significant tracts of the countryside were cordoned off. All the same, cars unwittingly drove through and workers were, in fact, blown up. The work on the pipeline was utterly exhausting, as we slaved away from 5 a.m. until 9 p.m., seven days a week. But it was worth it. With overtime and danger money, I saved $600, a small fortune at the time, every week. Few others managed as much as that, though; the minute they completed their two-week shift, the bulk of them, principally the welders – the aristocrats of the pipeline – flew to Las Vegas to gamble away their hard-won money.

After the contract with the Majestic Oil Company ended, Olympic Pipelines took Gary and me on, as by now we had experience. This time we were employed on the skid truck, a gigantic juggernaut and trailer almost the height of a house. The job was even more gruelling than the previous one. After the fencing crew had cleared fences from farms and the pipeline trench had been dug, we had to load the trailer every dawn with what looked like railway sleepers. This had to be done extremely accurately, because if the sleepers weren't aligned properly the load could shift and the skid truck would tip over. After they had been loaded, it drove along the trench while my friend and I had to toss two of them every twenty yards onto the ground to support the pipes before they were welded together, and the completed section manoeuvred into the trench.

At the beginning, I loved riding high up in the skid truck as we barrelled along dusty tracks in the backwoods. With the money I earned, I felt like a ten-cent millionaire, and, with all my worries about my life in Britain so far away, I felt as free as a bird. But, as bad luck would have it, the driver was a sneering, vindictive bigot and racist who resented my university education and our liberal ideas. A man with a wiry body and a flinty face as unyielding as a rock, he wore bleached jeans, a lumberjack's checked shirt and cowboy boots. After three weeks our relationship with him deteriorated dramatically, and he set out to break us. This he tried to do by driving faster and faster. For another three weeks we managed to keep up, until he shifted up from first to second gear. That was unprecedented, so we contemplated taking him to the union. However, eventually we concluded it was useless, as communication with him had irrevocably broken down, so we handed in our notice, even though it meant losing thousands of dollars.

When I got back from Canada, I felt that, despite having progressed by leaps and bounds thanks to the hours I was practising, I had reached a pivotal moment with the guitar. So I travelled down to London to seek guidance about what to do next. There, I contacted the Guildhall School of Music, who gave me the phone number of a Madame Kramer, one of their retired professors. When I contacted her, she suggested that I go and see her. The following day, I took the bus to her house in Swiss Cottage. She was an elderly, hunched Austrian with white hair, who had not only founded the Guitar Department at the Guildhall but taught several internationally acclaimed classical guitarists. To my consternation, she insisted that the position of my right wrist was completely incorrect and said that she would take me on as a pupil only on the condition that I learn a new technique. Feeling I had no alternative, I reluctantly agreed. But it was a major blow; apart from starting from scratch, it meant leaving Edinburgh – where Ruth had waited for me to return from Canada – to live in London again. At the same time, I made up my mind that I needed some vocation or other, seeing I was no longer willing to tolerate the isolation that becoming a musician entails.

While I was looking for somewhere to live, some of Jacob's friends offered to put me up in a red-brick Victorian villa that they had squatted in Crystal Palace. At the foot of a gently sloping hill, it was in an avenue lined with blossoming cherry trees. My room was an attic normally occupied by a student of theatre design, with light streaming through a Velux window onto a workbench laden with models of stage sets. Once I had settled in, still unable to work out a way to earn a living, I found my third job as a supply teacher of English in a school in Dulwich, by an odd coincidence in the same road as Alleyn's College, where my father had been educated.

The squat itself included 'Spin Dry' Dan and Bashir, the highly articulate but unctuous young Lebanese whom I had got to know two years earlier. Since then, he and I had been travelling in opposite directions politically. I had been a Marxist at university but was now interested in music and, to a lesser extent, writing; he had swapped Hornsey Art College for the London School of Economics, where he had now become a Marxist. As a result, I regarded him as a hard-line ideologue and he considered me to be a patronising cynic. It wasn't long until we were clashing rancorously every time we bumped into each other in the house, where, in keeping with his newly discovered democratic socialism, he was adamant a vote be taken on every trivial domestic issue. These arguments continued until one night, after a particularly heated one, he lost his temper.

'Right, fuck off, I don't want you here any more!' he exploded, beside himself with rage.

'No, I won't,' I countered. 'It's not up to you to say who stays and who goes. We need to vote on it, remember?'

Apoplectic, he seized a bottle and lunged at me. For several minutes, we wrestled with each other at the top of the stairs, until Ruth, who was visiting me, and other young women in the house succeeded in separating us. After that, understandably, the atmosphere between us was so poisonous that I couldn't conceivably stay there any longer, so, the following morning, Ruth and I collected my possessions and moved across the street to an all but identical house, which had also been squatted by friends of Jacob. As luck would have it, the two spacious, sunlit front rooms were unoccupied, so, because I wanted to have my own space, I took one. Ruth, who had just had a successful audition with a modelling agency in Regent Street and fancied giving London a try, took the other.

Like the majority of Jacob's friends, they were highly individualistic. Sebastian, a gangly twenty-four-year-old from Somerset with a sardonic sense of humour, sandy hair and a straggly red beard, had dropped out of art college, and frittered away his time drinking beer and watching cricket on television. Roger, who resembled Marty Feldman and was stunted with crinkled black hair, a beak-like nose, bulging eyes and black spectacles, aspired to being a photographer. But by far the most intriguing was Adrian, a raffish ex-public schoolboy who, in the 1950s, had been one of the first young Westerners to travel overland to India. There he had done Voluntary Service Overseas, before going to live in the remote mountainous kingdom of Sanskar, close to the Tibetan border, where he had lived for many years and married a local woman, with whom he had had a son.

Now, as their marriage had ended recently, he had come back to Britain for the first time in twenty years. In his early thirties, he was a bizarre sight in his Tibetan robe, tall maroon Tibetan hat and upturned leather boots. With his waist-length loamy-grey hair, drooping white moustache, slit eyes and high, pock-marked cheekbones in a raddled, licentious face, he even looked Tibetan. Like Sebastian and Roger, he lived on social security, and every afternoon he spent hours in a pub near the roundabout in Crystal Palace, drinking Guinness, smoking countless cigarettes, playing snooker and trying to seduce schoolgirls.

But, as if his story wasn't already remarkable enough, he was also given to flights of fancy. True, in India, he had indeed got to know the world-famous violinist Yehudi Menuhin, as a photograph of them together testifies. However, he asserted that he had gone there only because, when he was sixteen, he had somehow or other become acquainted with Stephen Ward, the osteopath, in Soho. It was Ward who had introduced John Profumo, the Conservative defence minister, to the prostitute Christine Keeler, and Adrian maintained he had wanted to avoid being called as a witness in Profumo's trial, a salacious event of national importance that helped bring down the Conservative government. And there was more: apart from claiming he had bedded an internationally renowned singer, he not only maintained that he had taken part in Formula One racing, he said he had even won a race in France in a nuclear-powered car.

His last few years were equally unusual. Once, the former girlfriend of Richard, with whom I had stayed in Cheat the Beggars, came down from Edinburgh to visit me. Almost inevitably, he ended up in bed with her, before he went to live with her in East Lothian in Scotland. There, funded entirely by her, he had renovated a cottage, although, when it was completed, he wouldn't allow her to move in. Instead, it had become his base in which to indulge his lechery. No woman was safe from him, and he had even deflowered the prettiest eighteen-year-old in the village, although he was twenty years older than her. At the same time, he was sleeping with the daughter of a local gypsy family, as well as drinking three bottles of gin a day, which he said he drank only to offset the effects of quinine he took for malarial fevers from which he had suffered for years. By now he was working as a hospital porter in the Royal Infirmary of Edinburgh, where, needless to say, he slept with a considerable number of the female patients – success which, it was rumoured, was due to him being 'hung like a donkey'. Then, aged forty, he died suddenly, although not of alcohol poisoning, as might have been expected, but from a heart attack while looking through a shop window.

I enjoyed living in Crystal Palace. When the others weren't at the pub, they spent the evening sprawled on frayed sofas in the huge, echoing sitting room, where, along with a table full of overflowing ashtrays, there was, for some reason that eludes me, a towering bank of obsolete televisions. Every Wednesday evening I took a bus across London to Madame Kramer's house in Swiss Cottage. Like many first-rate teachers, she was both authoritarian and demanding, but I was an exceptionally diligent student, and after school I practised for four hours a day. I had grounds for optimism. One night I attended Madame Kramer's yearly soirée, when her pupils assembled to give recitals. It was a revelation. Her star pupil, an implausibly gifted youth of nineteen who had been playing for only three years – only a year more than myself – was already a virtuoso guitarist. Encouraged, I redoubled my efforts, trusting that one day I would be able to play as proficiently.

To my astonishment, I also enjoyed teaching at the secondary school, which, if anything, was even more chaotic than that in Kennington. Regardless, it had its amusing moments. I had a habit of playing with keys in my pocket, and once, when I had forgotten to do up my zip, a teenage girl quipped, 'Sir, your violin case is open – do you think you could stop fiddling?'

And once, I lost my temper with a particularly obnoxious teenager in my class. With the redneck justice of Canadian pipelines still fresh in my mind, I pinned him against the blackboard. 'Behave, or I'll knock your fucking brains out!' I yelled, to everyone's amazement. Speechless, he didn't bother me again, but I was fortunate he didn't report me for assault, as would happen nowadays.

By now, however, I was beginning to be disillusioned with the guitar. The problem was that I had hoped that the classical technique I was learning would enable me to improvise with non-classical musicians; in reality it appeared to make that, if anything, more difficult. The end came six months later, shortly after Ruth, dispirited about our relationship and having made no headway with a career as a model, had returned to Edinburgh. One evening, exasperated by my inability to play a demanding piece, Madame Kramer ripped my fingers from the guitar.

'Mr Richardson, you are, and for ever will be, nothing but a fiddler!' she hollered.

To begin with, I was indignant. How dare she – I wasn't paying good money to be insulted! But it wasn't long until, reluctant as I was to admit it, I realised she was right. The truth was, I had never had any innate talent for the instrument and, irrespective of how many hours I practised, learning the classical guitar had been a doomed project from the start. It was the end of my career as a musician, which I recognised I had pursued because of a mental decision rather than an inner need.

Then, two years after I had last seen him, I received another telephone call from Michel.

'Hi, Patrick,' he said laconically. 'Want to go to Greece?'

'Definitely!' I responded. Weary of teaching and London's teeming multitudes, I thirsted for adventure, so, with my Canadian savings still largely intact, I handed in my notice and, in July, we flew to Athens.

The mood in the Greek capital was still highly charged, following the heavy-handed suppression of a student rebellion at the Athens polytechnic by the right-wing military junta, which had usurped power in a coup d'état seven years earlier. We stayed for only a few days before we took the ferry from Piraeus to the island of Ios in the Cyclades. It was a revelation, and I fell in love with Greece the instant I set foot on the ship. I loved the soporific judder as the boat glided through the coruscating jade Aegean. I loved hearing the babble of black-clad Greek women in the second-class saloon and observing heavily bearded, venerable Greek Orthodox priests with Byzantine noses as they mingled with bent, wizened men with waxed, Cretan-looking moustaches. I loved idling at the stern, gazing at gulls as they hovered expectantly in the foaming wake, and I loved the mysterious islands shimmering behind the white heat-haze on the horizon.

Apart from the port, Ios had only one village. At the top of an apparently unending flight of steps, it consisted of brilliant, meringue-white Cubist-looking houses. Further up, in its heart, a miniature, barrel-vaulted church perched on top of a monumental, precipitous rock. There were two cafés in its diminutive square, where weather-beaten old men sat at little square tables drinking retsina or playing *tavli* (backgammon). At the time, there was only a smattering of foreigners on the island – where there were virtually no cars and roads, let alone an airport – most of whom were hippies going to, or returning from, India.

For two months, Michel and I lived in a cave on a craggy headland at the eastern end of a golden beach. Shielded by a knee-high wall of boulders that shepherds had built to provide shelter from the frequently stormy *meltemi* wind, it was a tiny niche under an overhanging outcrop of rock. Michel and I slept alternately on the stony ground or the smooth rocky platform that mirrored the shape of the human body.

It was a never-to-be-forgotten period of my life. Every morning, Michel and I, along with a sprinkling of hippies camping on the beach, picked our way to a dilapidated taverna two hundred yards downhill in the bay to have breakfast. The owner, who, with his spectacles, stubbly grin, and seemingly glued-on moustache, resembled an ageing Groucho Marx, and his family had heated rows as they prepared everybody's two fried eggs. In a while, however, the shouting and bawling subsided, and the rest of the day they were so considerate with each other it was as if they hadn't had an argument in their life. At midday, when the sun was too hot to lie on the beach, I sat at the taverna's draughty windows playing chess with a cadaverous-looking, thirty-year-old American with a Mohican haircut and baggy cream trousers that he had worn during the year he had just spent in India. He had a wry expression and was inseparable from his dog, a colossal, black-and-white Great Dane that seemed perpetually perplexed by life; if a fly landed on his back, his massive head swivelled round and his slavering salmon-coloured jowls flapped, before he lunged at it with his prodigious nose.

Once or twice, a Greek in his mid-thirties who worked at the taverna and whose black ringlets reminded me of Medusa took us out in his red, yellow and white fishing boat. In addition, I swam three times a day out into the bay, until the shallow emerald water gave way to the dark-blue fathomless ocean, when, having tested my fear of the deep to the limit, I turned back. In the afternoon, the proprietor of the taverna allowed Michel and me to have a cold shower on the veranda; below, the shepherd, trying to avert his gaze from naked young women sunbathing on the beach, drove his goats into wild fig and bamboo groves before they wound their way up into rocky hills.

I particularly loved the late afternoons and evenings on Ios. By 5 p.m. the baking sun had progressed midway into the bay, now aflame with orange, and diamond-like sunbeams sparkled on the water. By sundown, the iridescent sky had mutated from rose to vermilion to magenta, and the tide languidly lapping the beach turned claret red. After the crepuscular light had faded, Michel and I would gaze into the fire we made out of driftwood, lost in our own thoughts, and observe darting geckos, or we would whistle to three young American women who flashed their torches at us from their cave on the other side of the bay. Travelling outside the United States for the first time, they were brimming with joie de vivre and were relentlessly jovial. One was a raunchy young woman in her early twenties, with meaty arms and chunky thighs. The second was an incorrigible flirt, with a sensuous mouth, awe-inspiring breasts, and a resonating guffaw. The third was equally sexy and had a similarly jocular sense of humour, although she had teeth like a horse.

But as a rule Michel and I crunched along the beach and along a gorse-covered headland to the village, a mile to the west. There, we idled through serpentine alleys to buy still warm, savoury *tiropita* (cheese pies) and *milopita* (apple pies) at the baker's, where the odour of newly baked bread wafted into the bougainvillea-scented air. Next, we played *tavli* with Christos, a burly, hairy Greek with whom we had become friends on the beach, and his long-legged, shaven-headed Dutch girlfriend. Then Michel wandered off by himself, while I browsed in the second-hand paperback bookshop. Situated directly under a sunless archway, it was owned by a choleric middle-aged man who lounged outside on his stool, scowling through grimy spectacles at anybody who dared touch the teetering stacks of dog-eared paperbacks piled to the ceiling. Afterwards I feasted on freshly caught fish and *risogalo* (rice pudding) in my favourite restaurant in the square, before Michel and I drifted up to the Ios Club. Up near a line of derelict white windmills that straddled a neighbouring ridge, it was a bar where foreigners gathered on the terrace in the cool of the evening to listen to classical music and watch the sun, like the top of an orange, dip into the wine-red sea. At last, about 10 p.m., it was time to go to Homer's Cave, one of the village's two discotheques, where we hoped to pick up two women.

Here, one night, I ran into Maria. A twenty-two-year-old Hungarian with wavy black hair underneath a headscarf, an ankle-length flowery dress and a black shawl wrapped around her shoulders, she could easily, with her olive skin and dark eyes, have been a fortune-teller straight out of a gypsy caravan. Over drinks, she divulged that she was a painter and that she suffered from recurring panic attacks. In addition, she showed me her sketches, which depicted haunted-looking faces staring out from dog-eared pages. At midnight, we tramped in silence back along the headland, before we cut down the goatherd's path to the moonlit beach and up to the cave. For an hour or so, we drank retsina and stared vacantly at the remains of the evening's smouldering fire. I was aching to make love to her, but, all of a sudden, she vomited all over my sleeping bag, then promptly went out like a light.

Regardless, within two days we were having a highly physical relationship. In the village, she had rented a cavernous room that was completely devoid of furniture apart from a king-size mahogany double bed, and during the day we made love on its crisp white sheets. One afternoon, we inadvertently left the door ajar, and the owner of the house, a stooped old woman in black, caught a glimpse of us as she shuffled by with her stick. She was visibly scandalised, as the Greek islands were deeply traditional in those days, and from that day on we made certain to lock the door.

Three weeks later, after I hadn't seen her in the square or Homer's Cave for two days, I bumped into a Greek acquaintance, who, with his straggling hair, leathery skin and imperious features, looked like an Apache warrior. He knew her well, as he was from Ios, where, he had told me, she came every summer.

'You haven't seen Maria, have you?' I enquired anxiously.

'Maria?' he answered. 'Why you ask for Maria? She's gone to take the *Naxos*.'

'What!' I cried, unable to believe my ears.

'Yes. I see her with her luggage at the port.'

'When?'

'Just now, an hour ago.'

'But … did she leave an address?'

'Oh,' he chuckled, looking at my crestfallen expression, 'you're in love with Maria! She's a strange girl. She finds a guy and then leaves him after a month. Why worry about Maria?'

I was so distraught that I tore down the steps to the port in an attempt to persuade her to stay. But the ship had sailed, and she had gone.

A month afterwards, tired of lazing on the beach, swimming and playing chess or *tavli*, we took the *Naxos* back to Athens. For two days, we toyed with sailing to Alexandria in Egypt, which in those days seemed as far away as Timbuktu. After a while, however, we opted – I can't remember why – to go to Syria instead.

Turkey was much larger than either of us had conceived. After hitchhiking through seemingly unrelenting, dried-up plateaux, we were preparing to sleep in a field outside Konya, when we learned that Turkey had invaded Cyprus. Emboldened by the military dictatorship in Athens, the latter was on the point of declaring *enosis* (union) with Greece, in defiance of the mainly Turkish community in the north of the island. Fearing war between Greece and Turkey, we decided that, rather than continue and run the risk of being stranded in Asia Minor, we would race back to Greece before the border closed. This was prescient; it was a hectic journey, but we made it back to Athens with hours to spare.

There, hoping the crisis would blow itself out, we took the familiar *Naxos* from Piraeus back to Ios. We had no sooner disembarked than we discovered all the ferries were cancelled henceforth. Unable to leave, while Greece and Turkey teetered on the brink of hostilities, we returned to our cave above Nico's taverna. Every sunset, we once more crunched round the beach and up over the headland to the village. Now it was blacked-out and the Ios Club had shut. Instead of playing *tavli*, octogenarians huddled by candlelight around radios in houses, listening to the latest bulletins on the BBC World Service, and twitchy young men sifted through lists of those being called up that were pinned to a tree in the square. Outside the harbour a Greek destroyer was anchored to defend the island in case of attack. Two weeks later, disgraced by the debacle in Cyprus, where the movement for *enosis* had failed miserably, the military junta in Athens collapsed, and it wasn't long before one-time prime minister Constantine Karamanlis arrived from exile in France to restore democracy.

Dropping Anchor

By the time I got back to Crystal Palace it was September. Set on leaving London once and for all, I turned my sights yet again to Canada. This time, instead of trying to find another job on a pipeline, I planned to go to Saskatchewan to teach English, which was also reputed to be ridiculously well paid. However, I wasn't only lured by the name – I had developed an unmistakable romantic streak – but it was near the Rocky Mountains, which I had long wanted to see. I was still deliberating about it when Sebastian and Adrian invited me to go with them for the weekend to Amsterdam to stay with friends. Without thinking, I jumped at the chance, as I had never been there, and it had a reputation as being one of Europe's most enlightened and intoxicating cities.

Their friends, Rob and Marijan, lived in an attic on the Achterburgwal, a narrow canal in the red-light district. After we dropped off our bags, Sebastian suggested we go for a drink in an Irish pub he knew near Centraal railway station. There we downed umpteen Pils and picked up three Welsh nurses, who accepted our invitation to the Achterburgwal for a 'party'. After we climbed the vertiginous stairs to the attic, we found that our friends were out. As drunk as a lord, in a rash attempt to gain access I clambered onto the steeply sloping roof. Suddenly, I lost my footing and, horror-stricken, found myself sliding down the tiles, with my shirt riding up my chest. Mercifully, a gulley broke my fall and, rapidly sobered up, I managed to worm through a skylight into the attic, where, rather than 'having a party', one of the nurses, who had a first-aid kit with her, had to swab and bandage my badly grazed ribs instead.

Despite that, I was so enchanted by the cobbled streets, canals and doll-like houses that, instead of going to Saskatchewan, I resolved to go and live in Amsterdam. There were several reasons. Disenchanted with conventional politics, I was convinced by now that the most radical form of action was to take the 'revolution' onto the streets, and the freethinking Dutch capital seemed a great place to make a start. It would give a boost to my writing, in which I was becoming more and more interested. It would be an unmissable opportunity to live on the continent, as opposed to simply visiting it. Lastly, Dirk, Jaap and André, Dutch friends of Rob and Marijan whom had I got to know in the Achterburgwal, told me that they had just *gekraakt* (squatted) a building in the Kerkstraat and asked me if I would like to have the garret there. When I had a look, I found that it was right in the centre of town, and it was a four-storey, semi-derelict gabled house propped up by three twenty-foot-high pillars.

Moreover, the garret, which was entirely constructed of wood, had no tiles on the roof, no floor, no window frames, no gas, no water, no electricity and no toilet. In spite of that, because I was bent on staying in Amsterdam, where there was an acute housing shortage and renting an apartment was prohibitively expensive, I accepted without hesitation. I had absolutely no idea how long I would stay – such thoughts don't enter your head when you are young – although never in my wildest dreams did I envisage that it would be for eleven years.

As soon as I moved in, André helped me lay an electricity cable and a water pipe across the roof of the adjacent attic, which was also *gekraakt*. At night, I cycled to building sites where I scavenged planks and window frames, which I carried back to the Kerkstraat on the second-hand bicycle I purchased in the Waterlooplein, a nearby flea market. These I hoisted up to the garret with André's block and tackle, which I suspended from a hook on the front gable. Leaving space for a trapdoor, I laid the floor with the planks and installed the ill-fitting window frames.

Helped again by André, I converted a black oil drum into a crude, highly dangerous *kachel* (traditional Dutch stove) that was lit by tossing a match onto petrol from a tank we rigged on to the wall.

To make a kitchen, I sawed a hole in the opposite wall for waste water to drain into a gutter, before I installed a camping ring, and a sink and a still-functioning refrigerator that I found in skips. For a lavatory, I bought a chemical toilet designed for caravans and installed it in a corner I sectioned off with worn, coffee-coloured curtains. As André hadn't yet repaired his lavatory, just before the chemical toilet overflowed I carried it down four flights of stairs to the front door. Then at midnight, I levered off a manhole in the deserted street and emptied the foul-smelling liquid into the sewer. Nonetheless, nothing could be done about the roof, which was covered with only a thin layer of bitumen, as retiling it was beyond everyone.

While I was making the garret habitable, I cycled to a cheap hardware store near the Rembrandtsplein, where I pilfered paint, brushes, nails, screws and other trifling items I needed. I had no qualms or scruples about it; as far as I was concerned, supermarkets and banks were exploitative institutions and were fair game. My petty thieving didn't end there; every Sunday, I cycled to a newspaper shop in the nearby Rembrandtsplein, where I hid the *Observer* inside *The Sunday Times* and paid for only the latter. After the third consecutive bicycle I bought in the flea market was stolen, I went out with André at midnight to a badly lit side street, where he taught me the 'sixty-second technique' – the time it took to break most locks with a hammer and screwdriver – and simply stole another one.

Dirk and Jaap were also hard at work rebuilding their floors in the Kerkstraat. Like many of the Dutch, they were ingenious when it came to anything to do with water, and above their windows they improvised miniature aluminium foil canals to carry away rivulets leaking from the ceilings. They were all students in their early twenties. Jaap, a suave, lanky business student with a condescending smile and an air of effortless superiority, was on the ground floor. Dirk, an ebullient Marxist with a boisterous manner and a jovial laugh who was studying sociology, was on the second floor. André, the helpful medical student, was on the floor below me. That left only the first floor, but, heaped with rubble and plaster, it was such a shambles that it seemed beyond repair.

It wasn't until two months later, after the rest of the house was at least habitable, that the subject of the first floor was broached again.

'We shouldn't leave it like this,' remarked Jaap, who, like the others, spoke astonishingly good English. 'It'll only attract tramps.'

Unaware of the irony of his words, and little suspecting what was about to happen there, we nailed a curtain across its door, put glass in its front windows, and forgot about it.

As winter set in, and it started to freeze in the garret, I spent much of my time in cafés. I wasn't the only one. Amsterdam had one of the liveliest café cultures in Europe, as there were numerous people in their thirties, forties and even fifties who were employed in bars at night and so had plenty of spare time during the day. The first café I patronised was De Reijnders, a cosy establishment in the Leidseplein, one of Amsterdam's busiest squares. It had a sandy floor, wooden chairs and tables, and huge mirrors reflecting light from low, pearl-coloured globes. In the centre there was a warm *kachel* with a pipe going through the ceiling, and at the back there was a billiards room with a green baize table. Many of the waiters, who, with their white shirts and black aprons, looked as if they had stepped straight out of a Parisian café, had old-fashioned handlebar moustaches and black hair parted in the middle. It was predominantly Dutch-speaking, and it was crowded with regulars, although foreigners occasionally dropped in for a look. Initially I knew no one, but I didn't mind, as I simply ensconced myself by the *kachel*, learning Dutch from a grammar book or scribbling short stories in my notebook. As twilight fell on the misty December afternoons, I spent hours observing passers-by in the Leidseplein, where Christmas lights were being hung in trees. Within a few weeks, I had been introduced to a group of people who came in after work. They were, again like most Dutch, affable and multilingual, and they spoke to me in English, but soon they reverted to Dutch, which I was still at a loss to understand.

Then there was the Amsterdamsch Litterair Café on Kloveniersgracht. It was similar to De Reijnders, but it was more restful, except for Sunday after-noons, when there was a jazz band. Up steps from the narrow pavement, its entrance was plastered with posters for jazz concerts and art exhibitions. You could eat there, and behind the bar was a blackboard with a chalk menu that changed from day to day. In the basement there was a cramped, but excel-lent, bookshop, although nearly all the books were in Dutch. The café had a less regular clientele than De Reijnders, and the majority of its patrons were artists, photographers or writers. Because they mainly spoke Dutch, however, I ensconced myself in the bay window overlooking the canal, idly watching bicycles drift by on the cobbled street, or gazing at billowing white clouds becalmed in the ultramarine sky.

Finally there was the chess café, the most famous in Amsterdam, just off the Leidseplein. On the corner of a street running over with Italian pizzerias, Indonesian restaurants and porn shops, it had a semi-permanent fug of smoke and was frequented by unkempt, unshaven men. The game was taken extremely seriously and players sat hunched over chessboards while onlookers stood round offering unsolicited advice or, after the game ended, arguing excitedly about a move. The standard was abnormally high, as many cafés in Amsterdam had chess sets for their customers, and the Netherlands – astoundingly for such a small country – had not only several masters but also two world-class grandmasters. I found playing there a humbling experience; even though I had given up the game after I left school, I still considered myself to be a formidable player, yet time and time again I was roundly defeated. Once, I even took the train to the internationally famous annual Wijk aan Zee tournament. Situated on the coast to the north of Amsterdam, it was held in some buildings in the lee of the vast Hoogovens steel and aluminium complex, whose gigantic chimneys belched plumes of acrid smoke high into the air. But I didn't enjoy the tournament, where clusters of lonely-looking men gazed at wall-mounted television screens on which games and end-positions were being played or analysed.

After hanging about cafés for a few months, I got my first job in Amsterdam. Four floors above Damplein, it was in the bakery of the Bijenkorf, the city's biggest, and best, department store.

In the beginning, I ferried cakes on a trolley from the bakery to the self-service café and restaurant on the third floor. The cakes, which were laden with freshly whipped cream, were mouth-watering, specifically those topped with strawberries, raspberries and blackcurrants. Then, when my short-term contract expired, I got another job in the Bijenkorf. This time it was picking the tops off strawberries in the bakery on the fifth floor, where so many different nationalities were working that no one could make head nor tail of what anyone else was saying.

One afternoon, after I had been asked to push a trolley laden with cakes to the restaurant, I heard the sound of shouting float up from the street, followed by the wail of police sirens. Curious, I hastened to the window and looked down. Far below, I could make out dozens of people scattering across Damplein, pursued by units of the *Mobiele Eenheid* (ME – riot police). It was the start of the *ontruimings* (evictions) of the Nieuwmarkt …

In the mid-1970s, Amsterdam's council had embarked on a major restructuring of the city. This entailed razing large swathes of the Nieuwmarkt, a deep-rooted community that the council had allowed to decay in order to build a metro and a motorway through it. The *krakers* (squatters), who had occupied scores of condemned buildings, rejected the plan out of hand. After negotiations between the two sides had reached deadlock, the *krakers*, in preparation for being evicted, had fortified many of the houses and constructed perilous walkways that connected the rooftops.

Of course, I identified with the *krakers* – being one myself – so, the minute I completed my shift, I dashed down to Damplein. By now it had returned to normality, although scuffles and skirmishes were taking place all around the adjoining red-light district, where demonstrators were hurling cobblestones at the hated ME, who were trying to seal off barricaded houses in the Nieuwmarkt. It was the first time I had seen the riot police in action, and, with their white helmets, visors, shields, batons and pistols, they were a chilling sight. Coursing with adrenaline, I was lifted off my feet and carried towards the Nieuwmarkt by a mass of onlookers and sympathisers with the *krakers*. Then, without provocation, the ME charged the crowd and indiscriminately started beating everybody with their batons.

Carried away with indignation, I reached for an orange in my pocket and flung it at one of them. All at once, a man standing beside me – presumably a plainclothes policeman – punched me on the nose. Caught unawares, and swabbing it with my bloodstained handkerchief, I withdrew to the rear of the mob, where I watched the battle rage for an hour. By nightfall the ME had successfully blocked off the Nieuwmarkt with lines of police vans. Beyond, the scene was like a medieval siege, with units of riot police trying to scale thirty-foot ladders to the rooftops, where dozens of masked protestors rained bags of flour, paint, water-bombs and tiles down on to the massed helmets below. Eventually, after another two hours of mayhem, the remaining *krakers* had been evicted, and cranes wielding giant wrecking balls ripped down the rooftop walkways before, to the taunts of the jeering multitude, they demolished the houses.

Shortly after the Nieuwmarkt *ontruiming*, I made my first friend in Amsterdam. Strangely enough, it was Jonathan, a striking-looking man in his mid-twenties who, with his classical cheekbones and a sensuous mouth, resembled Rudolf Nureyev. I hadn't particularly warmed to him when I had known him briefly in Edinburgh, where he had been a cult figure on account of his being assistant director of its most avant-garde theatre. He had taken one of its plays to the Mickery, an equally prestigious experimental theatre in Amsterdam, but, by the time its run ended, he had so fallen in love with the city that he, like myself, had chosen to stay on. Although he wasn't gay – he had a young son whom he hardly ever saw – he was camping out on the settee of two gay theatre directors, who lived in an all-white, tasteful apartment on a bend in the Prinsengracht. Now we discovered that we had a lot in common: both of us were exiles from Scotland; both of us were interested in writing; and neither of us knew many people in Amsterdam.

At first we met in the neighbouring Café De Prins, one of Amsterdam's so-called *bruin cafés*, on account of their dark brown wood and smoke-stained walls. Like all the others, it was easy-going and very casual, and, as it was tranquil in the afternoons, it was a good place to discuss our writing and relationships in general. A few months earlier I had begun *The Sound of Breaking Glass*, a collection of short stories about people who had impressed me in my life. He had recently completed a play, and he had just begun a relationship with Kika, a gamine, twenty-five-year-old actress with chestnut hair. The daughter of one of Dutch television's best-loved personalities, she lived in a modest terraced house behind the Rijksmuseum. Soon Jonathan moved in and, as they both enjoyed cooking, they often invited me round to dinner.

One day, she took Jonathan and me down to meet her father. After being divorced, he had become one of the first actors in the country to publicly acknowledge his homosexuality. Then he had given up his career to follow Bhagwan Shree Rajneesh, the cult Indian guru, and now he lived with his partner in the south of the Netherlands. There, surrounded by flat, poplar-lined fields, he lived in a sprawling farmhouse whose steeply sloping ochre roof almost reached the ground. A delicate-looking, theatrical man with cascading hair and a crusty, witty face, he delighted in telling jokes and amusing anecdotes. He had just come back from his guru's ashram in Poona, and he wore a sannyasin's orange-coloured robes, and beads and a locket containing Bhagwan's photograph round his neck. A year later, the relationship between Jonathan and Kika broke up, and he left Amsterdam to study at a college in England. After that, I lost contact with him and I thought – mistakenly – that our paths would never cross again.

After Jonathan left Amsterdam, I saw a great deal of Nico, a bony, gangling psychology student who lived in the adjoining house on the Kerkstraat. Like number 386, it had four floors, although my garret overlooked that of a timid, twenty-year-old philosophy student. But, unlike our house, it was an official *kraakpand* (squat), since everyone paid a nominal rent to the council, and it had mains electricity, gas and water. It was also organised on more collective lines, because the residents had knocked the two rooms on the ground floor into a communal kitchen cum sitting room that was almost as big as a church hall. Nico's room on the first floor was homely and spilling over with plants and LPs. He was very congenial, and he had an equally amiable ginger Alsatian, from whom he was inseparable. He had lived in Birmingham for several years and his English was so fluent he even spoke with a Brummie accent. On sunny days we knocked a tennis ball over a net full of holes that we stretched across the Amstelveld, a public space behind an eighteenth-century clapboard church on the other side of the Utrechtsestraat.

The Kerkstraat, an attractive street of early twentieth-century, red-brick gabled houses, had an unbeatable location between the Keizersgracht and the Prinsengracht, two of the city's four exquisite canals that curve in four long concentric circles around the heart of Amsterdam. Here, both canals were singularly enchanting, as they were crammed with houseboats and converted barges, while at the end of the street, only a hundred yards away, was the Magere Brug (the city's famed white drawbridge across the River Amstel), which still opens to allow barges and sailing craft through.

A hundred yards at the other end of the street was the Utrechtsestraat, a narrow thoroughfare full of inviting restaurants, high-quality delicatessens, casual boutiques and cafés. In the middle of the street, tram number four rattled east to the Rembrandtsplein, the Dam and Centraal station, and west to the Albert Cuyp, Europe's largest open-air market.

But I was also exploring the rest of Amsterdam. There was the Jordaan, in those days a down-at-heel quarter with little canals and bridges, and quirky shops specialising in tin toys and knick-knacks. There was the Museumplein, at the top of which was the incomparable Rijksmuseum and streets chock-full with art galleries and antiquarian bookshops. Nearby were the Stedelijk and van Gogh museums, which housed two of Europe's best collections of modern art. Opposite were the Concertgebouw, the home to the famous Royal Concertgebouw Orchestra, and the Café de Keizer, a grandiose Viennese-style café patronised by its musicians. There were the tourist areas, such as the Dam, the Leidseplein and the red-light district. Centred on the picturesque, tree-lined Achterburgwal, one of Amsterdam's most beautiful canals, it was so scenic that I often cycled there at night. There, I would hang over one of the miniature bridges, watching neon lights dance on the inky water and the tourists thronging the pornography shops, live sex shows and scantily clad prostitutes who, framed by draped curtains, sat on high stools in the red-lit windows that lined the narrow, cobbled canal.

All the same, however much I enjoyed the city's traditional attractions and the canals, it was underground Amsterdam that attracted me the most. Although the city had passed its peak compared to the days of the *kabouters* (the radical movement in the mid-1960s), in the early 1970s it was still an extraordinary place to live in. The counterculture had three predominant hubs – the Melkweg, the Paradiso and the Kosmos. The Melkweg was an avant-garde multimedia centre in an ex-dairy factory off the Leidseplein; the Paradiso was the centre for punk music in a nearby converted church; and the Kosmos was a centre for eastern mysticism near Centraal station on Prins Hendrikade.

At the beginning, because I couldn't stand the raw aggression of punk music and I had temporarily lost my interest in spirituality, I went to the Melkweg. It was a continual hotbed of activity. On the ground floor were a café–restaurant, a market with stalls selling second-hand clothes and bric-à-brac, and the *oude zaal* (old hall) for music concerts. Upstairs was a cinema where you reclined on cushions on the floor, the *theezaal* (tea room), and the *theaterzaal* (theatre hall) for dance and theatre performances. At the weekend, the market, which reminded me of the souk in Marrakech, was an astounding scene, with hundreds of hippies wandering about the stalls, or queuing at the tea counter for 'space' (marijuana) cake. To one side was a minuscule bookshop and, at the entrance to the market, the house dealer, the only person in the building authorised to sell marijuana, did a roaring trade at his table. The market was swarming with outlandish-looking characters, the best of which was the hippy who resembled an Afghan warrior. He had a fiery face, a bristly moustache, blazing eyes, along with shoulder-length, flame-coloured hair and baggy trousers, a flowing white robe, an amethyst waistcoat, shoes upturned at the toes, a turban, and a scimitar dangling from his jewel-encrusted belt.

As well as the Melkweg, the Paradiso and the Kosmos, there were other captivating places in Amsterdam. In the Vondelpark, joggers, cyclists and roller skaters wove in and out of paths congested with promenading lovers, and, in the summer, teenagers lay on the grass smoking marijuana, throwing Frisbees and strumming guitars. Further along, beside a gushing fountain and ducks preening their feathers near a pond, people reclined under sun umbrellas in an outdoor café or meandered past stalls selling junk and trinkets. In the middle of the park was an outdoor theatre where, on Sunday afternoons, there was a rock band, followed by the Friends Roadshow, an outrageous and talented American street theatre group who whipped up jam-packed audiences with their clowning and calls for 'the revolution'.

Then there was the annual, two-week International Festival of Fools. This took place in a number of venues. One was on the other side of the river from Centraal station, where magicians, acrobats and comedians performed on the stage of a huge open-air amphitheatre. Another was the Spiegeltent, a round pavilion with a canvas roof that was erected every year in the huge open grassy space that is Museumplein. Inside, it had dozens of mirrors, an ornate bar, an art nouveau chandelier and wooden booths radiating from a circular floor where Europe's best street theatre companies presented hilarious, subversive shows. The main venue for the festival, however, was the streets of the city itself, where, in every corner, there were jesters, jugglers and clowns on stilts, while transvestites wearing metallic-grey bodices, metallic-grey angels' wings, and metallic-grey hats made of upturned lampshades tottered along on twelve-inch platform heels.

Once, an incident occurred in the Albert Cuyp market that confirmed why I so loved Amsterdam and the Dutch. Every week, I wheeled my bicycle down past fruit and vegetables stalls to the fish section, where I bought the cheap mackerel on which I practically lived. One Saturday morning, after I'd wheeled my bicycle up to the busy main street, the cardboard box containing my week's provisions toppled off the back and spilled onto the road. Without braking, a man in a slow-moving line of cars deliberately drove over them, before he accelerated to a nearby set of traffic lights. Unluckily for him, he hadn't anticipated these would change to red. Livid, I was about to chase after him, but I didn't have to. The Dutch are famous for their love of cycling, and Amsterdam, with its traffic lights and lanes for cyclists, is one of the most bicycle-friendly cities on the planet. In the twinkling of an eye, passers-by who had observed what had happened, raced up and started hammering on his window. For an instant, I thought they were going to drag him out of the car and lynch him, before the lights changed and, visibly traumatised, he raced off at high speed.

When I wasn't in cafés or the Melkweg, I spent much of my time in the Moor. A casual, informal club in a seedy alley in the red-light district, it held classes in jazz dance and photography. In theory, it was private, although to gain admission you merely had to sign your name in a book. To the left of the entrance was a dimly lit bar with high stools around a counter; to the right was a cosy tearoom with low-hanging lampshades, where people in deep, snug armchairs played chess and backgammon in a fug of marijuana smoke at tables covered with imitation Persian rugs. It was at one of these that I ran into Jan and Ethan. Jan was a softly spoken Dutchman with soulful eyes who spoke English with a heavy Dutch accent and received a lavish state subsidy to support his career as a painter. Ethan was an American from Seattle who had been in the Netherlands for ten years. Prematurely bald with spectacles, he mumbled in staccato sentences through his unkempt, walrus moustache. He spoke fluent Dutch but, despite having a degree in ecology, could only eke out a paltry living doing translations.

Like myself, they were in their late twenties, and both of them were married, although I hardly ever met their wives. We would play chess in the Moor, and then go back to the Kerkstraat, where, over pots of tea and smokes, we talked until the early hours of the morning. We talked about everything: good and evil; freewill versus determinism; how to transform society; personal growth; relationships; football, music and sex. But our friendship wasn't merely cerebral; on Sundays we kicked a ball about in the Vondelpark before we adjourned to Ethan's nearby house for his specially baked apple pie. One particularly icy winter, when the canals froze over and looked more magical than ever, the three of us took the bus to Edam, where we strapped on long, wooden, traditional skates and glided round a pond. Regrettably, a year later, Ethan and his Dutch wife moved to the south of the Netherlands, where he had finally succeeded in getting a well-paid job measuring the environmental effects of a new dam on the habitat of local wildlife. Jan, who stopped going to the Moor, persevered in his career as a painter, and I lost contact with him. However, I was later flabbergasted to learn that for years he had been making fraudulent claims for social security – he had always struck me as having unimpeachable integrity – and had had to repay an enormous sum to the tax authorities.

I had other friends. Aldo was an Italian anarchist, poet and painter with long, fuzzy black hair and a beard who rented a cavernous studio on the Prinsengracht that was packed with his drawings, etchings and paintings.

In the 1960s, he had been part of the underground scene in Rome, but now he had been living for ten years in Amsterdam, to which he had fled in the early 1970s, after being incarcerated in an Italian psychiatric hospital for – or so he maintained – possessing merely a gramme of marijuana. Only five-foot-five and in his mid-thirties, he had receding bushy black hair and a bushy black beard, and he too patronised the Moor. Most of the time, he roosted on a stool in the tearoom, talking animatedly to strangers or drawing in pocket-sized notebooks. In addition, he frequently sang his own songs. First he would sound a tiny Buddhist gong and play a few plaintive notes on a flute, before he attacked the only three chords he could strum on the guitar. He obviously enjoyed being an exile in bohemian Amsterdam, and his songs, whose key words he repeated ad nauseam, expressed his implacable hostility towards the state and the Catholic Church, but he also sang of his unrequited love for a Dutch woman and his yearning for Italy, to which he couldn't return. By and large, he sang in Italian and, aware of its soft, sonorous vowels, he would linger lovingly over every 'a', although he every once in a while switched to Dutch, when, given the difficulty of pronouncing its harsh, guttural consonants, he sounded – to me, at least – rather comical.

He regularly came round to the Kerkstraat, where he cooked spaghetti and gushed about his love for the Dutch woman. He had an idealised image of me and was sure I was going to be a great writer.

'Patreek Reachardson, the 'enry Meeler [Henry Miller] of Amsterdam, leeving in 'ees garret in the sky!' he would cry theatrically.

The truth was, he was far more prolific than myself, and at intervals I caught a glimpse of him riding his rusty black bicycle to small, independent bookshops to sell his booklets and comic strips. These he published himself in Dutch under the title Vrije Vogel Pers (Free Bird Press), with the front page stamped 'Tristam Da Cunha, Trip around the World through Four Centuries'. Inside were dozens of sketches of expressionist-looking city skylines, silhouetted black under a low-hanging moon, and Chagall-like drawings of fish, birds, snakes and heads of people seated in toy-like cars. These mostly illustrated his rejection of the family and capitalism, but others, such as Psychiatry, or The Death of the Soul, were tirades against conventional psychiatry and labels such as 'schizophrenic'.

Then there were my Dutch friends. Rob and Marijan were the friends of Sebastian and Aidan on whose attic floor in the red-light district I had slept when I had first come over from London. Rob was a paraplegic confined to a wheelchair after he had broken his back several years previously while playing football. Marijan had a part-time job with the Vietnam Solidarity Campaign. By now they had moved to a more accessible, first-floor apartment behind the Mozes en Aäronkerk, the white baroque church on the Waterlooplein. Rob was admirably stoical about his condition, and he spent the day devouring European literature. Their best friends were Robbie and Tommy, two brothers who lived with their cats in a subsided apartment overlooking the litter-strewn Lijnbaansgracht. Opposite the Heineken brewery, the apartment was overflowing with rows and rows of LPs. Robbie was a benign, avuncular giant, who didn't seem to be interested in women and spent his free time watching football on TV, drinking beer and cataloguing on a computer his vast collection of beer mats. Although he was employed in the housing department of the council, he was staunchly left-wing and sympathised with the *kraak beweging* (the squatters' movement). Tommy, his younger brother, was a tall, spare, boyish-looking young man in his mid-twenties who worked alongside him in the council. He was less political than Robbie and, in his spare time, was the lead guitarist in a rock band.

They were both fond of cooking and they occasionally invited me round for a meal, although I went mainly to watch the Dutch football team, most of all when it was playing West Germany, its redoubtable arch-rival, in the European Championships or the World Cup. Because of the Nazi invasion of the Netherlands during the Second World War, Robbie and Tommy were, like many Dutch, vehemently anti-German. To their disgust, the Dutch routinely lost, even though they had an exceptional team at the time that reached the semi-finals and finals of both tournaments. One day, to his delight, Robbie found a girlfriend. The pair went out together for over a year, until suddenly she switched her allegiance and started going out with Tommy; amazingly it didn't affect the relationship of the two brothers, who remained almost umbilically linked. Then, thirty years later, Robbie tragically contracted motor neuron disease, from which he suffered with unforgettable, inspiring dignity for two years until a humane doctor mercifully helped him to end his life.

Last but not least, there was Barry, who owned a second-hand paperback bookshop on the Kloveniersgracht. An American in his fifties, he was as bald as an egg, apart from a few strands of hair brushed back on the sides of his bony head, and he had an aquiline nose and a deeply lined forehead.

From San Francisco, where he had known the Beat poets in the 1950s, he had fetched up in Amsterdam in the early 1960s. Now he perched every day on a high stool behind a counter overlooking the canal. He was hardly ever without a cigarette, and, with sharp intakes of breath, he was forever exchanging repartee with his faithful clientele. He had a jaded, world-weary air, and if you weren't careful it was easy to find yourself at the receiving end of his rapier wit and acerbic comments. The bookshop was long and only ten-feet wide and had shelves groaning with thousands of literary paperbacks. Barry was phenomenally well read, and if he didn't have the book you were looking for, it wasn't worth having. For a long time, he had owned the bookshop with a fellow Californian, until they had fallen out acrimoniously and his ex-partner had set up his own bookshop near Café de Prins. Barry spent hours every night drinking beer and listening to jazz with friends in the Litterair Café, directly opposite the bookshop and just round the corner from his apartment on the narrow, tree-lined Groenburgwal.

The bookshop had such a comprehensive selection of English and American literature that I bought all my paperbacks there. Since I had arrived in Amsterdam, I had been reading insatiably, chiefly outsiders such as Paul Bowles, Henry Miller and Charles Bukowski, and by now I was sure I wanted to write. In contrast to my decision to learn the guitar, this desire emanated from a profound inner compulsion that had been germinating for the last three years, but I must have inherited some of it from my mother. She had loved literature and poetry – she could recite whole stanzas by Siegfried Sassoon, Hilaire Belloc, Yeats and Wilfred Owen verbatim – since she was a teenager, when she was attracted to remarkably handsome young men in the literary world. One of her first boyfriends had been J.I.M. Stewart, who, under the pseudonym Michael Innes, later became critically acclaimed for his crime novels, and she had also been very close to Hubert Nicholson, of course, who had been friends with the perenially bearded G.B. Shaw, the Sitwells, W.H. Auden and Dylan Thomas. Another of her admirers had been A.J.P. Taylor, the illustrious historian and author who subsequently became, like his friend J.I.M. Stewart, a distinguished academic at Oxford University.

During the 1930s, when she had been a journalist, and again during the Second World War, women's magazines had even published a few

of her poems. Then, after she had a family, she had given up writing for publication, although that didn't stop her compulsion to write. In graphically written diaries she described how she had 'bathed naked at midnight in Lake Garda in Italy, where I lay in a moonlit vineyard eating grapes'; watched the sun 'dip like a tangerine beneath the horizon in the Bay of Naples'; and 'danced, in a blue frock the colour of a summer sky, with a handsome cavalry officer at Lake Balaton in Hungary'. Later, when she travelled abroad with or without my father, she inundated her friends with postcards overflowing with descriptions of 'glittering villages as white as wedding-cakes in Greece', 'ancient, black-shawled crones seated on donkeys' in Spain, and 'little withered men with faces like dried walnuts in Morocco'. If her friends were going somewhere she had been, she supplied them with detailed instructions on how to get there, how long it would take, where to stay, where to eat, what to do during the day and at night, and where to go thereafter.

My father and his family, beyond doubt, also played a role in my growing desire to become a writer. Before the Second World War he had also been a journalist, of course, and, later, editor of an agricultural magazine. But perhaps even more seminal was the influence of my grandfather, Henry Marriot Richardson, who always wore a bow tie and smoked a pipe.

As part of his trade union work, he knew the press barons Lord Beaver-brook, Lord Northcliffe and Lord Rothermere, as well as the writers H.G. Wells and G.K. Chesterton.

But, in addition, he had been a writer and dramatist, and had written thrillers such as *The Temple Murders* and plays such as *The Sword of Justice.* Some of the latter were staged in Manchester, and his books sold so well that the royalties, which his wife kept receiving for years after he died, subsidised the family's holidays in Dimchurch in Kent, where they lodged with the famous actress Dame Sybil Thorndike.

Now, set on completing a manuscript for the first time, I sat every day at my desk by the window working on *The Sound of Breaking Glass.* Even so, it was painfully slow going, as, at the same time, I was also teaching myself to touch-type, something I found so frustrating that in a fit of frustration I twice hurled the typewriter across the garret, and had to buy a new one. Sometimes, I did nothing but watch swallows screech through giant chestnut trees in the back garden, or gaze over the rooftops to the distant turrets of the Rijksmuseum. Sometimes, when my writing wasn't flowing and I was downhearted, I simply smoked some marijuana and sank into oblivion on my mattress on the floor in the corner. That summer the weather was dry and hot for six weeks, so I frequently sunbathed on my 'balcony'. Initially that was extremely hazardous, as it was in reality only the flat roof of André's kitchen, and there was nothing to prevent me from plunging forty feet below to the back garden. However, after I constructed a fence around it from cracked wooden doors I found in skips, it became such a suntrap that it was like being in the Mediterranean.

A year flashed past, during which, in addition to going the Litterair Café, I started patronising the Frascati, a café in an alley off the Rokin. Patronised by the fashionable media set, with its white walls and parlour palms it could have been something out of Scott Fitzgerald's *The Great Gatsby.* White globes suspended from the ceiling suffused the walls with a warm, mellow glow. Clean-cut young men with chiselled jaws, fair hair, and wearing cream tennis pullovers and striped blazers conversed languidly with suntanned, leggy women with blonde hair. Modish couples on stools at the bar sipped cocktails before going to the evening performance of the theatre next door.

I also went to the American Hotel, a stunning art nouveau establishment off the Leidseplein. Outside, it didn't look particularly special, but the Café

Américain on the ground floor, with its stained-glass windows, gold leaf frescoes and glittering chandeliers, was fabulous, and one of the most refined places in Amsterdam to be seen in.

Waiters in white shirts, bow ties and black aprons bustled about with silver trays laden with pots of coffee. In the centre was a glass hexagonal island, where a chef in a tall white hat presided over tastefully displayed dishes of salmon, roast beef, luscious fruit salads and succulent delicacies. But at the same time it was surprisingly democratic, with penniless students and scruffy artists at baize reading desks mingling with theatregoers in black ties who were heading for the Stadtsschowburg, Amsterdam's municipal theatre, on the other side of the tram tracks. Indeed it was such a prestigious place that aspiring young writers were reputed to ask reception to repeatedly announce their names on the Tannoy to give the impression they were in constant demand.

One night, I was ascending the vertiginous wooden stairs to the garret when I detected the glow of a lamp from inside the first floor, which had lain vacant for months. Curious to discover what was going on, I drew aside the drape over the door. Inside, all I could make out was a mountain of orange boxes stacked against the rough walls.

'They're for the ceiling,' a self-assured voice announced in flawless English.

All of a sudden, I found myself facing a broad-shouldered, powerfully built young man in his early twenties. He had unkempt reddish hair down to his shoulders, a reddish beard, and, as he balanced skilfully on two wooden beams, there was a twinkle of amusement in his brown eyes, and a playful smile flickered at the corners of his mouth.

'Who're you?' I enquired.

'Ruud. I'm moving in here,' came the reply. 'Didn't the others tell you?'

They hadn't, but I didn't hang about to find out more. Beginning at 5 a.m., I had a job shovelling concrete by arc lights on a construction site and I needed a good night's sleep. I didn't get it. Ruud, recently dropped out of university, burst upon the house like a bomb. Without any warning, wires, cables and ropes sprouted like mushrooms on the first floor and at times it felt as if the very foundations of the building were shaking as the sound of drilling, hammering and sawing reverberated through the Kerkstraat. Outside, a forest of planks piled up on the pavement, although by midnight they had been cleared away and it had been swept cleaner than before.

At last, after six weeks, Ruud had completed his rebuilding. The following evening, he invited us to dinner, and the four of us trooped into his room. The transformation was remarkable. Overhead, where there had been broken laths and dangling plaster, was a ceiling made from orange boxes. Frayed curtains sagged at the windows, and a threadbare carpet covered the floorboards. Boxes of rumpled clothes were stacked underneath bookshelves groaning with books, there were plants in every corner, and candles cast shadows over a chipped table set for five.

'Welcome,' declared Ruud, beaming.

During the meal, he proposed that we improve the rest of the house. It seemed a good idea, so, over the next months, we painted the front door dark brown and the pillars and windows pale green. We pumped three feet of water out of the flooded cellar with a generator that Ruud hired, and converted it into a bicycle workshop. We cleared out the back garden, which was buried beneath mounds of rubble, ten loads of which Ruud transported in a hired van to the nearby dump. Before long, in its place was a 'patio', complete with a table, chairs and a trellis that Ruud had draped with plants.

When we had finished, Ruud proposed that, because Sonya, Dirk's new girlfriend, was also looking for somewhere to live, we move operations a hundred yards further along to the only single-storey house in the street. Abandoned and derelict, it was virtually surrounded by concrete gaps choked with weeds, and rebuilding it would be a mammoth task. But everybody wanted to do it for Sonya. A five-foot-six, olive-skinned, twenty-eight-year-old of Lithuanian extraction, she had flashing eyes and intense features and she wasn't afraid to get her hands dirty. So we removed mountainous piles of debris, we unblocked the drains and sewage pipes, and we even cobbled together a makeshift shower, until in the end the house was habitable, although it was as damp as a marsh and plagued by mosquitoes.

One mild evening, we were lazing about in the 'patio', having a barbecue.

In the corner, a chicken rotated lazily on an improvised spit in a sandpit that Ruud had built. After a while, he and Dirk rose to their feet and disappeared, re-emerging thirty minutes later with two crates of beer.

'Where did those come from?' enquired Sonya.

'Ruud and I liberated them from the all-night supermarket,' answered Dirk proudly.

'Well, I don't agree with stealing,' she commented disapprovingly.

'We're not stealing,' he shot back, looking flustered. 'The system exploits us so we're getting our own back.'

'Look, if you don't like society, you should change it,' she said.

'You can't. First it's got to be destroyed.'

'Godverdomme!' Sonya cried. 'Those're just words.'

'So what do you suggest?'

'Get out altogether,' a no-nonsense voice interjected. The fire flared and lit up our faces as we all turned towards Ruud.

'What are you trying to say?' said Jaap caustically, snorting like a horse.

'Go travelling.'

'Where?'

'Africa, for example.'

Jaap flashed his bland, simpering smile. 'And where exactly do you intend to get the money to go there?'

'Work for it. '

'How?'

Ruud deliberated and, with a hint of impatience, helped himself to another beer. 'Jaap,' he sighed, 'if you want to do something you do it, you don't sit around and think of the reasons not to do it.'

Jaap stiffened. Then he drew himself up to his full height. 'Ruud,' he drawled disdainfully, 'if you are so keen on the idea, what's stopping you?' He wheeled to face the others and gesticulated. 'Or any of you, come to that?'

Ruud stared at the embers before he examined calluses on his palms. 'Nothing,' he mused. There was a pause, until he too turned and cast his eyes quizzically at everyone 'All right, what do you think?'

'I'm with Ruud,' answered Dirk.

'Me too,' added Sonya.

I was on excellent terms with them all, although Dirk, Jaap and André remained acquaintances rather than friends.

'So am I,' I said.

That night Ruud expounded his plan. It was highly ambitious. André wanted to continue with his studies, but Dirk, Jaap and Sonya would drop out of university. All of us apart from André would contribute a fifth of the cost towards purchasing a second-hand van. Then we would drive it across Europe to Greece, ship it to Egypt, and follow the Nile to the Sudan before we crossed into Ethiopia. First, though, there were practical tasks to be addressed. Sonya would handle all the visas, health certificates and necessary documents for the van. Jaap, Dirk and I would work to raise funds for the journey. Ruud, who professed to know 'a little' about cars, would buy and equip the van.

Within days the plan swung into action. It was much easier than expected. After Jaap's initial reservations, there were no great discussions. None of us knew why we set our sights on Ethiopia – it simply struck us as being different – or wondered what we would do when we got there or after we got back. Ruud and Dirk believed it would be a revolutionary act. Jaap reckoned it would be romantic. Sonya was only at university because she couldn't think of anything else to do. I had a job stripping empty houses for Nico's father, who owned a family construction company in Purmerend, a nearby dormitory town, and, because I had as good as stopped writing, I leaped at the chance of going travelling again.

Within a week, Jaap had found a job as a waiter and Dirk was employed in a bakery. I carried on working for Nico's father. Every afternoon, by the time we had returned to the house, Sonya had prepared an evening meal on the first floor, which had become the focus of operations. There would be a spray of fresh flowers and a home-baked cake on the table as well, and if she couldn't be present she wrote a note telling us to leave the dishes for her to do the following day. When the meal was finished, we pored over maps on the wall, calculating mileages and planning schedules. It was going to be an exceedingly challenging journey, as the region was politically volatile and beset with internecine conflicts, especially in Sudan and Eritrea.

Ruud wasn't worried.

'Providing we don't argue, everything'll be OK,' he proclaimed in his customary sanguine manner. Then he turned towards me with a winning smile. 'And don't forget we've got Patrick, who's an experienced traveller.'

Despite being flattered by his belief in me, I wasn't sure I shared his optimism. There were manifold things to go awry. Apart from myself, hardly anyone had been outside the Netherlands. Sonya and I were appreciably older than the others. Then there was the difference in personalities. Ruud radiated such authority you felt that anything was possible, while Dirk, who was the same age as Ruud, came over as a mere boy in comparison. Jaap, educated at one of the country's most famous schools, was poised and charming, but getting to know him was like peeling an orange, only to discover that it had an infinite number of skins. Nor was I easy to get on with, because I wasn't accustomed to living with others, and I could be very intense and moody, as Ruud, who clearly saw my weaker side, intuitively knew.

'Don't make life too complicated,' he said to me once, smiling sympathetically.

But the biggest obstacle was going to be the group's gender. Four men and one woman wasn't the ideal travelling combination, especially as everybody would be cooped up with each other for prolonged periods of time. Moreover, after only two months, Dirk's love affair with Sonya was already in trouble. When she was a child, her parents had packed her off to a convent near Rotterdam, after which they had pressurised her into marrying a comfortably off, but uninteresting, vet. He had taken her to his tranquil country practice, where he had provided her with a four-bedroom house, a garden the size of football field, and two cars. Three years later, bored and dejected, she had divorced him and gone to Amsterdam, where she had enrolled as a psychology student at university. There, she had first met Dirk, who had impressed her with his ebullience. Now infatuated with her, he smothered her with demonstrations of his love, a distinctly misguided thing to do with someone recently out of a failed marriage. Worse, the more maddening she found him, the better she got on with Ruud, whose infectious humour had her in stitches. Dirk, to his credit, sought to take it in good spirits, but his mirthless laugh hinted that, in the near future, there were going to be problems between the two of them.

One weekend, I went with Ruud to collect the van that he had settled on buying. It was a crisp spring morning and fluffy white clouds chased each other across the aqua-blue sky. For an hour, we cycled out of Amsterdam and along the River Amstel. Water lapped against barges lining the banks of the river, which gleamed like a mirror in the glaring sunlight. In the distance, triangular farm roofs jutted like pyramids over the flat horizon. Black-

and-white cows grazed in green polders, and herons stood one-legged in bulrushes. A farmer rode by on a tractor, his clogs caked with mud.

Abruptly, Ruud braked outside the crumbling fence of a used car depot. Inside was a jumble of vehicles with no wheels and their doors hanging off. Ruud approached a tumbledown hut, where a grimy mechanic was snoring by the window.

Ruud shook him by the shoulder, until he woke with a start.

'Wij zijn voor het Hanomag gekommen,' Ruud began.

'A Hanomag!' I exclaimed. They were the incredibly reliable vehicles made by the truck division of Daimler Benz.

'Goed, komt met mij,' the mechanic answered. He escorted us to the back of the yard. 'Kijk,' he said. 'Twee duizend gulden.'

My heart sank as he gestured to a grey, moss-encrusted van in a corner. It had no windscreen, a rust-eaten chassis, and one of its doors was missing.

'Ruud, you haven't bought this?' I enquired incredulously.

'Wait,' rejoined Ruud, 'you'll see.'

Amazingly, its engine still functioned, and, after we put our bicycles inside, Ruud drove it back to the Kerkstraat, where he parked it outside the front door. In the following weeks, using oxyacetylene tools he borrowed from the obliging mechanic whose workshop and garage was opposite the house, he cut out oxidised metal from the bodywork and welded in new panels. He dismantled and reassembled the dynamo, and fitted new shock absorbers, a new water cooler and a new distributor. He stripped the inside of the van, where he built a mini kitchen complete with cupboards, benches and a table. He rewired the electrical system, installed a short-wave radio transmitter, and constructed a stereo out of orange boxes.

Indeed Ruud appeared to be capable of doing everything. He could swim like a dolphin and play the guitar expertly, and he had even been one of the Netherlands' most outstanding junior tennis players.

Irrespective of the underlying friction between Sonya and Dirk, preparations for the journey forged steadily ahead. We paid off the Hanomag, which Ruud said was more or less ready. Sonya obtained nearly all the visas and booked the tickets for the ship from Piraeus to Alexandria. Jaap, Dirk and I earned sufficient money for us to be able to travel for three months. Five weeks before we were due to depart Ruud invited Sonya and me, the only ones not working at the time, to accompany him in the van to Luxemburg, where a friend of his had offered us some free spare parts. We were in high spirits as we drove down the motorway into north-east France. It was late summer and a fierce sun seared the undulating countryside. After three hours, Ruud proposed we branch off the motorway and find a secluded spot for lunch, and it wasn't long until we found ourselves in a world of drowsy villages, timbered farmsteads and farmhands driving cows along country roads. Two miles further on we pulled up in a hamlet, merely a church and a jumble of thatched houses with their windows shuttered against the heat. Outside a tavern there were stools under a sun umbrella. We sat down and ordered drinks, which the waiter deposited silently on the table before he slipped back into the cool interior.

It was only then I noticed how close Sonya was sitting next to Ruud, although I didn't pay much attention to it until Ruud stood up.

'We're just going for a walk,' he explained, as if it was the most natural thing on earth for them to do. 'We'll be back soon.'

Before I had time to say anything, they had hurried off down a peaceful country road that lost itself in an ocean of golden wheat. I settled down patiently in my chair and dozed off. I don't know how long I slept, but the moment I came to and noticed that Ruud and Sonya were holding hands and gazing into each other's eyes, I realised that my suspicions were confirmed.

Ruud pre-empted any questions I might have thought of asking.

'We did our best to stop it,' he declared without a hint of embarrassment, 'but we couldn't control ourselves any longer.'

Thrown off balance, I said nothing as we pressed on towards Luxemburg. Oddly enough, I felt relieved, as Ruud was undoubtedly better suited to Sonya than Dirk. We spent the night in Luxemburg, where Ruud and

Sonya shared a bed, and the next day we headed back with the spare parts to Amsterdam. However, as we drew up outside the Kerkstraat at midnight, I experienced a sudden sense of foreboding. Ruud and Sonya had decided to inform Dirk immediately about the weekend's events, so the minute they opened the front door, I scurried upstairs and went to bed. I had barely drawn the blankets over my shoulders when I heard the sound of sobbing and someone pacing to and fro, followed by voices descending the stairs; it was only then it occurred to me that Sonya had simply swapped Dirk's bed on the second floor for Ruud's directly below it.

During the following days, after Sonya gave up her mosquito-infested house to move in with Ruud, the house split into opposing factions. Jaap sided with Dirk, and attacked Ruud and Sonya roundly for their 'irresponsible behaviour'. Sonya defended herself by saying that her break-up with Dirk was bound to happen sooner or later, and it was preferable that it had happened now than in the midst of some godforsaken desert. Dirk, who, if anybody, was justified in feeling aggrieved, was kindness personified towards Ruud and Sonya. However it wasn't difficult to see it was purely a ploy to win her back. Most surprising of all was the reaction of Sonya, who made it plain that she couldn't tolerate Dirk any longer, and the nicer he was towards her the she worse she treated him.

For my part I sought to exercise a moderating influence and build a bridge between the two opposing camps. But it was hopeless, given that even the one relationship that remained intact, that is, between Ruud and Dirk, had crumbled. Two weeks after returning from Luxemburg, the van stood abandoned outside the front door, Sonya had cancelled the tickets for the ship to Egypt, and the memories of our communal meals and all the effort we had invested in rebuilding the house were quickly forgotten. If anyone from the two camps met on the stairs they passed in silence or exchanged a welter of bitter recriminations. I remained friends with Ruud and Sonya, who even proposed that only the three of us go to Ethiopia. For three weeks I mulled it over until, wary of going away by myself with just a couple, I thought better of it. In spite of that, I carried on going down for meals at Ruud's, and from time to time the three of us went out in the van. Indeed we got on so well that, once, after we parked in sand dunes on the coast, they made love so openly in the back that I had the distinct feeling they wouldn't have minded if I had joined in.

I was glad I didn't. One evening, while I was downstairs at Ruud's, I was taken aback when he let drop quite unashamedly that he had syphilis, which was already affecting his little finger. Then – I haven't a clue why – he and Sonya slowly but surely retreated into a world of their own. As they did so, my visits to them became ever more infrequent, until I ceased going altogether, although if I ran into them on the stairs they were always cordial and welcoming. Maybe it was because I felt resentful that Ruud never came up to visit me. Maybe he was put out that I no longer went down to visit him. Maybe it was because a friendship between a single person and a couple seldom lasts for long. Some time afterwards, Dirk and Jaap moved out of the Kerkstraat. Before they left, they asked Ruud to sell the van so that he could return their share of the money, so I too slipped a note under his door, requesting the same. Like them, I heard nothing, until one day, after I noticed the van was no longer outside the front door, I went down to André's and asked him what had happened to it.

'Oh, haven't you heard?' he replied. 'Ruud sold it. He and Sonya have split up and he's gone to the States.'

'What?'

'Yes. He's in Texas, working in a garage to make money to go travelling in South America.'

'So how much did he get for the van?'

'Three times what he paid for it.'

'So where's the money?'

'He took it all. Including Sonya's.'

'What?'

Incensed, that night I went down to Sonya's, where, as usual, she seemed pleased to see me. Although she didn't expand on why she and Ruud had parted company, contrary to all expectation she was supportive of him when I enquired about the money.

'I don't think we should blame him,' she began. 'You know, Ruud wasn't the big, powerful person you all thought he was. Actually, he was the same as the rest of us, except he hid his weaknesses. He thought the three of you were earning more money than you said you were, while there he was, working for nothing. So he took our money. Can you understand that?'

'I suppose so,' I responded grudgingly. Then, after a lull, 'So what are you going to do now?'

'I'm not sure. Stay on here for a bit and see what happens. But it's really good to see you again.'

She was so friendly that once again I started going down to eat with her. One night, after the meal was over, she was perched on the double bed by the door when she looked me straight in the eyes.

'You know, I've always found you extremely attractive, Patrick,' she said, smiling.

There was a strained silence as I scanned her face.

'What d'you mean?' I replied, lowering my gaze.

'I think you know what I mean.'

I wavered. From the moment I had first met her, I had been very attracted to her physically, and I admired her ebullient, tenacious personality. In spite of that, I felt that for me to now have a relationship with her, after she had just had one with Dirk and Ruud, would be somewhat incestuous. And Ruud had had syphilis ...

'I think it's too late for that,' I mumbled.

She must have been embarrassed about what she had said, as from that day forward we rarely saw each other. A few weeks later, without saying farewell to André or me, she too moved out.

Shortly afterwards, I went back to Edinburgh for the summer, and it was two months before I returned to Amsterdam. One Friday, when I was climbing the stairs in the Kerkstraat, I bumped into André, who told me that, through his brother, who had kept in contact with Ruud, he had heard what had happened to him.

'Well, once he had saved enough from the garage, he went to Cuzco in Peru,' he began. 'There, he hired a horse and set off by himself through the Andes. After three days, he fell off the horse, and landed on his leg with such force he knew it was broken. He lay in great pain for hours until some Indians came by and took him to a village. Because it had no doctor, they put his leg in a ...what do you call it?'

'A splint.'

'Yes, a splint. They took him to their house and gave him food, while one of them went to find help. The nearest town was two days away, and, as he lay there, he did a lot of thinking.

'He told my brother that, for the first time ever, he realised he was doing nothing with his life. There he was, alone with a broken leg in the middle of the Andes, with no career, no girlfriend and no friends. He fell into a huge depression, until he noticed a book by his bed. It had been there since he had arrived, but he hadn't paid it much attention. So he picked it up. It was the Bible, which he had never read, as he had always thought it would be boring. But when he opened it, he was gripped by it. It was – so he said – so … personal, as if every word were written for him. Suddenly, he didn't feel so alone any more, as the Bible allowed him to see – so he said – that we are all part of God's plan. He had found faith in something, at last.'

'So what's he doing now?'

'The last my brother heard, he was back at university, studying religion.'

I was silent for a minute, as I allowed the news to settle in. Then my thoughts turned towards Sonya, Jaap and Dirk.

'And the others?' I enquired.

'Sonya moved to Scotland or Ireland. She said she wanted to go and live in the mountains or by the sea, or something like that. Jaap's the same old … what's the word?

'Opportunist.'

'Yes, opportunist. The story goes that because he didn't know what to do, he decided to go into politics. So he wrote the names of the political parties on a piece of paper, put them in a hat, and chose the first one he pulled out. Now he is their assistant director of information.'

'And Dirk?'

'Oh, for a year he became the official dope dealer for the Melkweg!' André exclaimed, chuckling. 'He made so much money that he's not a revolutionary any more, and he's started his own dope café.'

A few weeks after everyone, apart from André, moved out, Christos and Aileen, his new Scottish girlfriend, came to live in the Kerkstraat. The burly Greek with whom I had become friends on Ios, he had thick, curly black hair and lived for rock music. She was a bubbly and feisty Glaswegian, with an oval face, crimped ginger hair, pearly teeth and a magnetic smile. They had got to know each other in the Cyclades, where he had been a *kamaki*, a predatory Greek who goes every summer to prey on Western European women seeking a holiday romance with a Latin lover. Like myself, they had both so fallen in love with Amsterdam that they had decided to stay. As neither of them had had anywhere to live, Christos had asked André, seeing that I was in Edinburgh at the time, if he could take Jaap's floor, and Aileen, who wanted her own space, had asked if she could take Ruud's. André had agreed, and two weeks later a large wooden board with 'House of rock and roll' daubed on it had been nailed onto the massive pastel-green pillars propping up the house.

By now an employment bureau had found me a job at Schipol airport, where I vacuumed jumbo jets and ran errands for Service Q, an employment agency. There were three shifts, and when the night one was finished, I frequently met up with Christos and Aileen at 11 p.m. in Café de Pels, another of Amsterdam's *bruin cafés* in a dark alley off Kloveniersgracht. Usually it was bursting at the seams, and the music was so ear-splitting that I couldn't bear it for long, although they lingered on to the early hours. In addition, I bumped into Christos in a record shop in the Utrechtsestraat where we often browsed in the afternoon. Nonetheless, apart from our mutual interest in rock music, we didn't have much in common. He never appeared to do any work, so I assumed he lived off Aileen – who, for some reason, I assumed was a cleaner – and the Netherlands' generous unemployment benefit.

As word spread among his family in Athens about the permissive life to be had in Amsterdam, they started coming over to join him. First to arrive was his younger brother, followed by four cousins, and soon an entire clan of his relatives was scattered over the city. Like Christos, whose nickname was 'The Bear' on account of his shaggy barrel chest, they were out of work and many of them lazed about all day in his apartment on the ground floor. In the afternoon, if I needed a break from writing, I went down to chat and listen to music. Christos was immensely hospitable and time and again invited me to share the meals he endlessly rustled up for his clan. They were as noisy as a flock of magpies, and much of the time it sounded as if they were having furious arguments, although, Greeks being Greeks, they were probably discussing the weather.

Before long, Christos, like numerous foreigners in Amsterdam, began dealing in drugs. At first, it was merely marijuana, although he slowly but surely drifted into petty crime such as trafficking in stolen passports. At last, as his lips became bloated, his eyes bloodshot, and his cheeks more and more puffy, I realised that he was dealing in cocaine. It was a perilous game to play in Amsterdam, because the international gangs who dealt in hard drugs were notoriously ruthless. To protect himself, he bought two deranged-looking Doberman Pinschers – the sure sign in Amsterdam of a drug dealer – and whenever anybody rang his doorbell, the dogs worked themselves into such a slavering frenzy they looked as though they were about to launch themselves through his gargantuan plate-glass front window.

At about the same time, he and Aileen began having increasingly acrimonious arguments. It wasn't surprising, given that he was hot-tempered and macho, while she was a fiery Glaswegian and, time and again, I woke up at night to hear the sound of furniture splintering and female screaming echo up from the ground floor. Elsewhere, her life was also on a downward spiral. One Wednesday, I was passing a topless bar in the Rembrandtsplein when a photograph in the window caught my eye. Looking out at me was a fresh-faced, topless woman with pert, petite breasts, a rosy complexion and a winning smile. Dumbfounded, I realised it was Aileen. But although the topless bars there were more reputable than those in the sleazy red-light district, it wasn't long until I discovered that their clientele were equally unsavoury. At 4 a.m. one Sunday, when Christos had gone back briefly to Greece, frenzied knocking on my trapdoor awakened me.

'Patrick, Patrick, please help me!' I heard her beg hysterically. I pulled the trapdoor up, to find her standing on the stairs. Dressed in black leather jacket and tight jeans, she had obviously just come home, and she looked in great distress.

'Why, what's up?' I enquired, half asleep.

'Quick! Quick!' she whispered in a trembling voice. 'There's a man outside the front door looking for me! I think he's got a gun!'

'Calm down, calm down!' I blurted out, instantly awake. 'Come up, and close the trapdoor.'

Without thinking, I threw on my clothes. I was no hero and, as there was no telephone in the Kerkstraat, I couldn't call the police – the last thing a *kraaker* would have done anyway. On the other hand, I had to do something. Armed with the sturdy four-by-four I used to prop open my trapdoor, I clambered down the few steps to the landing below. There, I urgently roused André and explained what had happened. He also quickly dressed and together we descended to the foot of the stairs, where somebody was hammering on the front door.

'Who is it? I grunted, trying to sound as tough as nails, but extremely glad André was on the step behind me.

'Open up!' an aggressive voice commanded in a foreign accent.

Hiding the four-by-four behind my back, I drew the door ajar. Outside, it was very dark – there was only one streetlight within a hundred yards – but I could faintly make out the outline of a man on the pavement. There was no sign of a gun, though I couldn't be certain he didn't have one, as his left hand was in his raincoat pocket.

'What d'you want?' I growled.

'Where's Aileen?' he demanded.

'She's not here.'

'Where is she?'

'She doesn't live here any more.'

'Where does she live?'

'No idea. She's moved.'

He glowered at the half-open door for fully a minute, until, obviously mollified, he stalked off into the inky darkness. That night, as a precaution, Aileen slept in my bed on the floor while I dozed beside her in my sleeping bag. I didn't enquire who the man was or what it was about; given her job, he was in all likelihood somebody she had short-changed, sexually or otherwise.

Songs of Sirens

I was in the Moor one night when I first set eyes on Margriet. In her mid-twenties, she was seated on a stool at the bar, and with her untroubled pale green eyes, crimped toffee-coloured hair, body-hugging jeans and flowery waistcoat, she exuded sexuality and looked pleasingly unconventional at one and the same time. We got chatting, as she spoke fluent English, and, a week afterwards, I ran into her again in the Egg Cream, a bohemian café in an alley near Centraal station where I often went for the delicious apple crumble. She was going round the tables, asking travellers who frequented the café to sign a petition.

'What's it all about?' I enquired, when she sat down next to me.

She took a deep breath. 'Well, I'd been living in London with Nick, my Canadian boyfriend. He's a professional photographer who's also done some underwater welding for people like Greenpeace. But because he's a bit of an adventurer, and because neither of us had a job or any money, he and I went to Casablanca in Morocco, where some people asked him to organise a large drugs run back to Britain. Don't get me wrong; I never had any part in it – I just wanted to be with him. Anyway, he spent two days welding ten kilos of marijuana into the bodywork of an old bus before we were driven back across the Straits of Gibraltar, and the whole way through Spain and France without being searched.'

Then customs officers in Dover, maybe acting on a tip, spent six hours taking the van apart, until they found the drugs. She had been sentenced to a year in Holloway prison and Nick had been sentenced to seven in Brixton. While there, she had started to have gynaecological problems, and had to have an operation. Nick's request to be repatriated to Canada to finish his sentence was rejected, so now she was organising a petition asking the authorities to reconsider their decision.

Of course, I signed it, and presently we were meeting up every Wednesday for a drink in the Moor, where she did a class in jazz dance. I found her very easy to talk to and, as she lived in Nieuw-Vennep, a sprawling village just outside Amsterdam, I began taking her on the back of my bicycle to Centraal station to catch the last train home. Then we began going together to films and the Melkweg at the weekend until, a month after I first got to know her, I invited her back to the garret. There we made love, but she made it plain what I was getting myself into.

'Patrick, I'm going to wait for Nick,' she warned. 'But seven years is a long time, so I don't mind having another boyfriend while I do.'

For several months, we had a wonderful, relaxed relationship. She had such a buoyant spirit, and her rippling laugh was so light that it was like hearing the coo of doves. She was independent-minded and at ease with herself, and I liked the way she didn't demand anything of me. She was also extremely sexy and matter of fact at the same time. She unfailingly asked me to wash myself before we made love, and one Sunday, when I was staying with her in Nieuw-Vennep, she caught me admiring her firm breasts in the mirror.

'Why do men make such a big deal about them?' she proclaimed, laughing. 'After all, they're only flaps of skin.'

Nieuw-Vennep wasn't far from Schipol, and after a while she, too, quite fortuitously, got a job there. It was in one of the tax-free jewellers in the departures hall, but as we were both busy working we hardly ever saw each other and met up only at weekends. If she had to work on Saturdays, we would meet on Sunday mornings in the veranda of the Victoria hotel at the head of the Damrak. There, we picked our way through buskers, beggars and the Turkish shoe-shiners who throng the entrance of Centraal station before we had breakfast in the magnificent art deco restaurant on the first floor. Then we took local trains for day trips throughout the Netherlands.

We travelled the length and breadth of Holland. Just to the north of Amsterdam were Volendam and Marken, two fishing villages on the Ijsselmeer, the apparently endless inland lake cut off from the choppy North Sea by the ten-mile-long Afsluitdijk. We would saunter along the Ijsselmeer, lingering at stalls to sample waffles and raw herring in brine or browse in shops selling Delft chinaware and lace with intricate designs. The inhabitants of both villages were famous for their devout religious convictions, and on Sundays they still wore their traditional costumes and clogs. The women had white aprons with black stripes, short-sleeved bodices, and hats with upturned wings similar to those in van Gogh's Breton-inspired paintings; the men wore striped shirts, baggy trousers and black astrakhan hats.

Further up the coast, there was Hoorn, a historic town that had green wooden houses, russet roofs, cobbled streets and a diminutive harbour overlooking the Ijsselmeer, while offshore, the cinnamon-coloured sails of ketches billowed in the stiff breeze. As well as going to Hoorn, we now and again took a train to Zandvoort, west of Amsterdam, where we hired bicycles at the station and cycled through dunes to the coast. At the end of the beach was a nudist section where we once dug a shallow hole in the sand, stripped off and made love. On another occasion, we took the train to the town of Harlingen, where we crossed by boat to Terschelling, one of the flat West Frisian islands off the north coast of the Netherlands. There, we lodged in a converted windmill, and every day trekked along windy beaches or cycled the length of the eighteen-mile-long island.

Smitten, for the first time in Amsterdam I felt content. I had settled down in the Kerkstraat, where I had weathered two numbing winters in the garret. The city and its sublime canals and architecture enchanted me more than ever. In addition, it was so romantic having a Dutch girlfriend, especially one with whom I was getting to know the Netherlands so intimately that, when we came back by train from one of our outings and I peered through the window into the bleak, rain-swept night, I almost felt at home there. Nor did

I mind, now, that I was merely an errand boy at the airport, given it was purely a temporary job and that, in time, something better would surely turn up.

Then, imperceptibly, things changed. At the start of our romance, I had accepted that it would be no more than casual, but more and more I became dissatisfied with being only a short-term substitute for Nick. I didn't show it, naturally, although I still lived in the hope that I might lure her away from him. For all that, even though her petition for his repatriation had come to nothing, it became obvious I wasn't getting anywhere with her, and in all likelihood never would. Eaten away with jealousy, I lost eight kilos in weight. Eventually, I could take it no longer, so, gaunt, run-down and demoralised, I asked her to meet me at lunchtime in a secluded corner of the arrivals hall.

'Margriet,' I blurted out, 'the situation is killing me. It can't go on any longer. You're going to have to choose between me and Nick.'

'Patrick,' she countered without hesitation, 'I explained to you at the beginning I would wait for Nick as long it takes, and that's what I'm going to do.'

Despite my begging her, and even breaking down in tears, nothing would make her reconsider her decision. It was the end of our relationship and from that day on we rarely met up, although, for old times' sake, we periodically still slept with each other.

I had been running errands for Service Q for four months when I succeeded in getting a job as a *kruier* (porter). I had been angling for one since I had started work at the airport. At the time, Schipol had no self-service trolleys, and passengers, rather than struggle with a mountain of suitcases, had to engage self-employed *kruiers*. These were in great demand seeing there were only thirty in the entire airport. Twenty-nine were black-haired Italians from Sicily; the other was a jovial Dutchman with ruddy cheeks, prematurely white hair and a mutton-chop moustache. Everybody was aware they were raking in money, principally through tips given by big-hearted Dutch holidaymakers, but, because they were like a mafia, nobody could ascertain precisely how much, and getting a job with them was about as rare as striking gold. One Monday, however, I got lucky. After a vacancy arose and they couldn't find another Italian, they asked me to fill it, as I was on very good terms with all of them and I spoke English, Dutch, French and elementary Russian.

The *kruiers* operated three ten-man shifts – one in the morning, one in the afternoon and one at night. For me, the morning shift was the worst. That year, it was an abnormally bitter winter, and leaving my bed at 5 a.m.

in the ice-bound garret was how I imagined going out of a tent into the Arctic. When I awoke, the frost on the windows was so opaque I couldn't see out of them, and my breath was so thick I could all but slice it in two with a knife. However, that was nothing compared to cycling along the dark, snow-crusted, cobbled streets that lined the frozen canals to a bus stop near the Leidseplein, where I caught the first KLM bus taking service personnel to the airport.

The *kruiers* had to watch the continually changing arrivals boards to gauge which flights to attend to, and at what time luggage was arriving on carousels in the two baggage reclaim halls. These we offloaded onto our trolleys, before, accompanied by our clients, we wheeled them past customs into the arrivals hall. There we deposited the luggage in the boots of waiting buses or cars, and raced back to the arrivals hall. Then, using our security key to unlock sliding glass doors on which 'NO ENTRY' signs were written in bold letters, we let ourselves back into the baggage reclaim halls.

If we moved extremely fast, and customs didn't search the suitcases, it took us five minutes to carry out the whole operation. After the shift was finished, we convened in an office upstairs, where we pooled the money we had made. Of course, we had to rely on each other being honest about what we earned, which, on an average day, was roughly 250 guilders (£150), a colossal sum at the time, especially for unskilled workers. That paled into insignificance, though, compared to what we made if we landed contracts to unload jumbo jets, for example when ice hockey teams from Canada landed for a Dutch tournament. Then, each *kruier* could earn up to an astounding 600 guilders (£360) in a day, although this didn't happen frequently, and during lulls we earned practically nothing. At such times, the Italians would huddle in the baggage reclaim halls, gossiping in a Sicilian dialect while I chatted to the Dutch *kruier*, with whom I got on famously.

I enjoyed working at Schipol. I enjoyed watching blonde KLM stewardesses stride purposefully through the airport in their trim, sky-blue skirts and jackets. I enjoyed observing the tall KLM captains chattering to each other as they marched along in their flat caps, looking as if they had stepped out of a 1930s poster for flying boats. I enjoyed seeing bronzed, good-humoured Dutch holidaymakers return from holiday in the Canary Islands or Majorca. But best of all was when Surinam, which had been a Dutch colony for three centuries, was about to gain independence, and its inhabitants were given the option of becoming nationals of their new country or citizens of the Netherlands. As the deadline for transfer of sovereignty loomed, thousands of them opted for the latter, and every day congested Boeing 737s landed from Paramaribo, the Surinamese capital. Soon the baggage reclaim hall would be thronged with excited families, and the *kruiers* needed man-sized, wire-mesh wagons to cope with cages of squawking parrots, cartons of spicy foodstuffs and wicker baskets overflowing with exotic tropical fruit that heaped up on the carousels.

A few months afterwards, to bring Schipol into line with rival international airports and provide a better public service, the authorities resolved to introduce self-service trolleys. The *kruiers*, understandably, waged a protracted campaign against them. It even made the newspapers, which carried photographs of the Dutch *kruier*, who was quoted as saying all the *kruiers* wanted was to 'verdien een goed boterham' (earn a good sandwich). This made us laugh, even though we recognised that, sometime or other, we would have to bow to the inevitable. It wasn't long until everyone lost their jobs, and the bulk of the Italians had to put up with demeaning, poorly paid posts with Service Q instead.

But that wasn't the end of the story. Like the *kruiers*, Service Q personnel had a security key to the baggage reclaim halls, where they were regularly going in and out on errands. Of course, it was an ideal opportunity to smuggle drugs, which the *kruiers* could have been doing themselves, but we had been earning so much that no one had even considered it. Now, humbled and earning only a pittance, a handful of the Italians could no longer resist the temptation. On the face of it, the operation seemed simplicity itself. A courier attired as a respectable businessman arrived in one of the two baggage reclaim halls, where he collected his suitcase and took it into one of the cubicles of close-at-hand toilets. Five minutes later, he was followed by one of the Italians, who slipped into one of the adjoining cubicles. The courier unlocked his suitcase and slid packets of cocaine under the door to the Italian. Then the 'businessman' strolled through customs with his suitcase, secure in the belief – or so he thought – that he was 'clean'. Meanwhile, the Italian took the cocaine to his locker upstairs and concealed it in his bag. Then, at the end of the day, he sauntered with it through customs, with whom, naturally, all the Italians were on first-name terms.

Unluckily for the Italians, they didn't know that customs had not only been monitoring them ever since they had begun working for Service Q, but every incoming flight from Colombia and other narco-states as well. Six months later, together with a score of baggage handlers complicit in the smuggling, the Italians were caught red-handed and arrested. They were tried and convicted of smuggling class A drugs, and, a year after they had lost their jobs as *kruiers*, each of them was sentenced to five years in prison.

Before that occurred, I had my second disastrous, and again self-inflicted, love affair within two years. One night, while I was on a flying visit to Scotland, I went to a pub in Stockbridge. I was standing in a crowd waiting to be served at the counter, when I found myself behind a young woman in a white sheepskin coat. After she had bought her drink, she turned round, and I found myself facing the most feminine woman I had ever seen. She had a baby face, a wide forehead, a dimple in her chin, a pert nose, wavy shoulder-length hair, and a soft, moist mouth. Underneath her sheepskin she wore brown corduroys and a navy-blue pullover, and there was something so tender about her that I simply ached to melt into her.

She told me that her name was Anna, that she was English, and that she was in her fourth year at art college, where she was studying tapestry. After an hour she said she was leaving, so I asked her if I could go round and visit her later that night. Caught on the hop, she agreed, and at midnight I knocked on a door in a poky tenement in a claustrophobic street behind the King's Theatre.

There, she told me that she had ended her relationship a short while ago with her boyfriend, who was also at Edinburgh College of Art and kept pestering her. We were still talking at 3 a.m. when the doorbell rang. It was her ex-boyfriend. The minute he saw me, he barged past us into the kitchen and I found myself facing an infuriated young man brandishing a knife. As luck would have it, he was so puny that, pushing aside thoughts about what she had ever seen in him, I managed to grab the knife and shove him out of the front door. After I locked it, we discussed what to do, until we concluded it was best to leave Edinburgh without delay. Although dawn hadn't yet broken, I phoned my parents to ask if I could borrow the second-hand VW camper van they had just bought. My mother agreed and, satisfied that the coast was clear, we took a taxi to their house to collect it. Then I drove across the Forth Road Bridge to St Andrews in north-east Fife, where we spent the rest of the night parked in a tranquil side street. I was longing to make love to her, but she was so shaken up that she promptly fell asleep.

The following day, I had to return to Amsterdam, but for the next two months, if I had a few days off, I flew over to spend time with her. Several times we drove up to stay with Sue, who still lived at the far end of Loch Rannoch. There, we went for long walks up gulleys where rushing streams tumbled down from the mountains and cut their way through bottle-green pine forests. When we were in Edinburgh, I stayed in her tiny apartment, where she slept in a bunk bed in her box-bedroom. To my frustration, she seldom allowed me to sleep with her, which I attributed to her still hankering after her ex-boyfriend. Of course, once I was back in Amsterdam, I wrote to her. Then her replies became ever more infrequent, until, two months after I had last heard from her, I wrote to her confessing that I had slept with Margriet, my erstwhile girlfriend, whom I still saw sporadically. This was merely a ploy to make her think that women found me desirable, but the following week I received a letter from her saying that, because she could never trust me again, our relationship was finished. Confounded, I requested compassionate leave and flew to Edinburgh to try to persuade her to reconsider.

Initially I believed that I had succeeded. For three or four days, I collected her every afternoon at the College of Art after her work was over, or we met at a restaurant at the foot of the castle. Then, five days after I arrived, we were leaving her apartment when she suddenly wheeled round towards me. 'Patrick,' she declared, 'I think it's better we don't see each other any more.'

'What?' I blurted out, caught off balance. 'Why?'

'I don't want to go into the reasons.'

'But I've flown over specially to see you! You have to!'

'No, I don't.' Shaking her head, she hurried to a bus stop outside the King's Theatre, a hundred yards round the corner, where I caught up with her.

'Anna, I only want to talk to you!' I pleaded in front of a startled queue.

'No, I never want to see you again!' she shouted, bursting into tears before she jumped onto a bus that had just pulled up.

Unable to accept what was happening, I pursued her onto the lower deck. 'Anna! Anna, come back!' I beseeched her, impervious to the stares of the disapproving passengers.

'Leave me alone! Leave me alone!' she sobbed convulsively, as she jumped off and onto another bus that had drawn up behind.

Yet again, I sprang on after her, until, realising that it was pointless, I stepped off the slowly moving bus. Then I watched helplessly as it gathered speed up the hill, before it and Anna receded into the distance.

Twice a year, my parents came over to Amsterdam, visits that my mother looked forward to tremendously. Being so maternal, she had been disconsolate after her children had gone to live on the continent, and, as if that wasn't already painful enough, she felt even more cut off from me, because she had had to become accustomed to my prolonged silences while I was travelling. Nor could she get in touch with me in the Kerkstraat, where there was no telephone. However, because for years she had remained astonishingly youthful – she continually said she felt as if she was still only twenty-one – she had always got on exceedingly well with young people, and, after my sister and I went to live abroad, to compensate she had a tiny coterie of women, quite apart from Julia, whom she looked on as her substitute daughters. Nevertheless, conscious of how much she missed my sister and me, every Sunday evening I cycled diligently to Damplein to telephone her from Centraal post office, an echoing, cathedral-like edifice whose ochre-and-white Moorish-style arches inside resembled those in one of M.C. Escher's architecturally impossible buildings. Before my parents arrived, I booked them into the Seven Bridges hotel, a cosy, family-owned pension on an intersection of four of Amsterdam's most enchanting canals, where, intent on welcoming them as much as possible, I would fill their room with bunches of daffodils.

The vast majority of their visits were relatively harmonious, and the only time there was tension in the air was when my sister, who had married a German and was living in West Germany only one hundred metres from the Dutch border, came up to join us. It wasn't difficult to see why. Not long before, she had had her first child, a girl whom my mother adored and spoiled terribly. One weekend, she and my sister had such a fierce altercation in the Rembrandtsplein about my mother's inordinate generosity – she had just returned from Spain with thirty pairs of baby shoes – that my mother ran off, swearing that she was going to throw herself into a canal. After traipsing around alone all day she turned up at the pension, but for hours the three of us were worried sick about her.

My parents only visited the Kerkstraat once, as my mother maintained that she found its stairs too vertiginous to climb. The truth was, she was doubtless too ashamed of me, even if she never admitted it, to go there. If her friends in Edinburgh enquired what I was doing in the Netherlands, she affirmed that I was a 'manager for KLM at Schipol airport'. Then, as the years wore on, she became more and more apprehensive about my future. One night, we were eating in the candlelit restaurant in the basement of the Carré theatre, a majestic, colonnaded white building beside the Magere Brug.

'Patrick, what are you doing with your life?' she enquired fretfully. 'You're close on thirty, you've no profession, no money, you're not married and you've no children. Who's going to look after you when you're sixty?'

A similar consideration had crossed my mind, although I had never particularly wanted to have children and, like numerous people in Amsterdam, I was muddled between living for the present and having a long-term goal.

'Oh, the future'll take care of itself,' I rejoined blithely.

My father, without fail, was exceptionally tolerant of me; he hadn't even commented on my appearance at the height of the Beatles' most extravagant sartorial phase when I, with my bell-bottom trousers, lilac chiffon neck scarf, and black velvet jacket, must have looked like a self-indulgent dandy.

'Oh, let him be,' he said. 'He'll grow out of it someday.'

Besides the visits of my parents, my sister and her husband Joseph also came up to see me. In fact, after Ruud and Sonya moved out, they had spent part of their honeymoon sleeping in Ruud's bed on the first floor, an experience they had treasured until I let slip that he had had syphilis. But I also visited them in West Germany. Every month or so, at the weekend, I took the tram in the Utrechtsestraat to Centraal station. There, I would have a cursory glance at the international departures board, where the names of such destinations as Milan, Vienna and Budapest never failed to fire my imagination, before I boarded the train to Germany. There were two ways to go. The first was to take the Amsterdam–Milan express to Cologne, where I would catch a regional train that trundled past decayed stations, forlorn factories and over-grown sidings to Goch, a sprawling village in the Nord Rhine-Westphalia countryside. The second was to go to Nijmegen via Arnheim.

I relished both journeys, but especially the latter. The intercity train, inevi-tably thronged with students studying textbooks, tracked a raised embankment where barges appeared to be sliding through broad open fields. The flat terrain was divided as far as the eye could see by dykes, and dotted with Friesian cows and grazing horses. Herons stood impassive in bulrushes, watching the train rattle by. In the distance, church steeples in villages with ochre roofs punctu-ated the horizon. After Arnheim the train switched direction, until it crossed a bridge over the Rhine, the scene of the ferocious Second World War battle immortalised in the film *A Bridge Too Far*. Here, a short distance before the train terminated at Nijmegen, barges as long as football pitches powered up and downstream, their flags whipping in the wind.

When we arrived at the station, my sister and Joseph would be waiting patiently to pick me up in their Volkswagen estate car. Then we crossed the border into West Germany to the small town of Goch and on to their house, one of a row of capacious bungalows tucked away in the countryside, only a hundred yards from a little-used border crossing with the Netherlands. Behind their house, and opposite a field of grazing thoroughbreds, was one of West Germany's handful of private boarding schools, where Joseph, who had himself been a pupil there, taught English. Run by the Catholic Church, it was mod-elled on the English public school system and had Gothic cloisters, dormitories and an imposing spire. Opposite was a grey customs post where West German police inevitably interrogated me and scrutinised my passport, despite the fact that I wasn't even crossing the border back into the Netherlands, while I hung around, muttering under my breath. In hindsight, it wasn't surprising I was pulled up time after time; with my shoulder-length black hair and beard, I must have looked like one of the Baader-Meinhof terrorists in *Gezocht* (wanted) posters plastered everywhere. Things were incomparably more relaxed, how-ever, in Siebengewald, a Dutch village with orange-tiled roofs immediately over the border, where tall, fair-haired young Dutchmen in tangerine shirts and white shorts played football next to busy tennis courts.

Although my sister and her husband's formative years had been the Sixties, when she had worn beads and Afghani kaftans and travelled to India and Morocco, and he had sympathised with the student movement during his exchange year at Edinburgh University, that astonishing decade hadn't changed them as fundamentally as it had me. Now, like numerous people, particularly those with families, her primary concern not unnaturally was for her husband, children and friends. She believed life to be a question of using common sense, and had little time for the role the subconscious plays or for investigating the dark night of the soul.

But, along with the influence of our parents, those permissive years had left her with broadly liberal ideals. She had great empathy in particular for gay men, who loved her anecdotes, stories and light-hearted sense of fun. Knowing that I had very little money, she was also unfailingly friendly and generous towards me, although she continued to have a distorted view of me. During my mother's afternoon teas in Edinburgh, she had by and large seen me only after I had been smoking marijuana, when she had surmised – not without reason – that I was too introverted for my own good. Now she had an idealised image of me as a hedonistic bohemian sowing his wild oats in Amsterdam, and, because I never disabused her of the notion, she had no inkling how insecure, unhappy and deeply troubled I could be.

There were plenty of pleasant diversions at my sister's. Every now and then, I pushed her baby daughter in her pram along deserted lanes in the flat countryside which, dissected by shallow ditches that separate fields of maize and lined with poplar trees, resembled a landscape painting by Courbet.

Intermittently, my sister and I went for long bicycle rides on the family's graceful, old-fashioned Dutch bicycles. Dotted here and there were farmhouses with steeply sloping roofs and backyards abounding with honking geese and yapping dogs. In fields, pigs grunted and hens clucked, and in autumn the lanes were bordered with bushes weighed down with black-berries. On Sundays, Joseph would drive us along a winding country road to visit his parents. Humble farmers who lived half an hour away near low, wooded hills, their farmhouse was at the end of a bumpy track flanked by apple and cherry orchards. Built of beige brick, inside it was shadowy and crawling with flies, with lace curtains semi-permanently drawn against the frequently baking summer heat. Down steps, a dark basement had rows and rows of his mother's home-made blackberry, raspberry and strawberry jam, and there was a huge refrigerator groaning with home-cured ham.

I enjoyed visiting the farm. Outside the farmhouse, there was a yard full of disused machinery, and a rusty, corrugated-iron barn piled to the roof with bales of hay. At the back were the family's two arable fields, where Joseph's brother, a part-time prison officer, once or twice allowed me to drive their tractor. Joseph's father was a portly, sixty-year-old man who still had a full head of fine, mousy hair. Although he hardly ever mentioned it, during the Second World War he had fought at Stalingrad, where he had lost a finger. Joseph's mother was a warm-hearted, motherly woman with spectacles, who clucked around like a hen as she served up plates of home-made sandwiches and sponge cake to us, his brother and two sisters, both nurses, who loved to return to the farm on Sunday.

I was on the Amsterdam–Milan express going down to spend the week-end with my sister, when I first noticed Hannah, a small but shapely young woman sitting on the other side of the passageway. She had a broad face, straight fair hair, sapphire eyes and heavy breasts underneath her blouse. Instantly attracted to her, I plucked up my courage.

'Got a light?' I opened in English, blushing at being unable to think of another way of engaging her in conversation.

'Yes, I do,' she said with a demure but encouraging smile.

She told me that she was from Düsseldorf, and was returning to Cologne, where she was a second-year student at university. Before I got off the train at Wesel, a town on the Rhine where my sister now and then collected me, I asked her for her telephone number, which she gave me. When I phoned her at the weekend, she sounded pleased to hear from me, so on Monday I took the train to visit her in Cologne, where she lived in a down-at-heel suburb chiefly consisting of Turkish immigrants. That evening, we downed innumerable beers in a local bar, and, an hour later, we made love in her bed.

After a short time, she was coming up at weekends to visit me in Amsterdam. She was ten years younger than me and she had a somewhat reserved personality, but I liked her bashful innocence and sweet smile, and I couldn't get enough of her voluptuous body. I would pick her up at Centraal station and take her back to the Kerkstraat, where we made love in the armchair with sawn-off legs by the window overlooking the attic next door.

I also took the train down to Cologne to see her. There, she would be waiting faithfully for me behind the station in her rusty Opel car. One Saturday, I noticed a poster for a show at the university theatre. To my amazement, the student who had directed me, Ian Charleson and Hilton McRae in *Saved* at Edinburgh University, was performing in it. After graduation he had turned his back on a career in conventional theatre and become one of Europe's most outstanding street theatre actors. When the show ended, I took Hannah backstage to meet him. With his shaven head, earring and toned chest, he looked like a convict, and I was heartened to learn that I wasn't the only one of our contemporaries at university who hadn't become a businessman, media tycoon or politician.

As well as going to visit Hannah, I returned twice a year to see my parents in Edinburgh, where, to raise some much-needed money, I had long since sold the flat I had bought from the potato pickers. While I was there, I had a drink now and again in a local pub with Ruth, my sylph-like ex-girlfriend. She was as enigmatic and unworldly as ever, and one night she recounted what had happened to her since we had shared a house in Crystal Palace. Even at that time, she had been interested in the occult; now she was also attracted to witchcraft and shamanism.

'After we broke up, I went back with my new boyfriend to live in Cheat the Beggars Cottage, which was empty,' she began. 'One day, after he went out, I heard noises coming from the floor above. It struck me as weird, because nobody was living there, although from time to time it was used as a holiday let. When I went upstairs to find out what the sound was, I discovered that it was furniture being moved around by a ghost. It was the father of the Black Dwarf, a dwarf who had lived either in or near the cottage.' She paused. 'It's true,' she insisted, seeing the scepticism on my face. 'If you don't believe me, look it up – he was the inspiration for the main protagonist in Sir Walter Scott's novel *The Black Dwarf*. Anyway, now his father lived there and, after I first met him, I often felt his energy behind me in the kitchen, where we used to dance together to Mike Oldfield's LP *Tubular Bells*.

'A few months afterwards, my boyfriend and I decided it was time for us to move on. So we moved to a broken-down castle that a friend of mine rented on the west coast of Scotland. Long ago, it had been a fortified keep, and it had three-foot-thick walls and was surrounded by gnarled trees where a flock of cawing crows nested. Among them was a raven, one of three pairs that lived in some woods close at hand. Then a farmer had shot its mate, so now it lived with the crows, which had adopted it. I also became friends with it. It was amazing. Every day, I used to watch as it left the copse, accompanied by the crows, who flew alongside to protect it, to visit the other ravens.'

Apart from seeing Ruth, I visited Sue in northern Scotland. By now she and the gamekeeper had moved from Loch Rannoch to outside Tomintoul, near the Grampian Mountains and the second highest village in Britain, even more remote than Loch Rannoch. There, in yet another cramped white cottage, she, her daughter, the gamekeeper, and her newly born son by him lived with a menagerie that included three cats, two dogs, a goat, rabbits, hens and a donkey. It was the last time I saw her for three decades, although when we did meet up she recounted what had happened in her life. In Tomintoul she had become attracted to the art of falconry and had started travelling round falconry meets and various Highland games. Then her nine-year-old relationship with the gamekeeper broke up, and after her father had died and bequeathed her a house in York, to everybody's astonishment she had gone, along with her children, to Essex to train – of all things – as a pilot. She had been awarded her licence, and, in yet another change of direction, she had settled in a cottage in the west of Ireland. There, she had become interested in antiques, and had found a job taking tourists round stately country houses before she did an MA in historic house studies. Meanwhile, her daughter became a traveller, though her son stunned everyone by going to London where he joined the Metropolitan Police.

BOOK III

Wanderings West and East

In September, Michel, whom I hadn't seen for two years, turned up out of the blue at the Kerkstraat. As usual, he was merely drifting about.

'Fancy South America?' he enquired laconically.

I needed no persuading. I wasn't looking forward to another interminable, freezing winter in the garret, and it struck me as a heaven-sent opportunity to put the still fresh memories of Anna and Margriet behind me. Not only that; Hannah also swore to be there for me when I returned, although I warned her that I didn't have the faintest clue when that would be. So, in case the Kerkstraat was demolished while I was away, I stored my records, which, through contacts of my father I'd had shipped over from Edinburgh shortly after I had arrived in Amsterdam, with some of my Dutch friends. I could do nothing, however, about my books, by now an exhaustive collection of avant-garde European, Japanese and Latin American fiction stacked in six unstable piles at the end of my mattress. Then, a week later, Michel and I flew from Geneva to Lima in Peru.

Michel and I spent the next twelve months travelling the entire length of the Andes. At first sight we must have come across as a singularly unlikely travelling partnership; we had nothing in common — he wasn't interested in books, films, art or world affairs — except that both of us rejected society and delighted in travelling for the sake of it. In reality he was the ideal foil for me. I was complicated and dogmatic; he was straightforward and hardly ever expressed opinions about anything. I was impetuous, combative and hot-headed; he was relaxed, unflappable and happy-go-lucky. I had firm ideas about where I wanted to go; he had virtually no preferences, and, bar four occasions in the three years I was to travel with him, was content to follow me there.

But he had changed since I had first chanced upon him. Despite still being able to endure hardship and discomfort better than anyone I have ever known, now he habitually seemed to have a cold, a cough or some trivial ailment. Furthermore, he had a perceptibly widening bald spot, which, joke as he might about it, he was unequivocally concerned about. Nor did he have the success with women he had once enjoyed. A few years earlier he had had a love affair with a German woman who had a young child. She had become the love of his life, but, for some reason he never clarified, she kept him at arm's length, and since then he hadn't had a relationship. Of course, he was still unusually laid-back, but his obsessive, almost salacious interest in women indicated, to me, at least, that he felt increasingly incomplete without one.

The mid-1970s were a very dangerous time to be travelling in South America; practically everywhere right-wing military regimes were in power. After being stopped continually by gun-toting soldiers at roadblocks, we drifted down through Peru and Bolivia to northern Argentina. There we had heard rumours that, under the particularly vicious junta that had just overthrown the legally elected President Allende, people were already disappearing (the *desaparecidos*). Nevertheless, unaware that we were stepping straight into the middle of the 'Dirty War', during which, so it later transpired, over 30,000 students, intellectuals and trade unionists were killed, we decided to continue south. We were having breakfast in a café near the railway station in Jujuy, where we had just purchased tickets for the midnight train to Buenos Aires, when a headline in the provincial newspaper caught my eye.

'BORGES EN JUJUY!' it blared.

I shot bolt upright. At that time, he wasn't as iconic a figure as he is now, but he was still widely regarded as a great writer, and he was one of my favourite authors. On scanning the paper further, I learned that he was giving a lecture that evening on 'The Role of Myth in World Literature' in the Auditorio del Ministerio de Bienestar Social. According to my map, it was only four blocks away and, with mounting excitement, I calculated that I could hear the lecture, have a meal, and still have time to catch the train.

Because Michel wasn't interested in the lecture, I set off to buy a ticket. The Auditorio was at the head of a street lined with espaliered orange trees. When I arrived, there wasn't a living soul in the ticket office or foyer. Trying to track down somebody to help me, and ignoring a 'NO ENTRY' sign, I opened the lecture theatre door. Inside, it was dark, although at the foot of a steeply banked auditorium two technicians were helping a blind, senescent-looking man with a white stick up to a floodlit stage. A thrill coursed through me; I would have recognised those pallid features anywhere – it was Borges himself, doing a trial run for the lecture.

A slide projector was flashing images onto a screen behind his head, and a loudspeaker system crackled. Hoping that the technicians wouldn't notice me, I sidled down to the front seats for a better view. By now Borges had sat down at a table. He was in his late seventies, bald, and his skin was white and spectral. As he spoke, his mouth revealed what appeared to be a row of perfect false teeth and his eyeballs stared ahead vacantly. 'Uno, dos, tres,' he said, tapping a microphone.

I had no sooner been seated than a voice bawled 'Luces!' and the lecture theatre was engulfed with light. One of the technicians turned round and spotted me.

'Hey, you!'

I can't imagine what possessed me, but to my surprise I found myself stepping across tangled microphone cables and mounting steps to the stage. 'Hello, Señor Borges!' I said in English, which, from BBC television interviews I had seen, I knew he spoke fluently.

There was a silence until the hint of a smile flickered over his pallor. 'That wouldn't be an Englishman speaking, would it?' he enquired in the overcorrect, formal English of non-native speakers.

'Not really. I was born in Sussex, though I was brought up in Edinburgh,' I answered, trying to ignore the technicians who were glaring at me.

'Ah, I know it well!' he continued, this time in an Irish accent. 'Edinburgh and Geneva, two of the loveliest Calvinistic cities in Europe. Did you know that the name Edinburgh may have originated in Northumberland?'

'No, I didn't ...'

'Well, some say that Edwin, the King of Northumbria from 616 to 632, built a town on the Forth that became known as Edwin's Burgh.'

'Really!' I blurted out; Borges was famed for his erudition but still ...

Thankfully, the technicians, satisfied that I represented no danger, had retreated to the front row to unload sound equipment.

'So how did you like my Scottish accent?' Borges continued.

'That was Irish, not Scottish!' I chuckled.

'Forgive me.'

Before I knew what was happening, he proceeded to recite an extract from a poem in a language that I couldn't identify. As his quavering voice echoed through the hall, the technicians ceased clattering about and listened in awed silence.

When he had finished, he leaned across to me. 'I wonder if you can tell me what language that is?' he enquired.

'Hebrew?'

'No, Saxon. That was Beowulf, needless to say. You doubtless know that Saxon comes from Friesland in the Netherlands?'

'Yes, actually, I do,' I nodded. 'I've been living there for the last four years and ...'

'Ah, so many fine Scotsmen!' he exclaimed, taking no notice. 'Hume, Adam Smith, and ... who wrote *The Confessions of a Justified Sinner?*'

I was still combing my memory when I spotted two menacing-looking soldiers striding down the aisle towards us.

'You know, every time I see the name Argentina I think of you,' I volunteered, improvising the first words that came into my head.

'You are too kind. Have you read my stories?'

'All of them!'

'I have done my best, although I must apologise for their poor quality.' Borges was renowned for his humility, authentic or otherwise.

'No, really, you're too modest.'

A playful expression flitted across his countenance. 'Perhaps you are familiar with the story of what occurred when Goethe visited a brothel in Hanover?'

'No, but I'd love to hear it.'

The long, convoluted story, which I have forgotten, lasted for five minutes, until he questioned me about my journey in South America and my life in Amsterdam as a writer. At last, after what seemed a lifetime, a man in a stone-coloured suit came down the gangway, mounted the steps onto the stage, and leaned over him. 'It's time to go, Señor Borges,' he said in a hushed voice. 'You have an appointment at three.'

'Very well,' responded Borges grudgingly. Holding on to the arm of the man, he rose unsteadily to his feet. To my apprehension, the two soldiers, waiting in the front row, had stood up and were moving in my direction.

'You will give my greetings to Robbie Burns, won't you?' said Borges, smiling from ear to ear, as the man guided him down the platform steps and up the auditorium.

Desperate to retain the link with my protector, I tagged along behind. Then, as they turned right through a door, I turned left into the bright sunlight and, watched charily by the two soldiers, strode up the street.

At 7.30 p.m., I was back at the Auditorio, where I managed to get one of the last tickets, before I entered the lecture theatre. There was still half an hour to go, but it was bursting at the seams with people, although I was alarmed to see that most of them were high-ranking military officers in spruce, laurel-green uniforms dripping with gold braid. I found a seat midway in the back row. Behind, a soldier with a Kalashnikov stood at a door, eyeing me warily. At intervals, the door swung open, whereupon all the military, believing that it was Borges, rose to their feet and a host of faces swivelled round, to discover that it was merely another officer.

I had been sitting there for ten minutes when I heard an ominous voice say, 'You with the bag, come with me!'

I glanced up. A stunted, weedy-looking man in civilian clothes was hovering at the end of the row, waving an identity card. His jacket was half-fastened, and in a holster I caught a glimpse of a revolver.

'Oh God!' I groaned.

Blushing with embarrassment, I made my way to the aisle. Outside the hall, two more plainclothes policemen were waiting. The weedy-looking man motioned to the lavatory. 'Go inside and empty your bag!' he commanded.

I hesitantly pushed open the door, which banged behind us, leaving the four of us standing alone near the urinals.

Ignoring alarm bells jangling in my head – they could batter me to a pulp or even shoot me and nobody would be any the wiser – I saw red. 'Look, I'm a journalist for *The Times* of London!' I roared, oblivious, given my scruffy appearance, of the sheer improbability of such a claim. 'Believe me, I'm going to describe everything that's happening in this shithole country of yours!'

Disregarding my outburst, the weedy-looking man inspected my bag and passport. Then he handed them back to me. 'You may return to the hall, Señor Richardson,' he uttered with a polite nod.

Feeling utterly humiliated, I returned to the lecture theatre. I was halfway along the row when Borges emerged from a side door leading to the stage. Escorted by the man in the suit whom I had observed earlier, he had barely taken a step when, applauding rapturously, all the officers once more stood up. At the foot of the stage, television cameras whirred, cameras clicked and flashlights popped.

Two minutes later, Borges, who had been led to the table on the stage, lifted his hands. 'Gracias, señoras y señores!' he began, motioning for the applause to die down. 'Tonight, I want to dedicate this lecture to our military, which has fought so bravely to save us from the subversion that is threatening to overwhelm us. Our country ...'

The remainder of his introduction was drowned by another tumultuous ovation as, yet again, all the officers rose to their feet. After they settled back in their seats, I leaned back, more composed now. So this was the other side of Borges ...

For a long time, the literary world had speculated that it was only his reactionary opinions that had prevented him being awarded the Nobel Prize for Literature. Indeed, in a barber's shop, just seven days earlier, I had chanced upon a magazine interview with him, in which he was quoted as calling for a military coup in the USA to 'stop the communists taking over'.

All of a sudden, I couldn't take it any more. I didn't care what I missed; I was seized with a desire to retain the memory of the delightful, blind old man I had sat with alone at a table, not the mouthpiece of a barbarous regime culpable for God only knew how many *desaparecidos*. To the bewilderment of the three soldiers, I stood up, impulsively shoved my way along the aisle, and stormed out of the building.

For the next four months Michel and I travelled up to the north of South America, before we flew back to Europe. When I finally reached Amsterdam and boarded the tram from Centraal station to the Kerkstraat, my heart was in my mouth. While I had been away, I had left instructions with my parents and friends about where to forward mail. Nonetheless, our route had been so unpredictable that I hadn't received any for a year, and I had no way of telling if the garret had been razed to the ground. As I rounded the corner from the Utrechtsestraat into the by-now familiar street, I heaved a sigh of relief – there were the huge pastel-green pillars propping up the façade of the house and, high above, my beloved garret still nestled amongst a jumble of aerials and ochre-gabled roofs.

I settled back into the Kerkstraat and after a short time it felt as if I had never been away. I had hoped that being away for a year in South America would solve some of my seemingly intractable, perennial problems. These included my persistent failure to sustain a relationship, my deep-seated self-doubt and my apparently hopeless inability to find out what to do with my life. I was, however, quickly disenchanted; travelling from one place to an-other, irrespective of how long, changes nothing, and I felt that I was back at square one. But at least something new was emerging from my experiences. Although *The Sound of Breaking Glass* was less than half completed, I had been to so many riveting places and had such unforgettable experiences in South America that, for the first time, I began to write about my travels. Until then I had never considered it, as, assuming what I wrote would be published, I wanted to avoid being responsible for ruining places that I loved. Now I found this argument unconvincing; in time, I told myself, others would write about these places, and, anyway, if readers took as much time and trouble to get to them as we had done, they would probably treat them with the same respect.

About this time I started going on Friday evening to a yoga class in the Kosmos, one of Europe's biggest, and most pre-eminent, East–West spiritual centres. A majestic, white, four-storey building on the waterfront, it was, like the Melkweg and the Paradiso, a hive of activity. In the basement was a book-shop with books on astrology and eastern religions, along with a Japanese-style vegetarian restaurant and a cavernous white sauna with cushions, plants, a twenty-foot-long cage with canaries and, outside in the open air, a minuscule icy pool. On the ground floor there was a teashop and an extensive library, with encyclopaedic sections on the occult, the supernatural and the world's most famous mystics. On the first floor was a stupendous cream-and-maroon hall modelled on a Tibetan monastery, where all the events and courses were held. These included sitar recitals, lectures by internationally honoured Indian gurus and yoga teachers, and classes in t'ai chi, yoga and aikido.

In those days, yoga was still mistakenly perceived as a dubious Indian activity where hippies sat in the lotus position staring at a candle. The teacher was a vain Dutchman in his forties with ash-grey hair tied in a ponytail, long sideburns and a drooping moustache, who, to the delight of his adoring female students, wore only a loincloth in his class. Afterwards, I had a herbal drink in the teashop or browsed in stalls that sold Buddhas, incense and miniature spirit levels that you pinned on your lapel to 'measure your karma'. At 11 p.m. it was time for the *swingavond* (disco) in the main hall. At the time, Bhagwan Shree Rajneesh was hugely popular, especially with young German hippies who inundated Amsterdam at weekends. He was renowned for instructing his sannyasins to cast off their inhibitions, and, once the music started, the hall became a maelstrom of swirling orange dresses and robes. I would smoke some marijuana and stay until midnight, watching the dancers weave seemingly infinite patterns in the air with their arms. Then, when my senses became so heightened that I only wanted to be alone, I cycled back along the River Amstel to the Kerkstraat, spellbound by the matchless beauty of the doll-like gabled houses and the canals.

In fact I found the Kosmos so interesting that I resolved to try to get a part-time job there. At length, after several months, I succeeded. It was no more than washing dishes in the vegetarian restaurant in the basement for three evenings a week, and the pay was derisory, but it suited me. I could write during the day, and it provided me with a free meal in the evening, along with unrestricted access to lectures, yoga classes, the sauna and the showers – the latter of inestimable importance, seeing that the garret's only washing facilities consisted of a grime-encrusted sink that I had retrieved from a skip.

I also got a kick cycling there via the Zeedijk, the heart of Amsterdam's hard drug scene. Running over with seamy Malayan, Vietnamese and Chinese restaurants controlled by Chinese Triads, it demarcated one of the boundaries of the red-light district and was essentially a no-go area for tourists and the Dutch alike. For a thrill, I would cycle to the beginning of the street, take a deep breath, and pedal hell for leather past the Surinamese and Moluccan look-outs who loitered about alleyway corners to warn cocaine and heroin dealers should the police arrive. Trying to stamp out the traffic in heroin in Amsterdam seemed an impossible task for the authorities, because, like a bubble, every time it was suppressed in one area it simply resurfaced in another one. The police, consequently, appeared to be resigned to confining it to the Zeedijk, where the battle against narcotics had long since been lost.

When I had been at the Kosmos for only four months, everybody was dismayed to discover that the kitchen, which prided itself on its nutritious vegetarian food, seemed to be a surprisingly insalubrious place in which to work. First the Canadian cook was diagnosed with cervical cancer. She and I had established an instant rapport, as she was unpretentious, unlike some of the other cooks, and she was an avid reader who knew I was an impoverished writer living in a garret. She was also exceedingly popular in the Kosmos, and everyone was shaken to the core when her cancer metastasised like a wildfire and she died barely a few months later.

Then, a month afterwards, everybody in the kitchen started phoning in sick, and I began getting boils all over my body. I assumed, understandably, that these were caused by bacteria from the mammoth aluminium pots and saucepans that I had to scrub every night. Naturally, everyone in the Kosmos had their pet theory regarding what to do about the boils. I should do more yoga or take up shiatsu, t'ai chi or aikido. I should begin to meditate. I should eat less cheese and more broccoli, carrots, ginseng or tofu, and so on. Perplexed, I consulted a doctor, who informed me that I merely had a common infection caused by the common bacteria staphylococcus aurous; he prescribed some antibiotics and, within a week, the boils completely vanished.

As another winter drew in, I made up my mind to do something, once and for all, about the garret, where I found the winters ever harder to endure. Of course, after Dirk, Jaap and Ruud had left I could have swapped it for one of their floors, but when I was visiting Edinburgh, Christos and Aileen had moved into the first and second floors and, although that still left the third floor free, I had opted to stay in the garret, as I had put so much time and energy into rebuilding it and, in spite of everything, I had grown accustomed to living there. Now I had made my bed and I had to sleep in it, seeing that, while I had been in South America, Christos had commandeered the third floor to use as a storeroom or to put up visiting Greeks.

It wasn't that I hadn't done my best to tackle the biting cold. When I had first moved in, I had lined the window frames with thick strips of newspaper. During the winters I'd had the *kachel* going full blast, in addition to three bars of an electric heater that I had rescued from the street. Then, to make the garret at least look warmer, I had painted the wooden walls and beams yellow and white respectively. In desperation, I had even divided the garret into two with a threadbare velvet curtain before I retreated into the half overlooking the back garden. None of this had made any difference, so now I asked my father, who had learned a lot about carpentry when he had converted the loft in the bungalow into my bedroom, to come and help me insulate the garret properly. At the time, he and my mother were staying at my sister's in West Germany, so before he arrived, I raked through skips for hardboard and laths, and bought rolls of silver insulation from a hardware shop. Then, once he did, to create an insulating wall he and I nailed the hardboard to the beams, the laths onto the hardboard, and the insulation onto the laths. Next, we lowered the ceiling, and repeated with the insulation what we had done with the walls. It was a major undertaking, but, working eight hours a day for a week, it was finally completed.

To my intense disappointment, all the heat continued to vanish the minute I turned off the *kachel*. However, our labour wasn't entirely useless; now the garret, with its reflecting insulation, looked like the interior of a spaceship. Furthermore, the insulation acted as soundproofing, and that winter, as I sat at my typewriter looking out over the tops of towering trees that dominated the back garden, it felt as if I were living in a cocoon. André below was as quiet as the grave. Christos practically never used the third floor, and all I could hear was the muffled throb of Bruce Springsteen and the E. Street Band, his favourite rock group, echoing up from the ground floor. Every three or four weeks, Hannah came up from Cologne. In a little while, winter elided into spring and the sky dissolved into showers and kaleidoscopic rainbows. At the back of the house, the sun shimmered on puddles on the balcony, and pigeons cooed in ivy on the garret next door. At the front, blossoming chestnut trees in the gaping space to the side of the garage were decked with what looked like purple candlesticks.

One Saturday I took the train down to my sister's house in West Germany, where I had arranged to meet Hannah and introduce her to my parents, who were once again staying there. Unknown to me, however, she had met a young journalist who worked for *Der Spiegel,* the German magazine. Now, sitting on the double bed in my sister's bedroom, she informed me that, as I had never seemed to be serious about her, our relationship was over. I was distraught; despite not being in love with her, I had grown deeply attached to her. Two weeks later, smoking continuously and drinking every night for the first time in my life, I was still so overwrought that I phoned my mother and asked her to come up to Amsterdam to see me.

When she arrived, she was shocked to the core at the state I was in. She did her best to console me, as she always did whenever a girlfriend jilted me. But unburdening myself to her didn't help; I was beginning to find the apparently irredeemable failure of my relationships, along with the prospect of spending a fourth, long, freezing winter in the garret, almost unendurable. It wasn't surprising therefore that when Michel turned up for the second time at the Kerkstraat that October and proposed that we go travelling to South-east Asia, I jumped at the opportunity. Yet again, the Kosmos pledged to keep my job in the kitchen for me, and I stored my records with some of my Dutch friends.

A week later, Michel and I flew to South-east Asia, through which we roamed for the next ten months. Then, after he decided to return home, I climbed to Mount Everest base camp, before travelling to Ladakh in northern India which, some backpackers had told me, had just opened its doors to the outside world and was supposed to be the new Shangri-La for travellers.

I was eating breakfast in the courtyard of my guesthouse, directly underneath the towering white, semi-derelict palace in Leh, the tiny capital, when I got chatting to Marie. A petite Frenchwoman who spoke English with a heavy French accent, she was in her mid-thirties, and she had an olive complexion, big hazel eyes, shiny jet-black hair in a fringe, and a sensuous pout. She told me she had been married to a dentist, with whom she had had a ten-year-old daughter. Now they were divorced, and she worked in the European Parliament in Strasbourg, where she edited a magazine for the Council of Europe.

She had been travelling round India for six weeks, and now had only a fortnight remaining in Ladakh. Nevertheless, by the second day, we were having a highly romantic love affair. Every morning, we breakfasted on newly baked Tibetan bread before we wandered to the market in the main street, which was crowded with women selling vegetables. Squatting on the pavement, they had black plaits down to their waists, and they wore ankle-length maroon robes, striped woollen aprons and towering, witch-like hats. At midday, when the town emptied, we took buses heavily laden with Ladakhis, chickens and goats to adjacent villages. There, we trekked across inhospitable plateaux dotted with grazing wild horses, and scrambled up to monasteries nestling on craggy ledges. There was Shey, the one-time summer palace of the Ladakhi kings, and Tikse, which had Ladakh's most prestigious library of sacred Tibetan books. But best of all was Stok, where, lured by chanting, we wended our way along passageways to an incense-filled prayer hall. Inside, underneath scarlet and gold frescos and richly embroidered tankas, monks on cushions sat next to a tier of gold Buddhas, pounding drums and blowing long horns.

After Marie returned to France, I set off for the annual festival at Hemis, Ladakh's most famous monastery. Forty miles away, it housed Ladakh's largest, thirty-foot-long *tanka*, a tapestry which is exhibited only every eleven years. I set up camp in a willow grove near an eddying stream, and headed across fields where Ladakhis, many of whom had marched for days to reach the monastery, were drinking Tibetan beer in tents and watching archery competitions. The men, with their coarse maroon robes, woollen leggings, tall felt hats and leather boots with upturned toes, reminded me of Adrian, with whom I had lived in Crystal Palace. The women wore heavy woollen dresses covered with ceremonial silk shawls, and Tibetan hats with black wings studded with turquoise.

When I arrived at the gigantic doors of the monastery, an astounding sight confronted me. Inside, jammed into a courtyard and lining the roof, hordes of excited people were watching ten-foot-tall dragons and grotesque, grinning skeletons perform slow-motion, mesmerising dances. Then, to crescendos of clashing cymbals and beating drums, Tibetan Buddhist deities with demonic masks turned somersaults and chased saffron-robed lamas, before they harangued the shrieking crowds.

As autumn neared, I felt it was time to return to Europe, so I booked a flight from Bombay to Athens, where I had asked Marie to write to me. Sure enough, there was a letter in the post office, although it was distinctly non-committal. She wrote that she had received my letter from India, but suggested that I only pass by Strasbourg if it was on my way back to Am-

sterdam. It wasn't, but I found a bus going to the Netherlands via Strasbourg. Two days later, I found myself by the side of the motorway outside
Strasbourg as the bus accelerated into the distance. I crossed a bridge, and
found Marie's address in La Petite France, a warren of narrow passageways
and neglected eighteenth-century houses. She wasn't in, so I pinned a note
on her door and settled down to wait in a red, neon-lit bar below.

An hour later, Marie, noticably caught napping by my unannounced
arrival, peered round the door. 'You can't stay here,' she mumbled with a
crimson face, 'it's a bordello!'

Her apartment was on the floor above, overlooking a stream lined with
weeping willow trees. The sitting room, which was in a minimalist style,
had no furniture other than a piano, a bookshelf weighed down with art
books, a Tibetan *tanka* on the wall, and cushions on the floor. In her daughter's cramped room there was only a mattress and a few toys.

Over a glass of wine she explained why she had been so taken aback by
my sudden appearance on her doorstep.

'My life's crazy at the moment,' she began. 'I didn't mention it to you
in Ladakh, but for several years I've been going out with a philosopher
called Jacques who teaches part-time at the university. He can't decide
what sort of relationship he wants with me. When I first met you in Leh,
we'd split up, but after I got back from India we started going out again.
But he's always playing around with his female students, so I've been seeing a freelance photographer. Now Jacques, who's divorced, feels threatened by him, so he wants me to go and live with him in a cottage in the
south of France and look after his two children. It's all extremely difficult.
I've got my daughter to consider, and I can't do what he wants, just because he wants it.'

Her complicated love affairs notwithstanding, Marie took a week off
work and drove me in her little car to black-and-white-timbered Alsatian
villages. There we relaxed in the mellow, autumnal sun, sipping Gewür-
ztraminer wine. She also took me up to a ski resort in the Vosges Mountains, to show me the hotel that her parents, who were away on holiday, owned. Every evening we dined in romantic, inexpensive restaurants
in the backstreets of Strasbourg. Then, one Saturday, she obtained special
clearance and ushered me round the striking new state-of-the-art premises
of the European Parliament. Despite that, security men shadowed us eve-

rywhere, although that wasn't surprising, as, unaware the king of Spain was on a visit, I was wearing my Basque beret, and could easily have been taken for a Basque terrorist.

Blown off Course

One night, a few weeks after I got back to Amsterdam, I went to the Melkweg. I was loitering outside the bookshop in the market, tapping my feet to the hypnotic reggae throb of Bob Marley, when the owner emerged. A good-looking, blond-haired man in his late twenties named Alistair, he was on his break, and within minutes we were chatting away as if we had known each other all our lives. He was British, in contrast to the majority of visitors in the Melkweg, who were chiefly Dutch or German, and he was fascinated to hear about my experiences in South-east Asia, where he had travelled widely. I have never come across anyone with whom I clicked so effortlessly, and had so much in common. Although he was born in Kenya and I was born in England, both of us had been brought up and gone to school in Scotland. Both of us had been to Edinburgh University and travelled in developing countries before going to live in Amsterdam. Both of us were penniless writers living in broken-down houses, and we both loved foreign films, learning languages, and playing chess and backgammon. The principal difference was that he was gay – though you would never have suspected it – and I wasn't.

After an hour, he had to return to the bookshop, but before he did he offered me a part-time job in it at ten guilders an hour. That was good money, so I promptly accepted, as I needed extra cash to boost my measly wages in the Kosmos. The bookshop was in reality nothing but a wooden hut crammed with postcard stands, marijuana pipes and cigarette papers, along with five shelves of books on feminism, ecology, gay literature and a tiny selection of his favourite novels. For two years, Alistair had had to concede it was sales of postcards and marijuana paraphernalia that kept the bookshop going. Still, this was purely a means to an end, because, like myself, his main interest in life was writing. A year ago he had completed a collection of short stories called *A Box of Dreams* and I had finished my account of travelling in South America. Within weeks, he was coming around on Wednesdays to the Kerkstraat for our 'Doomsbury Group' evenings – an ironical allusion to the Bloomsbury Group – when we exchanged feedback on how to enhance our manuscripts, which publishers still kept returning to us. I considered his stories, which were very anthropomorphic, highly original; he was effusive in his praise for my manuscript, and he was in paroxysms of laughter at the passages meant to be funny and transfixed by those meant to be profound.

Before long, we were as thick as thieves. He would close the bookshop at 2 a.m., and we would wander across the Leidseplein to buy croquettes from vending machines. Even at that hour the city was extraordinarily lively, with droves of people spilling out of cafés, clubs and restaurants. After that, I returned to the Kerkstraat, while he went to gay discos until 7 a.m., before cycling home to write and sleep until the bookshop reopened at 9 p.m. that night. At weekends and Wednesdays, when it was closed, we went to art-house films in the cinema. Our favourite was the Movies, an intimate art deco cinema near Centraal station that had claret walls, claret seats and claret curtains. But we also went to horror films, mainly in the Tushinski, a cinema near the Rembrandtsplein, where, mimicking everybody else, we gasped in mock terror and munched popcorn from tubs the size of flower pots. Although it generally screened the latest blockbusters, it was even more stunning than the Movies, as all the carpets, light fittings and tiles were original art deco.

Then, afterwards, we played chess or backgammon in our favourite café on the Keizersgracht or discussed the films we had just seen.

The most important person in Alistair's life in Amsterdam, apart from myself, was Fritz. Diminutive, with a hangdog expression and heavy bags under his soulful eyes, he was a retired, seventy-year-old Jewish law professor who owned a three-storey gabled house in Van Eeghenstraat, one of the city's most exclusive streets behind the Concertgebouw. As was to be expected, he was very erudite, but he was highly cultured, too, and he had converted the ground floor of his home into an art gallery, where he allowed the coterie of gay, young South American artists with whom he surrounded himself to mount exhibitions. At the back, a conservatory overlooked a rambling, overgrown garden with mammoth chestnut trees and a frog-infested pond. On the first floor, at the top of precipitous wooden stairs, was an antiquated kitchen off a long, narrow sitting room overlooking the Vondelpark. Here, amidst bulging bookshelves and piles of yellowing newspaper cuttings, he lounged about in his stained silk dressing gown, grinding his teeth, drinking whisky and puffing away at cigarettes in his silver cigarette holder.

Alistair and Fritz, who was indisputably his surrogate father, had a love-hate friendship. Since he had been a teenager, Alistair had been attracted to spirituality. After he dropped out of university, where he had studied anthropology, he had travelled overland to India. There, he had flirted briefly with the Bhagwan Shree Rajneesh movement, and, subsequently, in Amsterdam, he had become interested in rebirthing. Fritz, whose rationality and logical approach to life nettled Alistair, pooh-poohed all this as hocus-pocus. Worse, he had nothing positive to say about Alistair's writing. Even so, he had his good points. He was exceedingly generous towards him, and allowed him to write in the conservatory, sleep in the spare bedroom, and borrow his Mini whenever he wished. In return, Alistair, Fritz's undoubted favourite amongst the gay men who helped out at the Van Eeghenstraat, did the shopping. Alistair also enjoyed cooking, and he spent hours in the kitchen preparing gourmet meals for Fritz, who had a highly refined palate and discriminating taste for wine. Every so often, Alistair would invite me to join them for dinner, when they and a host of guests, such as the paunchy, bearded cook who had opened the Netherlands' first cookery bookshop, sat eating, drinking and arguing for hours at the candlelit table in the book-lined sitting room.

Fritz was unusually radical for a man of his age, and was on the board of the Melkweg, where he was an outspoken advocate of gay rights, abortion, euthanasia and the legalisation of heroin. He even favoured lowering the age of sexual consent to twelve, a scandalously low figure even by freethinking Dutch standards. He had written one or two minor legal texts, in addition to articles for the *NRC*, one of the Netherlands' most authoritative newspapers. Regardless, he was perpetually aggrieved that he wasn't more respected by academia or that more of his work hadn't been published. Now he spent hours writing letters of complaint to editors of newspapers, along with those airing his opinions about every subject under the sun. I was indebted to him for what he did for Alistair, even though I for my part found him self-centred and egotistic. After an hour of his monologues I rapidly flagged, and generally I steered clear of Van Eeghenstraat.

The third person in Alistair's life was a thirty-year-old, auburn-haired woman called Inie, with whom he had an unusual, platonic friendship. She lived in a rented apartment in a broken-down quarter of north Amsterdam, but inside it was very attractive, with chrome-coloured floorboards, a chrome-coloured sofa, a white table and chairs, plants and a black *kachel*. She was very assertive and uninhibited, and when the three of us went to the cinema every fortnight, she persisted in making such strident comments during the film that I sometimes squirmed with embarrassment.

Intermittently, she invited Alistair and me around to dinner. She had studied drama, but, after graduation, she eked out a living giving polarity massage and rebirthing sessions. She was direct to the point of being confrontational, and her insistence in pursuing what she perceived to be 'the truth' meant that her meals could resemble group therapy sessions. I personally found this wearing, but Alistair, who thrived on self-analysis, couldn't get enough of it. She had almost never had a relationship with a man, far less one of any length of time, although she had a long-standing circle of loyal female friends. She also knew Fritz, who had initially invited her to meals in Van Eeghenstraat. However, he held her responsible for encouraging Alistair's interest in mysticism and gradually they fell out so rancorously that he never invited her again.

Once a year, Alistair's parents, who lived in a bungalow in the suburbs of Perth, came over to visit him. Both of them were decidedly conventional. His mother, to whom he was very close, was a hearty, outgoing Scottish woman with a contagious sense of humour and throaty laugh. His father, a bald, dull, unimaginative man, had worked in insurance before he retired; now he was happiest pottering about their house in his cardigan and slippers. Their trips to Amsterdam weren't an unqualified success. One Wednesday, Alistair took them to the Melkweg, but they were so shocked by the company of semi-naked drag queens dancing *Swan Lake* in the *oude zaal* that he had to hurry them out. On another occasion he got round to telling them that he was gay. The revelation was received considerably better than he had expected; his mother putting his mind to rest that it made no difference to her before adding as an afterthought that, given he had never brought a girlfriend home, she had known it since he was a teenager. However his father was devastated and, beyond question, viewed his son's homosexuality as a reflection on his own masculinity.

His younger brother also came to see him. They were as different as chalk and cheese. He was a brawny, likable twenty-four-year-old who had left school early, done a lot of manual jobs, and hardly been outside Scotland. In spite of that, they were close, as he patently looked up to Alistair for his worldliness and sense of adventure, and Alistair felt keenly responsible for his younger brother. Nevertheless, in many ways, I was Alistair's family. He was seven years younger than me, but the age difference was irrelevant. We had similar accents and, after I unintentionally started imitating his infectious laugh, people from time to time even mistook us for brothers.

A few months after I began working in the bookshop a once in a lifetime opportunity opened up for Alistair. Europe was changing and the counterculture era was at an end. The Melkweg, aware of its outdated image, decided to convert the second-hand clothes and bric-à-brac market into an avant-garde art gallery and offered Alistair a lavish sum to run a new bookshop just behind it. Ecstatic, he jumped at the chance. As soon as his convoluted legal and financial negotiations with the board were satisfactorily completed, we gaped in wonder as the wooden hut was flattened and the new bookshop was built from scratch. First, a floor-to-ceiling glass partition was constructed to separate it from the modish, all-white gallery. Then the floor was laid with glittering silver linoleum. Last but not least, the walls disappeared underneath gleaming white shelves.

Alistair was clear from the outset about what he wanted. 'I'm not going to fill them with best-sellers,' he said unequivocally. 'I'm simply interested in having a high-quality bookshop, and if it doesn't make it, too bad.'

A month later, the new bookshop opened with a champagne reception.

Named the Labyrinth, after the book by Borges that I had introduced Alistair to, it had the same stock as before, except in greatly expanded sections.

LABYRINTH BOOKSHOP
MELKWEG

Fijne selectie boeken & de beste ansichtkaarten

OPEN
14.00-17.00 wo t/m za

Gratis entrée via Marnixstraat 405
t/o Cinema Bellevue
Café & exposities

Kunst/Reizen/Anthropologie/Filosofie
Foto-Film/Politiek/Vrouwen/Literatuur
Alternatieve levenswijzen/Stripverhalen

's Avonds open voor Melkweg bezoekers/leden

Post adres: Labyrinth Bookshop, Melkweg,
Lijnbaansgracht 234A, 1017 PH Amsterdam, Holland
Tel.: (020) 268797

Alistair, with a new spring in his step, couldn't believe his luck. Every night, dressed in pale blue trousers, yellow shirt and cerise tie, he perched on his high stool behind the till, drinking cognac, chatting and laughing like a drain with his trusty circle of friends who also hung around the Melkweg.

There was the forty-year-old, gay Argentinian punk who, with his shaven head, chains and black leather jacket, looked very intimidating, although he was actually highly intelligent and spoke five languages fluently. There was the gregarious, effervescent Dutchwoman with a freshly scrubbed face and gusty laugh who, with her raven-coloured tresses, made me think of a lioness. There was the handsome young Dutchman who had been one of Alistair's former lovers and whom he still lusted after. Strictly speaking, I was just Alistair's employee, and for three nights a week I tidied up the books, swept the floor, and kept an eye on a mirror high up in a corner to deter thieves. For all that, I felt more like his partner, and I regularly accompanied him in Fritz's Mini to De Boekerij, De Bezige Bij and other book distributors outside Amsterdam.

The following year was a halcyon period for him. Although he had sympathised with the *kraak beweging*, when he had first arrived in Amsterdam, he had slept on the floors of his numerous friends. Then, unlike myself, he had managed to get on to the council's waiting list for accommodation. To begin with, he had been given a one-room apartment near the Albert Cuyp market, but shortly afterwards he had been allocated another one in a picturesque, two-storey gabled house on the edge of the Nieuwmarkt. That hadn't lasted long, as the council was forever repossessing them for redevelopment, and I had as good as lost count of the number of times I helped him transport his meagre possessions from one run-down apartment to another. But finally he was given a permanent one in the Jacob Van Lennepkade, a decaying street overlooking a polluted, rubbish-strewn canal and a disused factory in west Amsterdam. Its main room was beset with mosquitoes, but at least, unlike my garret, it had a tiny kitchen and lavatory. Alistair was delighted with it, so he painted the walls salmon pink, laid out his mattress under a mosquito net he suspended from the ceiling, and set up his typewriter by the window.

There was more. For the first time since I had met him, his emotional life was going well. He had fallen in love with Conrad, an impossibly beautiful, twenty-year-old Australian with soft pink lips who had just come to Amsterdam and was the image of Tadzio, the dazzling gentle youth in Visconti's film *Death in Venice*. Now, in place of the unsatisfactory trysts he had had in gay clubs or in bushes in the Vondelpark at 5 a.m., Alistair had a meaningful relationship. He introduced Conrad to Fritz and all his friends. He gave him five hours' work in the bookshop, which was now so profitable it was also opening in the afternoons. He even invited Conrad to stay in the Jacob Van Lennepkade, where the three of us frequently played backgammon for more and more outrageous stakes until dawn, when Conrad had lost so much we had to stop.

I, too, was the most content since those exhilarating days when I had first arrived in Amsterdam. For a year, after I had got back from Strasbourg, Marie, who had split up yet again with Jacques and was no longer seeing her photographer, had been coming up to visit me in Amsterdam, and I had been going down to see her in Strasbourg. There she had moved from La

Petite France and, for financial reasons, she was sharing an apartment with Jacques, with whom she maintained a loosely defined, platonic relationship. Nestling high up amongst a profusion of red rooftops, it consisted of spacious rooms connected by long, winding corridors, and this, plus the fact that he was only there once in a blue moon, meant that they hardly ever saw each other. Her light, airy room was to the front, affording a superb view of the cobbled main square and the soaring steeple of the cathedral. Once again, it was in a minimalist style, and for furniture and decoration there was only a white double bed, beautiful gentian and violet gauzes over the window, and Indian rugs on the floor.

But inescapably, given the distance between Strasbourg and Amsterdam, something in our relationship had had to give. Taken to its logical conclusion, I would have had to, in due course, go and live in Strasbourg, or she and her daughter would have had to relocate to Amsterdam. In reality both options had been unrealistic. I didn't want to move from Amsterdam, where I was a half-hearted, poverty-stricken writer with little to offer a woman and a child other than life in a primitive garret with no proper washing facilities and a chemical toilet. She was set on staying in Strasbourg, where she had a highly remunerative professional job and her daughter was at school. In addition, after the novelty of our romance had waned, both of us had been aware that it had never been serious enough for either of us to contemplate such a move. At length, ground down by the travelling between the two cities, in an attempt to finally resolve matters between us, we had gone for a walk in undulating countryside outside Strasbourg. It was a suffocating autumnal day, and only the faint pealing of church bells and shots from a party of hunters crawling like ants across faraway fields disturbed the deafening silence. The decision about what to do was a great deal easier than we had expected; in the middle of a field of ripe yellow maize, we decided that we had no choice except to break up, but remain good friends.

I was less heartbroken than I generally was when one of my relationships fell apart; in fact I was now more content than I had ever been in Amsterdam. With two part-time jobs, I had settled into a rhythm there that suited me, and gave me enough money to subsist on. In Alistair, I had the best friend I had ever had, and a soulmate with whom I could go to films, play chess and backgammon, and discuss books and relationships until dawn. Moreover, I

still adored the sights, sounds and smells of Amsterdam: the lime-green wil-
lows hanging low over the canals in spring; the odour of roast chestnuts from
stalls in Damplein; the ethereal tinkling of bells from Munt tower; the tunes
being ground out from old-fangled *draailiers* (hurdy-gurdies); the cheerful
clanging of trams; and everywhere the sweet tones of violin and piano sona-
tas that drifted from the houses.

There were other reasons, too. I still enjoyed working in the Melkweg, where there was without exception something enthralling to see or
listen to. During my breaks in the bookshop, I would go to the Oude
Zaal, where many undiscovered, although subsequently famous, African
and Afro-Caribbean bands played. It was also the venue for outrageous
'happenings'. One in particular is branded in my mind. First on stage was
Patti Smith, in those days still a little-known young punk poet. Next was
Ken Kesey, who recounted how, hallucinating on LSD, he and his Merry
Pranksters had travelled across America in their psychedelically painted
ex-school bus.

Last came an emaciated, peaky-looking man wearing a suit, tie and fedora. He was the image of a used-car salesman, but it was the cult writer William Burroughs.

'Good evening,' he began. 'I want to read you something I've written recently. It's called "Bugger the Queen".' Then, to general hilarity, he read out a poem that described Queen Elizabeth II being buggered by her corgis.

The Melkweg wasn't the only venue for scandalous events. One night I helped Alistair set up a stall from the Labyrinth in the Paradiso for the One World poetry festival. Inside, on a stage in the tenebrous hall, poets such as Yevtushenko, the controversial Russian dissident, recited from their work. A twelve-member reggae band succeeded them until, at 2 a.m., flashing strobe lights illuminated a gargantuan silver globe suspended from the ceiling. While the multitude gasped in disbelief, it sank to the dance floor, where the upper half rose to reveal a perspiring, naked coal-black man with a fifteen-foot-long python coiled around his neck. As the music reached a crescendo and the hall was wreathed in grey smoke, he performed an erotic, funereal-paced rumba. Then he unwound the snake from his sweating torso and released it into the screaming audience. Obviously, everyone scattered until, too stoned to care, they enveloped him again and danced the night away.

But the most intoxicating events of all in Amsterdam were the *ontruimings* …

At the start of the 1980s, with the city's housing shortage worse than ever, the *kraak beweging* had reached its zenith and, in scenes of virtually unparalleled chaos in the Netherlands during peacetime, the *krakers* were now in a state of open war with the police. In fact, although, as a pacifist like my father and grandfather, I unreservedly rejected the idea of anybody being hurt, far less killed, I, along with numerous *krakers*, even sympathised with the Baader-Meinhof gang, the left-wing terrorists who sporadically used the city as a safe haven. Nor were we the only ones, as they had a not in-considerable number of supporters among anarchists in Christiania (the self-proclaimed autonomous commune in Copenhagen) and *hausbesetzers* in West Berlin, which, with its gratuitously brutal, baton-wielding police, looked as if it was sliding towards authoritarianism.

Now, whenever I heard a helicopter overhead – the sure sign of an *ontruiming* – I tore down the stairs, jumped on my bicycle and, tracking the clattering blades, pedalled furiously to see what was happening. There were at least five major actions, each resulting in serious riots. 'De Groote Keizer' was three gabled townhouses on the Keizersgracht that *krakers* had converted into a fortress, where they were – falsely – reported to have weapons and set up an illegal radio station to summon support when an eviction loomed. The 'Weteringschanz' was to one side of Centraal station, where ten twenty-foot-high hydraulic cranes were needed to evict *krakers* occupying newly built apartments next to St Nicholas Church. Koningin's Dag (Queen's Day), which is a national holiday to celebrate the birthday of the queen of the Netherlands, was when demonstrators chanting the slogan 'Geen woning, geen kroning!' ('No house, no coronation') utilised the investiture of Queen Beatrix to demonstrate against the acute lack of housing. In the actions, thousands of rioters roamed the centre, tearing up cobbles on the sides of the canals or bombarding columns of ME vans with stones as, sirens wailing and blue lights flashing, they hurtled down to Damplein. There was no denying that it was exhilarating and, pulsating with adrenaline, I now and again risked going to the front of the clashes. As a rule, though, I remained a passive onlooker at the back of the crowd, and took great care to avoid becoming corralled into a cul-de-sac by the ME.

Two other *ontruimings* stand out. The first was the 'Stopera' on Waterlooplein. For four years, after flattening the decaying houses there, the city council had allowed the resulting open space to be used for allot-ments and a flea market. When the council resolved to clear it to build a long-planned opera house, a pitched battle ensued. All morning the ME struggled on the Blau Brug (blue bridge) over the Amstel to thwart protestors from reinforcing their comrades on tear gas-enshrouded Waterlooplein. It was only four hundred yards from the Kerkstraat, and ultimately other *krakers* and I admitted defeat, spending the remainder of the afternoon trying to outflank them via side streets.

The second was the 'Vondelstraat', the most dramatic eviction of all. In February, *krakers* reoccupied a building in a street near the Vondelpark that had already been evicted. When three ME platoons attempted to storm it, they were driven off by hundreds of increasingly militant *krakers*.

To defend it, the *krakers* overturned vehicles and used material from a construction site to erect barricades across the tramlines of two main thoroughfares. Over the weekend, the two sides held fraught negotiations, and after these came to nothing, the government concluded that the sole way to resolve the impasse without loss of life was to call in the army. On Monday morning, I couldn't believe my eyes as a column of tanks, armoured vehicles, and ME units from around the country stormed the barricades. Seeing the tanks rear up over them, with their commanders' arms akimbo, was reminiscent of the arresting images I had seen of the Red Army entering Berlin in 1945.

Meanwhile, there had been a transformation in the lives of my parents, whom my sister and I continued to visit every summer and Christmas in Edinburgh. As time had rolled by, she and I had grown to dislike the bungalow. I had come to reject what it and the barren, treeless suburbs symbolised for me, after my experience of living in semi-communal squats for a decade. She had found it too restricted for her rapidly growing family, which, besides her daughter, now included her twin boys. At length, we had persuaded our parents to move from the bungalow – which later my father said he had only bought because he wanted my sister and me to have a garden – and with the inheritance Eva had left my mother they bought a new residence in the centre of the Georgian New Town. Snapped up by my father at a time when property in Edinburgh was still absurdly cheap, it was magnificent. A double upper, first-floor flat, it had an echoing hall with elegant spiral stairs up to the first floor; a huge nineteenth-century kitchen with granite-grey flagstones, an original, black iron, nineteenth-century cooking range and a long, pine kitchen table; and two colossal drawing rooms, each with original cornices, floor-to-ceiling astragal windows and floral-patterned sofas grouped around marble mantelpieces. The green drawing room had apple-green walls, a dark red carpet, elegantly draped burgundy velvet curtains, and a polished mahogany table and cabinets. The brown drawing room had tangerine walls, a dark brown carpet, an antique sideboard and writing bureau, a six-foot-tall gilt mirror, and elegantly draped brown velvet curtains over immense, floor-to-ceiling astragal windows. On the second floor, overlooking the street to the front, there was a master double bedroom with a pale green carpet, a white dressing table and bookshelves, and uninterrupted vistas to the River Forth and the hills of Fife; an attic bedroom with a dormer window; and, at the back, two double bedrooms with stupendous views over the New Town to wooded Corstorphine Hill and the Forth Bridge.

One night, a few months after they moved into their new abode in Howe Street, my mother telephoned me in the kitchen of the Kosmos. The instant I heard the panic in her trembling voice I knew that something awful had happened, as I had given her strict instructions to use the number solely in an emergency. 'Patrick,' she said, close to tears, 'not long ago I found a suspicious lump in my breast. I went to see the doctor, who arranged for a biopsy and I've just got the results. I've got breast cancer.'

I instantly requested compassionate leave, and that weekend I flew back to Edinburgh. My mother wasn't one to conceal her feelings and she was beside herself with worry. Every day, I drove her, heavily sedated with Valium, and my father up to the Royal Infirmary for more tests. These revealed that an appreciable proportion of her lymph nodes had been affected and she was notified that she had to undergo a radical mastectomy, the standard procedure in those days. Although it was imperative that the operation was carried out at once, there was a two-month waiting list. In desperation, she contacted her favourite cousin, a senior consultant in oncology at a leading hospital in Manchester. He was an intimate friend of the head of oncology at the Royal Infirmary and, within a week, she was admitted to hospital, where the professor himself carried out the operation.

After it was finished, she had to stay in hospital for three weeks, as her right arm was severely swollen because of a blockage in her lymph glands. Every day, my father and I visited her in her ward. As if she hadn't taken in the enormity of what had happened to her, she was in good spirits. However she required an enormous amount of encouragement, and we reassured her, with no real grounds for doing so, that her prognosis was favourable. During those terrible, terrible two weeks before the operation, I had read *Getting Well Again* by Carl Simonton, an influential, if controversial, oncologist with a groundbreaking, holistic approach to cancer. A self-help guide to overcoming the disease, it made clear how essential it was for cancer patients to maintain a positive outlook and decrease the stress in their lives. I found it highly persuasive, so I did my utmost to convince my mother of its contents, and, as my father and I were going out of the door, I would turn to her and raise my clenched fist to give her courage. Afterwards, when he and I were back at the house, I told him how convinced I was of the need for a radical trans-formation in the dynamics of our family. This would mean, in particular, he and my sister desisting from attacking her over her excessive weight, and all of us, myself included, ceasing to use her as the butt of the family's humour.

After the operation, she appeared to be making a remarkable recovery, and I had to return to Amsterdam and my part-time jobs in the Kosmos and the Melkweg. There, Alistair's life was also entering a new phase. His flat in the Jacob van Lennepkade had become a misery, because his neighbours in the apartment above were drug-dealers – acquaintances of Christos, to nobody's surprise – and there were so many people tramping up and down the stairs twenty-four hours a day that he couldn't sleep. His constant battles with the bureaucracy and income tax authorities were wearing him down. Conrad had dumped him, saying he didn't want to be 'pinned to the wall like a butterfly', yet whenever he dropped in on Fritz in Van Eeghenstraat, there was Conrad, ensconced like a cuckoo. Worst of all, sales in the bookshop had nosedived. Now Alistair was drinking a bottle of cognac every night, and after he closed at 2 a.m., he started going to the red-light district to have another drink with his friend, Eddie, an American writer and publisher of *Inns and Outs*, an underground magazine, before going on to buy some cocaine from a nearby dealer.

Occasionally, out of curiosity, I accompanied him to see Eddie, who lived in a cluttered fourth-floor garret in the middle of the red-light district that doubled as his office. Renowned for having developed a unique method of liquefying psilocybin mushrooms, like numerous foreigners in Amsterdam, he had lived a remarkably picaresque life. He had been a restaurant manager in Hong Kong, a features writer for the *Bangkok Post*, a 'kept man' in Sin-gapore by a Chinese drag-queen prostitute, and a journalist for the *Tehran Journal*. As if that wasn't enough, he had hung out with Tennessee Williams, with whom he had travelled to Malaysia and Singapore, he had published Al-len Ginsberg, Lawrence Ferlinghetti and other Beat poets, and he had shared a platform with William Burroughs and Patti Smith at the One World poetry festival in Amsterdam.

Copious amounts of cocaine, self-evidently, didn't do Alistair any good. After the bookshop closed, he cycled home and, under the illusion his creative juices were flowing, pounded away at his typewriter, simply to discover that, when he came to at 2 p.m. the following afternoon, he had written more or less the same sentence umpteen various ways. He himself contended that cocaine wasn't addictive, but he seemed to be powerless to stop using it. But, like myself, he was becoming ever more aware of what Amsterdam could do to you. At the beginning, with its unfettered access to sex, drugs and pornography, it had promised so much. It was brimming with beautiful or artistic people. Its cosmopolitan cafés matched any in Paris or Vienna. It had peerless concert halls, art galleries and museums. For all that, we were starting to realise at last that, for numerous foreigners, Amsterdam was a dangerous illusion, a seductive quagmire that sucked you in and before you knew it you couldn't extricate yourself. So far, unlike many ex-pats and exiles, we had escaped comparatively unscathed. They, on the other hand, unable to distinguish between freedom and licence, had become dealers, drug addicts and casualties or were languishing in prison. Worst of all, living there was like being in a time warp; once you were outside it, you swiftly learned that the real world – where reactionary governments were everywhere rapidly gaining ground – was a much more unforgiving place.

If things weren't going well for Alistair, they weren't going much better for me. I for my part never took cocaine or heroin. Furthermore, in all likelihood I was the only male foreigner to live in Amsterdam for a decade without going to a pornographic show in the red-light district, whose porn shops, strip-tease joints and live sex-shows I found increasingly degrading. All the same, I was close on forty, and the novelty of working in the Labyrinth, where I could no longer disguise that I was merely a glorified dogsbody, had long since ebbed. However, I couldn't envisage an alternative to working there or washing dishes, which I had had enough of, in the Kosmos. It hadn't been for lack of trying. The administrative staff and teachers at the Kosmos had been unfailingly well disposed towards me, as they knew that I was a struggling writer living in a garret. However, I found it difficult to admit that to visitors and the outside world I was only a dishwasher. The impact on my subconscious was far-reaching, and one night it hit me how low my self-esteem had sunk when I realised that I regarded waiting on tables, which I occasionally was allowed to do, as a promotion. Shocked, I had applied to be the manager of the bookshop in the basement when a vacancy had arisen. Exaggerating my responsibilities in the Labyrinth, I had told the interviewing panel of how experienced I was in 'managing a bookshop'. To my bitter disappointment, I had been passed over in favour of one of the staff, a bearded, thirty-year-old ambitious German who was, admittedly, bubbling with inventive ideas, and just happened to be the partner of one of the influential cooks.

It was the same with my housing situation, where I couldn't see any option but to continue living in the garret. I couldn't afford to rent an apartment, so I had kept my ears to the ground in case something else might crop up. For the first few years, I had also hoped, despite my attachment to the garret, that I might get a floor in the *kraakpand* next door if one became vacant. Nonetheless, when one did, which was seldom, without fail it went to somebody else, as I was away travelling so much. Now, accordingly, I was resigned to living in the garret, where the sound of mice scuttling under my mattress no longer bothered me. Every two weeks, I automatically emptied my chemical toilet in André's lavatory on the floor below. When tea leaves and other waste from the kitchen blocked the gutter, I took it for granted that I had to clamber out of the front window and, dicing with death, sweep it out with a broom.

Then there was my relationship with the Dutch and the Dutch language. When I had moved to Amsterdam, I had started studying my Dutch grammar book in Dutch-speaking cafés, as I hadn't swapped London simply to live in the world of English expatriates. Regardless, for the first four years I had made little headway in learning the language, not because it is difficult to learn – which it isn't – but because I so seldom had an opportunity to practise it. The Dutch are famously bilingual, and I only had to say 'Dag' for them to reply 'Good morning' in fluent English. At the outset, it hadn't mattered. I hadn't needed Dutch, as English was the lingua franca in the Bijenkorf, where the greatest part of the staff in the restaurant were of different nationalities, and in the Melkweg, where a substantial proportion of the visitors were foreigners who spoke English. After I started working in the Kosmos, I had to speak Dutch, as those who ate in the restaurant were mostly Dutch. Nevertheless, I found it such an ugly language that I could scarcely bring myself to speak it. Nor was it just the language. When I had first arrived in Amsterdam I had gone to cafés hoping to meet new people, principally women, and have exciting new encounters. Initially I'd had some success, notably in De Reijnders and Café de Prins, although now I never encountered anyone new, which merely left me feeling melancholy, disheartened and yearning for a successful, long-term relationship. Finally there was my circle of Dutch friends, but whenever I dropped in on them, after they spoke English for a while, they habitually reverted to Dutch, leaving me feeling marginalised and frustrated at my inability to express myself.

But, first and foremost, there was the abject failure I felt as a writer. Although I had been writing for a decade, much of what I had written was about how to 'find myself' and 'the truth' rather than how captivating it was to live in Amsterdam. The result was that all I had to show for it were six fragmentary short stories in the still unfinished *The Sound of Breaking Glass*, and my unpublished manuscript about my travels in South America. At my mother's suggestion, to get advice about what to do with the latter, I had posted it to J.I.M. Stewart, the Oxford don and writer who, of course, had been one of her first – in all probability *the* first – lovers, and who had always occupied a special place in her heart. He had evidently felt the same, because for the last four decades he had sent her a copy of his latest book (of which he wrote over fifty), and they had exchanged Christmas cards.

After he read the manuscript, he had written me an encouraging letter, advising me to persevere. So, following our 'Doomsbury' evenings, I had spent two years rewriting it, and Alistair had revised *A Box of Dreams* before we had posted them off again to publishers. Even so, we had kept on receiving only rejection slips. Both of us, but especially me, had found these hard to take, and I had been incensed when one of Britain's pre-eminent publishers returned my manuscript with a note commenting that it was 'little more than a series of delightful picture postcards'. So I had fired off a letter to the managing director, demanding to know if he was aware that 'one of your presumably junior editors is writing such discouraging letters to aspiring young writers'. I hadn't received a reply and, too thin-skinned to tolerate any criticism except that of Alistair, I had put the manuscript away in a tea chest, and now I was hardly writing at all. It wasn't surprising, therefore, that when Michel appeared unheralded at the Kerkstraat for that third, and final, time in October and proposed we go travelling to Africa, I promptly agreed.

We travelled through Central Africa until we headed east to Zanzibar, where I collected Marie – who was coming out to see me as well as visit

Tanzania's game reserves – from the island's tiny airport. Although our love affair had ended, we had stayed in contact, and twice, because she had split up with Jacques for the umpteenth time, she and I made love for old times' sake in the shallow jade sea off the east coast.

After we visited the game reserves, she had to return to France, while Michel and I crossed the border into Kenya. Then we travelled up the coast to the island of Lamu, from where we sailed on an Arab dhow for two days back down to Mombasa.

At last, six months after we had departed, we arrived back in Nairobi, where a decision had to be taken about what to do next. For the first time since we had begun travelling together, we felt jaded. Regardless, I was curious to see Egypt, but Michel, as usual, was bent on going back to Belgium. This time, though, it was for a different reason. Before he had departed for Belgium his oldest and favourite sister had been admitted to hospital, complaining of stomach cramps. As there was no mail from either her or his parents in Nairobi's poste restante, he had sensed that something was badly amiss. His intuition proved, as always, to be correct; as soon as he opened the door of his parents' house outside Antwerp he discovered she had died the previous week of bowel cancer.

After Michel returned home, I flew to Egypt. By the time I got back to Amsterdam, it was spring. When I turned into the Kerkstraat, I found that, once again, my beloved garret was still there, and all too soon I was back working in the Melkweg and the Kosmos.

Homeward Bound

One Friday, I was loitering behind the counter in the bookshop when there appeared Margriet, my one-time lover. She had changed remarkably little since I had last seen her, seven years previously, and over a drink in the café she recounted what had happened to her and her boyfriend. True to her word, she had waited for him, and after his early release for good conduct they had gone to Vancouver, his home town. They had got married, but, astonishingly, given their long wait, they had split up only three years afterwards. She had elected to stay on in Canada, however, where she had made close friends and revelled in the outdoor lifestyle. She had remained single and, because she loved children, got a job at a rehabilitation school as a childcare worker. Now she was in Amsterdam briefly to see her sister and parents, and she was visiting the Melkweg for old times' sake. Incredulous at the odds of us bumping into each other, we embraced and, before she left, pledged to always stay in contact.

Margriet wasn't the only spectre from my past that reappeared in, or near, the Melkweg. One afternoon, when I was on my way to open the bookshop, I bumped into Jacob, who, it transpired, occasionally came over to Amsterdam to see friends. I had long since lost touch with him, as I had scarcely ever gone back to London after I had moved to the Netherlands, but he seemed to be as ebullient, but needy, as ever. That evening, over a *rijsttavel* (array of Indonesian side dishes) in a restaurant off the Leidseplein, we caught up with each other's news. I told him about the journeys I had undertaken with Michel, whom he hadn't seen for a long time either, while he described how he had quit his job as a gardener and drifted around aimlessly until he had gone to live in Paris, where he was now training to be a translator. To his mother's chagrin, her other son had joined the Moonies, a religious cult whose headquarters were in South Korea, where he was living after he had married a Korean woman in one of their infamous, 1,000-strong wedding ceremonies.

After the meal Jacob asked if, as his friends were away, he could stay in the garret for a few days. By now I had become distinctly possessive about it, and I not only regarded it as too small to share with anybody except lovers, but – if the truth were to be told – felt that I no longer needed him. To my eternal shame, I therefore said no; as you might expect, given his and his parents' hospitality towards me, he never forgave me. It was the last I ever saw of him, although, still afflicted by guilt of the way I had used him, years later I attempted unsuccessfully to contact him. Then, I was taken aback to hear that his parents had got divorced, and his mother had gone back to Paris, where she was now living by herself in an apartment she had bought with her alimony. Somehow, I tracked down her telephone number, so I rang her and once, when I was passing through the French capital, I even looked her up. She was living in a cramped, but exquisitely furnished, flat in a narrow street in the exorbitantly expensive Île de France, only a stone's throw from Notre Dame cathedral. But I thought she was markedly cool towards me and I left feeling saddened, as she gave me the impression of being a sadly diminished elderly woman, with the days when she had so graciously presided over the generous breakfast table in the garden in Marbella now merely a distant memory.

Two decades afterwards, I gleaned via the internet what had happened to her two sons. Jacob had completed more prestigious translating courses before he had become an eminent professor of modern languages at a famous university in Italy and – judging by the way he came across on a YouTube video – matured into being a very impressive and dignified-looking scholar. His younger brother, who had learned Korean and Japanese, had studied East Asian philosophy and been awarded his doctorate at Stanford University before he had been given a chair in Asian history at some equally illustrious Australian university. I couldn't believe what I was reading, as the lives of the barefooted, charismatic hippy whom I had met by chance during that never-to-be-forgotten day in Sicily, and his once-gawky brother who had been expelled from his public school for smoking marijuana, had turned out so differently from how I had imagined.

Before my trip to Africa, I had started going every Tuesday afternoon to a class my yoga teacher gave in her airy, newly converted studio in the Jordaan, along with two she held every Friday night in the Kosmos. I was killing time in a neighbourhood café, waiting for it to begin, when I heard a soft female voice say in English, 'What'd you like to drink?'

I glanced up to discover a ravishing, dusky young woman leaning over me. She was about twenty-five years old, and she had slender legs, a tapering waist and shoulder-length black hair swept back from her face. She wore peacock-blue jeans, a plum chiffon scarf across her turquoise bodice, and she moved her lithe body with such effortless grace that she reminded me of a dancer. She told me her name was Penny, she was English, and she had been living in Amsterdam for several years. After a while, she was summoned to serve somebody else, but as I was going out of the door she invited me around to a meal the following night. Still taken by surprise, twenty-four hours later, I took the tram to Javastraat, a narrow, neglected, shady street on the way to the Tropische (tropical) museum. I had no sooner entered her apartment than I found myself pinned against the wall as she went down on me. Within minutes we were on the floor engaged in the most passionate lovemaking in my life, and before long I was totally besotted with her.

But it wasn't merely sex that drew her to me. The more I got to know her, the more my heart melted. Although she could have passed for some Polynesian beauty, she had in fact been born of a Guyanese mother and a semi-illiterate English father who lived on a council estate in the East End of London. She had left school at sixteen without any qualifications, and, after her parents divorced she had drifted to Amsterdam, where she had had a love affair with an Israeli hippy and a small-time drugs dealer. They had had a child, but she had split up with him after he had begun selling arms, although she kept in touch with him when he wasn't in Israel 'on business' or in Goa, 'chilling out'. She knew only a smattering of mothers in the neighbourhood, and she had hardly any money, which she earned by working three afternoons a week in the café while her five-year-old son was at playschool. The rest of the time they were trapped in an apartment whose bedroom was so cramped there was scarcely space for a double bed.

I was also enamoured by her ostensibly spiritual philosophy. One day, I asked her if she had any ambitions.

'Things only happen if they're supposed to,' she responded, looking at me as if I had said something distasteful. 'To realise our potential we need to take the energy of the universe and match it to the intelligence of our bodies. We can't force things. We need to slow down and give in, instead of resisting, and we need to live for the moment, for the here and now, and not for the future.'

I was aware, naturally, some of her beliefs were little more than mumbo-jumbo, but her last few words struck a chord because, like numerous people in the Kosmos, I believed that the need to live in the present overrode the need to make long-term plans. Two weeks after I first ran into her, I introduced her to Alistair in a café. To my surprise, he wasn't impressed.

'Patrick,' he warned after she had left, 'she's lovely, though she strikes me as muddled, and a lot of what she says is cliché-ridden hippy jargon. I think she's bad news for you, and I hope you know what you're getting yourself into.'

I ignored his warning. It made no difference to me that we had nothing in common apart from lovemaking, and we couldn't discuss books, films, politics – or anything at all, come to that. It was immaterial to me that, in our free time, we did nothing except sit round the Javastraat smoking marijuana, instead of going to the Vondelpark or the cinema. The most important thing was that she desired me as much as I desired her, and so devouring was the passion that consumed me that I was as addicted to her as a junkie is to narcotics. She stayed the night only once or twice in the Kerkstraat, I suppose because, as a mother with a young child, she found the conditions there too basic and unhygienic, although she never said so. Our sole distraction was when her older sister, with whom she was close, came over from London for the weekend. Articulate and intelligent, she had been married to a music producer at ITV before they separated. Now she was on the dole and living in a council flat on the 'front line' in Notting Hill, where she and her Rastafarian friends from the adjacent West Indian community were forever clashing with police about their right to smoke marijuana, an integral part of their culture. If anything, her older sister smoked even more than Penny, and within minutes of her arrival the apartment would be wreathed in a haze of fumes.

Even so, it wasn't long until I realised that Penny's spiritual philosophy was purely a legitimisation, albeit an unconscious one, of her whims. The problem was she wanted to see me only when it suited her – principally for sex – and I had to take it or leave it if my plans didn't fit around hers. On one occasion she proclaimed, 'Patrick, my love isn't something that can be turned on and off like a tap – it's a gift to you, and you shouldn't misuse it! Having a relationship isn't only about having sex, it's about creating a sacred space, where spirit can enter and guide us! We can't know when the time is right to see each other, and when it's not – we have to tune into our frequencies. What matters is feeling deep within, not thinking or agreeing or disagreeing with each other!'

All the same, I wasn't an easy lover either. Penny had a life of her own, however limited, what with her son, the other mothers and her part-time job in the teahouse. I, conversely, now regarded my existence, apart from my friendship with Alistair, as hollow and meaningless. My writing had stalled. I was still washing dishes in the Kosmos. In the bookshop I continued to do little more than sweep the floor and tidy the bookshelves. As a consequence, I wanted only to be with her the whole time. Of course I strove to conceal how reliant I was on her, but I found it ever more difficult to disguise that, for the second time in my life, I felt like a suffocating man desperately grasping an oxygen mask. Nor did my relationship with her son help. Cooped up for a good part of the day in the poky apartment, he was a fractious child, and at night, resenting the newcomer competing with him for his mother's love, he kicked me again and again as we elbowed each other for space beside her in the double bed.

That summer, as usual, I went back to Edinburgh. Before I departed from Amsterdam, I had forewarned Penny that I had invited Marie, whose relationship with Jacques had started up yet again, and her daughter to stay at my parents' house for a fortnight. Penny hadn't been overjoyed about it, although I made clear that Marie and I were simply friends and I was only carrying out a long-standing commitment to her, as for years she had wanted to visit Scotland. One evening, Penny telephoned me to say she had begun seeing a tall, blond-haired hippy who had just arrived in Amsterdam from Goa in India. Distraught, and trying to suppress my jealousy, I once more sought to reassure her about the innocent nature of my relationship with Marie. Then, two weeks afterwards, when I went back to Amsterdam, I tore round to the Javastraat to try to salvage things. I had just closed the door when Penny divulged she had slept with him.

'Couldn't you have at least waited until I came back, and we had a chance to talk about it?' I said despairingly. 'After all, I was away for less than four weeks!'

'Patrick, we don't possess each other!' she blurted out. 'Why can't both of you share my love? We need to get rid of rigid rules, we need to step outside of ourselves and be free. Let's put the past behind us and come into awareness of the present moment! We need to open our minds and channel the built-up energy we possess into oneness!'

Unable to accept the situation, I saw nothing of her during the ensuing month. Then – I never found out why – her romance with the hippy fizzled out as precipitously as it had begun and, after he returned to Goa, we started sleeping together again. Nevertheless, by now I was even more insecure about where I stood with her, and the battle between my attempt to stay positive and my inner desperation, which she couldn't but help notice, began to consume me. Late one night, on the second occasion she stayed in the garret, we smoked some marijuana. It was a mistake as, afterwards, I only wished, as usual, to sink into oblivion. She, on the other hand, wanted to make love and she was so put out when I lay there, pretending to be asleep, that she flounced out of the garret.

The following morning, when I hurried round to the Javastraat to try to make amends, she was still peeved. 'How could you do that to me, when all I wanted was to give you the gift of my love!' she cried.

As October slid into November, she began talking about taking her son to India for the winter. Naturally, I did my utmost to persuade her not to go, and when this was unsuccessful I promised her I would be there for her when she got back. Then, one Tuesday, without saying a word, she was gone. All at once, it was like the end of the world, and, yet again, as it always did when my relationship with a woman fell apart, I felt as if I were spiralling down into the black, familiar vortex. So, for the second time, I consulted a psychiatrist.

He listened solicitously as I described my life to him before I broke down and wept. I disclosed everything – about the garret, my meagre income from the Labyrinth and the vegetarian restaurant, and my seeming inability to sustain a relationship with a woman or find a role for myself. After I was finished, he explained there was nothing a fundamental change in my lifestyle wouldn't cure. Although this hardly touched on the reason for my desperation, and why I relied on women so much for my happiness, I realised he was right. At long last I was forced to recognise that, after eleven years in Amsterdam, my life was going nowhere. I was tired of living in a broken-down garret, tired of washing dishes and tired of trying to make ends meet. I was tired of the hordes of people in Amsterdam, tired of its drug-ridden counterculture and tired of living in a shifting world of drop-outs, outcasts, junkies and émigrés. I yearned for a sense of security, for a career, a steady income and a decent place in which to live. I yearned to be amongst hard-working, down-to-earth people, and live in a place where there were mountains, rivers and forests. I yearned to be able to speak my own language, and be in my own culture, however much I was repelled by its class-consciousness. So I decided to leave Amsterdam and return to Britain.

There, I told myself, I would find a stimulating job with a human rights organisation or Channel 4, the exciting new television channel. I would give up cigarettes and marijuana and I would live a healthier life. I would spend more time with my mother, who looked as if she had made a complete recovery after her operation, but had who knew how long to live. A week later, eleven years after I had gone from London to Amsterdam for the weekend, I walked out on my books and records in the garret and returned to Edinburgh, where my father agreed to let me stay in his pied-à-terre in St Stephen Street. Then, only six months after I had been back in Scotland, I received a letter from Penny. It was the first I had heard from her since she had gone to India. When we had been in Amsterdam, we had already talked about the need for both of us to find a more salubrious place in which to live. At the same time, she had disclosed that her sister's husband, a music producer at ITV, owned a cottage in Gordon, a remote village in the Scottish Borders. Despite being divorced, he and her older sister had remained on good terms and he had agreed when she had asked if Penny could stay in it. Now, Penny wrote, she was temporarily leaving her son with his father, before she flew over to see if she and her son could live in Scotland, and she wanted to know if I would collect her at the airport.

Clinging to the faint hope that our relationship might yet be revived, I answered that of course I would. Three days later, I borrowed the Volkswagen and, with my heart pounding, drove to the airport. The instant I caught sight of her, all my love for her flooded back. How could an impoverished, twenty-five-year-old unmarried mother put down roots in a tiny, remote village in the middle of nowhere after living for years in cosmopolitan London and Amsterdam? She would be totally alone, apart from her son. She had no education, no skills, and no work experience, apart from waiting on tables in a teahouse. She would be the only person of mixed race in the Borders, she would have to beg for social security …

The plane had been delayed and, as it was too late to take her down to

Gordon, she accepted my offer to stay overnight. Over something to eat, I also proposed tentatively that she live with me instead of going to Gordon.

'Thanks, but no,' she responded, with a smile.

'Well, you can stay here whenever you like,' I continued, trying to sound as nonchalant as possible.

'Patrick,' she retorted, 'you mustn't plan your life around me. Still, you can help me move to Gordon if you like.'

I swallowed my pride and that evening, despite her warning, we again made love. For the following five days, bewitched by her all over again, I chauffeured her around charity shops, where I loaded up with tawdry, second-hand furniture before we drove down to Gordon. Once or twice, if it was too late to undertake the long, two-hour journey, she stayed the night in St Stephen Street, where she would make love to me in a way nobody had ever done before.

The cottage in Gordon was in a row in the main street, which looked out to the distant Cheviot Hills. It had been unoccupied for several years, and it was dilapidated and antiquated, so she was pleased when I volunteered to decorate it. It was a daunting undertaking, because, although the cottage seemed very small from outside, there were two rooms on the ground floor and three rooms above.

During the day, we had virtually no contact with each other, as I was busy painting and she was making the sitting room and kitchen habitable. But while I was painting, it rapidly became obvious that, for some reason I couldn't fathom, I got on her nerves. Every night, accordingly, I slept on a mattress in the bedroom upstairs and she slept in the one downstairs.

A week later, after toiling from 8 a.m. to 8 p.m., I had finished. 'What d'you think?' I hazarded, pleased at how quickly I had painted the cottage.

She paused, before she looked me straight in the eyes. 'Patrick,' she rejoined tartly, 'somehow … you're too speedy and your energy's not right.'

Disguising my hurt, I drove back to St Stephen Street. Two days afterwards, at midday, the phone rang. It was Penny, who, as the cottage had no telephone, was phoning from a public telephone box.

'Patrick, I'm not well,' she said urgently. 'Could you come down and take me to see a doctor in Edinburgh?'

I could tell she was in a real state, so I hurriedly arranged to borrow the Volkswagen, and dashed down to Gordon. There, I collected her before I took her to a municipal health clinic in Edinburgh. It was in a converted church hall, where there was a snaking queue waiting to be seen. Two hours later, after tests, we were thunderstruck when a doctor told us she had highly infectious tuberculosis and had to be admitted straight away to hospital. As soon as she had dressed, I took her to a sanatorium in Morningside. Every day, I bought a bunch of flowers, chocolates and magazines before I visited her in an isolation room off a general ward. After two weeks, she was discharged and I drove her back down to Gordon. She looked drawn and wan, and, although her lungs had for long been wheezy through smoking too many cigarettes and too much marijuana, now her breathing was short and laboured.

After we arrived at the cottage, she made it clear that she expected me to leave.

'Look, I think I should stay here,' I remonstrated. 'Someone needs to take care of you.'

'Patrick, I'm dead tired and I need to rest,' she said.

'I know. But you can't stay here by yourself!'

'It's all right. I'll contact you when I'm feeling better,' she replied emphatically.

Feeling utterly helpless, I returned to Edinburgh. Two weeks fled by without me hearing from her. I couldn't phone her, of course, so I deliberated over whether to drive down to Gordon, until, wanting to avoid antagonising her further, I thought better of it. Then, one morning, I received a letter with a Dutch stamp on it. Inside was a scribbled note from Penny saying that, because she had felt 'like a fish out of water' in Gordon, she had moved out of the cottage and taken a plane back to Amsterdam. Scarcely believing what I had just read, it dawned on me at last that Alistair had been right; for the second time, I had come close to losing myself in her, and I swore to myself – a promise I kept – that I would never set eyes on her again.

The enormous change in their lives notwithstanding, my parents had simply transferred many of their habits to their new abode. As she had done for two decades in the bungalow, now my mother sat every night on the sofa by the fire in the green or brown drawing room, writing lists. She wrote lists of the tasks she had to complete. She wrote lists of children of her friends to whom she wanted to give Christmas presents. She wrote lists of what she had to pack for Germany or Spain and lists of people she wanted to invite to parties. She wrote lists of people to whom she wanted to send postcards and lists of people she had to phone. She even wrote a list of the changing sizes of the shoes of her fast-growing grandchildren. Then, after she had completed her lists, she emptied the contents of her handbag onto the carpet, and tidied them up before she stuffed them unceremoniously back in again.

In the meantime, my father sat in his armchair next to her, as he had done every night for three decades, interminably reading newspapers or watching the news on television. By now my mother was no longer so interested in politics and, as in the bungalow, my father was disgusted by her insistence that sensationalist tabloids be delivered on Sunday along with his heavyweight broadsheets. It was the same with television. Because she was so people-oriented, she enjoyed watching soap operas, comedy shows and detective series; because he was so cerebral, he preferred documentaries, current affairs and the news. Their dissimilar tastes led to frequent disputes, and if she wouldn't watch the programme he wanted to see, he stomped out of the room despite her pleas to stay and keep her company.

But what *had* changed was the relationship my sister and I had with them. The wish they had expressed before we were born, namely that he have a daughter and she a son, had been fulfilled. But it had had unforeseen repercussions. By now it had become plain, once and for all, that my affinity lay with my mother and that of my sister with my father. This was no doubt partly because of the age-old Oedipus complex that exists between mothers and sons, and the Electra complex that exists between fathers and daughters. But there was far more to it than that. No longer troubled by her obesity, I had come to appreciate her unparalleled warmth, enormous vitality and selfless generosity. We also empathised with each other; she with me because, in contrast to my sister, who had had a relatively smooth passage in life, I was so vulnerable on account of my broken love affairs and chronic inability to find a role for myself; me with her as I now understood why she – many a time, admittedly, with her complicity – had become the butt of the family's humour.

I had also become conscious of her unconditional love for me, irrespective of the scrapes I habitually got into. There was nothing she hadn't been willing to do for me. One evening, during my second year at Edinburgh University, I had been walking up a tough street in the East End, when two youths approached me. I had stepped aside to let them pass, but one of them had deliberately barged into me. I had carried on up the street, but he and his friend had spun round and, shouting 'Fucking wanker!', pursued me up the hill. Caught off-guard, before I knew it I found myself involved in a furious fracas, until two policemen from a passing squad car managed to separate us. The three of us were arrested, and I had spent three hours in a police cell in the Royal Mile, until I was allowed to telephone my parents. At midnight, my mother had arrived, beside herself with worry, and paid for me to be released on bail. The two youths and I were charged subsequently with a breach of the peace, although, as the magistrate considered it to have been an unfair contest, they were fined, while I, to my immeasurable satisfaction, was merely given an official warning.

Then there was the time when I was hitchhiking back to Edinburgh up the AI from London. It was a miserable evening, and I had become stranded on a deserted dual carriageway outside Morpeth, a cheerless industrial town north of Newcastle.

At midnight, I had tramped back to its outskirts, where I had managed to locate a public telephone box where I asked my mother to come and pick me up. This would involve her making a round trip of more than two hundred miles, yet she agreed of course and, having collected me at 3 a.m., daylight was breaking when we pulled up outside the bungalow.

My sister, on the other hand, was far closer to my father. By now she too had developed an outgoing personality, albeit a milder one than that of my over-emotional and, at times, domineering mother. In fact, having apparently inherited my father's dispassionate calmness and my mother's fun-loving gregariousness, she seemed – unlike myself – to have struck the ideal balance that they had so singularly failed to find, although her stiff shoulders and persistent headaches perhaps suggested she wasn't as imperturbable as she seemed. She too had built up a substantial circle of friends, who found her light-heartedness and long stories entertaining. The result was that, far more than my father and me, who were both shy by nature, she had to vie for the very limited social space left by my mother. It was hardly surprising, there-fore, that they quarrelled so much. Furthermore, there was the undeniably extravagant way my mother continued to indulge my sister's children, and every now and again, during their rows, my sister threatened never to allow her to see her grandchildren again, which distressed my mother terribly.

For all that, my sister, to her eternal credit, never gave up on my mother, and every year she invited her and my father to spend up to three months at her roomy house in the peaceful, rural countryside of Nord Rhine-West-phalia. This was to enable my mother to be with her grandchildren, although the arrangement, naturally, had advantages for my sister, as my mother could share the considerable work that goes with looking after three children under the age of three. At times that must have seemed all but unmanageable. One morning, when my sister was changing the nappies of the twins on a table in the bathroom, she became distracted and one of them tumbled headfirst to the floor to her left. Horror-struck, she bent down to pick him up, where-upon the other fell head-first to the floor to her right, but fortunately neither of them even suffered concussion.

My father and sister attributed my rapport with my mother to my seeing far less of her than they did. This explanation contained some truth. When I had lived in the Netherlands, I had seen her only three times a year – twice in Edinburgh for two weeks, and once a year in Amsterdam for only three or four days at a time. But now I was living barely four hundred yards down the hill from Howe Street, I saw a great more of her, and consequently I too had heated rows with her. These were chiefly caused by what my sister and I regarded as her excessive maternalism, which we found smothering. She was incessantly inviting me to go up to the house for a meal. She wanted me to meet her for a coffee, or go with her and my father for a run in the car at weekends. Worst of all were the phone calls with which she bombarded me. Sometimes, she rang me three times a day, but no matter how much I entreated her to desist, the following day the phone would go and a voice would say, 'This isn't a phone-call, it's only to say …' and it would start all over again.

And I, as headstrong as my sister, was equally capable of emotional blackmail. At least twice, after I had failed yet again to make her understand how unwelcome these phone calls were, I stood in the hall of Howe Street, banging my head against the wall at the seeming madness of it all. Unlike my sister, though, I wasn't afraid to make up with my mother after we had had a row. We also shared many values. Whenever my sister, Joseph and her children came over from West Germany, where they were still happily married after thirty years, the family assembled at mealtimes round the huge pine table in the kitchen. There, my sister, who addressed most of her remarks to my father, repeatedly commented on how inferior everything in Britain was compared to West Germany, while my mother and I sat exchanging glances and raising our eyes to heaven. My sister was right, although these trenchant comments offended my mother and me. Both of us were of the opinion there was more to life than the Teutonic drive for perfection, which we regarded as the other side of the coin, and we preferred to concentrate on what the British had to offer, such as their irreverent, self-deprecating sense of humour, friendliness and informality. Moreover, we considered it tactless for my sister to accept my mother's hospitality and proceed to denigrate Britain in her presence. For several years, I argued the point with my sister and my father, who also disparaged everything British, but ultimately I gave up.

My increasing identification with my mother's values meant that, over the years, I had repudiated those of my father. The fact is, by the time he was fifty, he had become emotionally crippled. What may or may not have happened between my mother and Karl, the German prisoner of war, had possibly initiated my father's emotional withdrawal from her. Now, whenever she attempted to show him affection he recoiled in repugnance; years later she confided in me unhappily that he hadn't touched her sexually, if at all, for forty years.

Nevertheless, my mother continued to adore him, and, after she died, he revealed to my astonishment that she had constantly feared he might leave her for another woman. He maintained this was something he had never been tempted to do, although for decades the rest of the family teased him about what he did or didn't get up to when he went down on 'business trips' to Middlesbrough, where his company had a mammoth industrial plant. That wasn't all. On one occasion, during the Royal Highland Show, where his company had a pavilion, my mother espied his secretary, who was devoted to him, pinching his bottom. However, he was almost certainly faithful to my mother, if only because, had he got to know another woman, he would doubtless have been too nervous to do anything about it.

Decades later, I asked him why he and my mother had stayed together, when they gave the impression – to me at least – of having made each other so unhappy.

'Unhappy?' he said, caught off balance.

'Yes, unhappy.'

'I never perceived it in such terms,' he rejoined tartly, avoiding, as ever, having to divulge his feelings.

'So you never thought about getting divorced?'

'No, never. In those days, no one even considered it.'

But he had become equally cold with the rest of the family. Instead of addressing us by our first names, he would refer to 'your mother', 'your sister' or 'your brother'. If we touched him, he would cringe and exclaim, 'Take your hands off me, take your hands off me!' He couldn't bear being photo-graphed, and if we tried, he would hold his hands up in front of his face. If we asked him a personal question about, for example, his happiest memory in life, he would reply defensively, 'I don't know. I never ask myself such questions.'

The seeds for him being so emotionally crippled, my mother, my sister and I were convinced, lay in his childhood. The Richardsons had originated in north-west England, where my paternal great-great-grandfather had been a QC and the mayor of Bolton. However, an uncle of my father who was interested in the family's genealogy maintained that the Richardsons were related to Empress Eugénie, the wife of Napoleon III and empress consort of France. For years, the rest of the family dismissed this as hokum, along with the rumour that, via my paternal grandmother, my sister and I were descended from sailors in the Spanish Armada whose ships had foundered off the west coast of Ireland. In fact at least the first Spanish connection was indisputably true; my grandfather, apart from being a Richardson, was a Kirkpatrick, and hence related to Doña Maria di Montijo y Kirkpatrick, a twenty-six-year-old Spanish countess who, known as Eugénie de Montijo, had married the French emperor.

Whatever the truth of the matter, Henry, my paternal grandfather, had lived in Manchester, where he was a journalist, writer and trade unionist. By the time my father – who, like the rest of the family, had unusually dark skin and black hair – was born, his mother was aged forty-four, and, with four children already, was worn out by childbearing. It was even rumoured his parents had merely conceived him to pre-empt Henry from being conscripted in the First World War, as fathers could claim exemption if they had two sons or more.

When my father was a year old, the family moved to London. He had never been close to his siblings, except possibly to his youngest sister, because she was nearest in age to him. But he had excelled in his studies, and when he was awarded a scholarship to Dulwich College, for the first time in the history of his junior school everybody was given a holiday. For all that, because his parents were too well off, he had to go instead to the less famous – although still highly regarded – Alleyn's. It was a bitter pill to swallow; nevertheless, here he also distinguished himself, and, at the age of eighteen, he won the school's divinity prize for Greek history. Nonetheless, owing to his retiring nature, within the family he was perpetually in the shadow of John, his older brother. A cocky, handsome boy with blue eyes and golden locks, he was, in contrast to my father – who of course hated sports – also very athletic; because he loved playing tennis with his father, who was addicted to the game, it wasn't surprising that he was the apple of his parents' eye.

It was just the beginning of fortune's tendency to favour John at my father's expense. After Henry, who was extremely fit for his age, dropped dead of a heart attack – on a tennis court, needless to say – my father suffered another blow shortly before the Second World War. In 1938 the National Union of Journalists paid for John to complete his course in agriculture at Reading University, where, naturally, he captained the tennis and cricket teams. Meanwhile, my father was forced, owing to lack of support from the union, to forgo his cherished ambition to go to the London School of Economics, which had already accepted him. Then hostilities were declared, but whereas John was able to avoid being called up because he worked as an administrator in the Ministry of Agriculture, my father, on account of his principles, had to spend the war as a farm labourer in Sussex.

My father incontrovertibly never recovered from these family injustices. When Henry died, he didn't even attend his funeral; when I questioned him about it in subsequent years, he couldn't even say where he was buried. Given that both his parents and all his brothers and sisters were atheists, and none of them believed in such ceremonies, this wasn't as surprising as it seems. In addition, my father, at only eighteen, had scarcely had time to get to know him. But, in reality, it was part of a pattern that was to last his whole life. Two decades later, John and his wife, whom my father hadn't laid eyes on for twenty years, came up to Edinburgh to stay with Mona, who had been living there since before the war. When John tentatively suggested that they drop in on us, my mother consented. She had never warmed to him, as she regarded him as insufferably arrogant; she was also fiercely protective of my father, and hadn't forgotten the favouritism shown to John by Henry and Ethel. Still, just as she had been willing to forgive Ethel for ostracising her and my father for twenty years, she was prepared to give him another chance. But the visit wasn't a success; she found him as conceited as ever, and my father was conspicuously ill at ease in his company. It was the last contact we ever had with him and his wife.

Mona was, in fact, the only family member my father ever saw, and even then it was at my mother's instigation. Like both my grandmothers, Mona had deplored my father eloping with my mother, her best friend, and for several years, like them, she refused to speak to her. All the same, my mother, who always preferred harmony to conflict, subsequently revived their friendship, and now and again we dropped in on Mona's family in their bungalow in Colinton, a leafy suburb of Edinburgh at the foot of the Pentland Hills. Mona had three children, the youngest of whom was a bashful thirteen-year-old with black hair whose sultry looks I couldn't help noticing although I was only twelve. Nevertheless, both she and her older sister – so she told me years later, to my astonishment – thought that we considered ourselves superior and, as they had hardly any money, they resented us being 'better off'. By and by, they moved to a small traditional village twenty miles south of Edinburgh, but my mother was as good at maintaining friendships as she was at forging them. Indeed she was one of the last people to see Mona alive, as she died of a heart attack only hours after they had been for a walk in the Pentland Hills.

In some ways, my father had cause to see so little of his family, which was even more dysfunctional than most. My father, of course, had eloped with my mother. His youngest sister had married three times, and her third husband, who turned out to be bisexual, had sexually abused her two sons – who were to commit suicide – from her previous marriage. The second-oldest sister had been unusually promiscuous and abandoned her young daughter to live in the USA. Last but not least, Mona's oldest daughter shocked her parents, even though it was the beginning of the permissive Sixties, by having an 'illegitimate' child that she gave away for adoption.

Nevertheless, his reaction to his mother's death speaks volumes about the depth of his alienation from his family. After he had left home in Dulwich, he had seen Ethel only once over the next sixty-six years. This was even more remarkable, given that she regularly came up to Edinburgh to visit Mona. A highly literate, uncompromising communist, she had always been very striking, with strong, square-jawed features, black eyebrows and tortoiseshell clasps tucked in what looked like a helmet of prematurely white hair. Even in her sixties, she was fashionably attired in a black suit, a white blouse, silk stockings, pearls and high heels. She also continued to be deeply unconventional. For a long time, she had shared the house in Staines with her cousin and her cousin's two homosexual sons. Then, in her seventies she had learned to ride, become a vegetarian and begun to practise yoga. Even in her eighties she still volunteered to sell the Communist Party's *Daily Worker* on street corners, until, owing to ill health, she had gone to live with my father's younger brother on his farm in Somerset.

One evening, several years after we had dropped in on her in Staines, my parents and my sister and I were watching television in the sitting room of the bungalow. As usual, my father had his head buried in a newspaper. All at once, the telephone rang in the dining room. My mother left the room to answer it. When she came back she looked very upset.

'Tim, your mother's just died!' she exclaimed.

'Is that so?' he replied indifferently. Then he turned the page.

My father, however, regarded his alienation from his parents and siblings – along with his lack of emotion – as entirely normal. Years later he said to me, 'You have to remember that I had a strict upbringing, like many middle-class children of Victorian parents. At that time, it wasn't common to express your feelings. Anyway, my parents were unapproachable figures who simply weren't interested in their children. My father, who was forever either reading or writing, was the worst. If I didn't finish my Brussels sprouts, which I abominated, he wouldn't permit me to leave the table. So I refused, and time and again I had to sit there for hours.'

But by now he was not only emotionally crippled, he was without a doubt also disappointed about his career. Over time, of course, he had risen to become his company's publicity manager. This involved editing its monthly newspaper, but the job was so unchallenging that he spent a considerable amount of the day reading newspapers or looking words up in the dictionary. Apart from providing him with a seemingly infinite vocabulary, it was an enormous waste of his talent; with his training in classics at school, coupled with his logical, analytical brain, he would have made a first-class barrister. Instead, wearing a businessman's trim, conventional suit, he had to queue every day for the bus to the office – not at all what he must have visualised when he had been a young journalist until the Second World War brought his youthful ambitions crashing down. Furthermore, this must have been all the more galling when he compared himself to John, now a successful farmer who lived in a lovely, rambling house on his two-hundred-acre farm in the Somerset countryside.

But he was even more embittered by politics. Like his father, who had opposed the First World War on the grounds it was being fought between two imperialist blocs, he was an intransigent communist. As a young man in the early 1930s, he, like numerous intellectuals, had envisaged that the Russian Revolution in 1917 would usher in a new, more equitable social and economic order. Instead had come Stalin's murderous purges, along with the show trials in Moscow and their sham confessions. During the Second World War, of course, he had been a pacifist, even if, as he maintained subsequently, it was simply because he wanted to stay alive, rather than because of high moral principles. Then, in 1953, came the workers' uprising in East Germany, and the invasion by the Soviet Union of Hungary in 1956 and Czechoslovakia in 1968. But by now he had invested so much of his faith in communism that it was too late for him to jettison his lifelong principles and admit that Marxist-Leninism had gone off the rails.

He attributed this failure, along with that of socialism, to its leaders, whom he berated for their incessant 'betrayal' of its ideals. But it was irrelevant, as his belief in socialism's values had become purely theoretical, and by now he had only antipathy for the human race. He stubbornly refused to believe that millions of kulaks in the Soviet Union in the 1930s and millions of peasants during Mao Zedong's Great Leap Forward in the 1960s had died of starvation, or he argued that, if they did, their deaths were justified because they were 'bourgeois elements'. He also derided as 'distortions of the western media' reports that Pol Pot's communist regime had murdered millions of teachers, lawyers and doctors in Cambodia in the 1980s. For years he had despised Americans – even though he had scarcely come across any – and he vilified the United States, which he blamed for every negative global event.

But communism shaped him in more ways than one. In accordance with Marxist theory, he believed in the need for a critical approach to society. He made the mistake, however, of extending it to every other aspect of life, including personal relationships. As a result, he disparaged everything and was incapable of uttering a word of praise or encouragement. Once, when I was at university, I spent a week helping him decorate his pied-à-terre. After we finished, instead of thanking me, he pointed to a two-inch patch in the ceiling that had been beyond my reach.

'You missed up there,' he commented brusquely, without the slightest trace of irony.

The consequence of my father's emotional and sexual withdrawal from my mother, along with his disappointment in his career and his bitter disillusionment with politics, was that, in addition to food, she had turned to me for solace. If we were at a party and she was having a conversation with a friend, she dropped it like a hot potato the moment I started talking to someone else. When we were with my father, she addressed most of her remarks to me. But the biggest indication of her increasing emotional dependence on me was her 'contracts'. Every six months, to help her diet, she drew up a piece of paper which she asked me to sign and date. Before long, she would shed several kilos so swiftly that her body couldn't sustain it and she merely regained her original weight. As time passed these 'contracts' contained so many exceptions that they became a charade, although, to please her, I pretended to take them seriously. One went: 'This is to promise my son that I won't eat any biscuits, puddings, sweets, sugar, cakes, pies, bread or ice cream, except at Christmas, Easter, birthdays, during the summer holidays in Spain and Greece, at an unavoidable party, on a plane, ship or in hospital. I will also do my best to stick to my diet, and get down to and remain at 11 or 12 stone, signed _____'

I, for my part, found my power over her embarrassing, and it wasn't surprising that my father, even though he was largely responsible for what had happened, had become jealous of me. To his credit, he strove to disguise it, but, even so, his resentment on occasion burst into the open. One night, shortly after my parents had moved into the centre of town, I appeared unannounced at a party in the New Town to which we had all been invited. All of a sudden, as I found myself following my father, my sister and my mother up the stairs to the elegant drawing room, he turned round and spotted me behind him.

'What are you doing here?' he spat venomously, as if his mask had slipped and he hadn't had time to exercise his customary self-restraint.

On another occasion, when my sister was visiting Edinburgh and my mother had gone out for the evening, he and I began a discussion about the council's plan to ban cars from Princes Street that rapidly escalated. He was adamantly opposed to the plan, and, after I asserted – correctly – that it was generally acknowledged to be a good idea, he flared up like a volcano.

'Get out, get out!' he bellowed, until my sister insisted he apologise.

His increasing abusiveness wasn't restricted to the family, as he was also becoming progressively unpleasant towards other people. At sophisticated dinner parties to which my mother's innumerable friends invited them, he quickly became inebriated. Then, he would become involved in fierce arguments, which several times ended with him thumping his fist on the table and shouting vituperatively, to my mother's mortification, 'Scum, scum!' at the other guests.

For all that, their marriage had many happy moments. Every year, my mother held a party in the big, echoing house, which they had both grown to love. Then, the long pine table in the kitchen would be laden with savouries, the two drawing rooms with their roaring coal fires would once again be bursting at the seams with my mother's and sister's friends, and, as in the bungalow, everyone would be chatting away, laughing and joking. By now he had taken early retirement, and every year they still travelled to the Greek islands or she chauffeured him in the Volkswagen camper van down through England and France to southern Spain, where they spent three blissful months. It wasn't until years later, after they died, that I became aware to what extent, in fact, it had been the presence of my sister and me that had generated so many problems between them, and how well they had got on together in our absence.

BOOK IV
Into the Whirlpool

The more time rolled by, the more obvious it became that the cherished hope I had fondly entertained for a new life in Britain was an illusion. I was too inexperienced to find a job in television and my application to join a human rights organisation in London was turned down. I couldn't put roots down in my father's pied-à-terre, for which I felt increasingly beholden to him. I found the sunless, baleful skies abhorrent, and the Scots seemed so dour and downtrodden compared to the good-natured, free-spirited Dutch.

My mother, predictably, was ecstatic at having me back in Edinburgh. Whenever I visited my parents' house, she would be leaning over the banisters on the top landing, and her face would light up with joy as she watched me ascend the stairs. Not unexpectedly, she was eager to help me try to settle down, and she generously offered to buy me a flat. For months we looked at properties. Once, one came up in St Stephen Street, the only place in Edinburgh, with its offbeat antique shops and bohemian atmosphere, which was even vaguely reminiscent of Amsterdam, and we were both dejected when her offer to buy it wasn't accepted. She couldn't figure out why I had such an aversion to Edinburgh. One Thursday, when we were at the east end of Princes Street, I told her how sombre and depressing I found its rainy streets.

'Good God, how can you say that?' she cried, pointing along the regal sweep of Princes Street towards the soaring spires of St Mary's Cathedral at the West End, a mile away. 'Look at the castle, and the superb architecture. It's one of the loveliest cities in Europe!'

My correspondence with Alistair didn't improve matters. He had been devastated after I had walked out on Amsterdam, and every week five-page letters dropped through my letterbox saying how much he longed for my laughter and our seemingly endless conversations about life, literature and relationships. I replied by return and, consumed by nostalgia and forgetting why I had ever left the Netherlands, described how I missed our friendship, the sunny summers and Amsterdam's cosmopolitan crowds and cafés. Two years after leaving it, I started flying back to work in the bookshop for several days a month. It was amazingly easy to do. The garret, which still had all my books and records, looked as if it had been frozen in time. André was still on the third floor with Happy, his cat. Christos and Aileen were still on the ground floor, as were their Doberman Pinschers. Before long, when the time came to return to Edinburgh, it felt like being wrenched out of the womb.

In the meantime, there had been a major change in Alistair's life, as he had been introduced to a gay, forty-year-old Dutchman called Willem who held rebirthing courses throughout Europe. Alistair, of course, had been attracted to spirituality since he was a teenager and, when he was younger, he had been to Poona in India, where he had stayed in the ashram of Bhagwan Shree Rajneesh. When Inie mentioned that she was attending Willem's course in the north of the Netherlands, and that he wasn't simply another cult guru but someone who seemed to possess genuine spiritual insights, Alistair began going as well. Soon he was travelling to courses Willem held in London and Wales, and within a few weeks, despite him being ten years older, they became lovers.

Elsewhere, though, things were deteriorating, above all in the bookshop. By the early 1980s, Amsterdam, like the rest of Europe, had changed, and the idealism of the 1960s was on its deathbed. Recession was far and wide, and there had been a dramatic drop in the number of visitors to the Melkweg. The policy of replacing the market with an art gallery had come to naught and now it was a white, sterile, deserted space. The result was that the bookshop was on the point of going bankrupt, so, in a last, desperate effort to rescue it, Alistair mooted that I become his partner. It was something that I had hoped for several years he would suggest, but, after much reflection, I declined, as I thought that now it was too big a financial risk.

Assuming that it was going to collapse, we toyed with all kinds of ideas. One was to share flats in Edinburgh and Amsterdam, which would enable me to continue the Edinburgh 'experiment' while having a base in Amsterdam. Because I couldn't find a flat there, however, we dropped the idea. Next, we contemplated opening a second-hand paperback bookshop in Edinburgh's Old Town. Alistair even flew across to look for premises, before we concluded it had too many already. Then, while I was in Amsterdam on one of my monthly visits, came the long-awaited news that our house in the Kerkstraat was finally about to be demolished.

But there was more. Amazingly, anyone who had lived there for more than a decade had the right to be rehoused by Amsterdam city council, and they could choose between three offers of economical, subsidised apartments. This applied to André as well as myself, because I had never notified the council that I had left the garret. It ought to have been marvellous news; now, if I accepted one of their offers, I could at last have a place to live actually built of bricks and mortar, with a real lavatory and kitchen, and mains water and electricity! Instead I found the revelation destabilising. I was as rootless as ever in Edinburgh; I was still living in my father's flat in St Stephen Street, and I hadn't found a job, far less a new vocation. Surely this was a sign the Edinburgh experiment had fizzled out and I should return to live in Amsterdam, where, even if the bookshop were in financial difficulties, I would at least have a job – at least until it folded – and a proper house to call my own?

A week after I came back from the Netherlands, I climbed the street to my parents' house, where I intended to tell my mother I was contemplating going back to live in Amsterdam. I had no sooner sat down in the kitchen than she pocketed a set of keys.

'Come with me,' she said excitedly, 'I've something for you.'

I followed her two hundred yards down the street to St Stephen Street, where we climbed four flights of stairs to the top of a nineteenth-century tenement.

'Look, I've bought this for you!' she proclaimed, as she unlocked the door of a lovely, sunlit flat with four compact rooms opening off a central hallway. 'We saw it yesterday morning. I was sure you'd love it, so I put in an offer straight away. It was accepted the same afternoon.'

I was overwhelmed. It was an ideal size. It was in the only street in Edinburgh where I wanted to live. It was less than four hundred yards down the street from my parents. In fact it was everything I had dreamed of. All at once, from having nowhere to live, I had two flats, or I could have, if I took up one of the council's offers in Amsterdam. But now I couldn't conceivably return to Holland, so I vowed to myself that, to repay my mother's generosity, I would live in the flat for at least a year.

One night that winter, on the spur of the moment, I called in on my parents. When my mother opened the front door, I found that they and Julia, my first love when I was seventeen, were on the point of leaving. My face dropped. After my abortive attempt to win her back at my party twenty years ago, my mother had remained in contact with her and had come to treat her as a surrogate daughter. Through my mother, I knew she had worked as a secretary, although she continued to be attracted to acting and she had been in several plays staged by an amateur dramatic society. I also knew that she had been living for ten years with a doctor called Chris – who, according to mother, treated her abominably – in the south of England, where they had a daughter. Whenever I had run into her at my parents' house, I had still found her so ravishing that I had been drawn to her like a moth to a flame. Aware what a lost cause it was, however, and nursing my resentment at my mother for putting me in this situation, I had invariably stalked angrily out the door.

Now she was apparently up spending time with her parents who still lived in North Berwick.

'Look, why don't you stay and be nice to Julia for once?' my mother ventured, seeing the look of consternation on my face. 'Your father and I are going out for the evening, so you won't be disturbed.'

I hadn't seen her for nearly a decade, and she had not only retained her matchless looks, but she had also matured into a singularly mature, graceful-looking, forty-year-old woman. She seemed more at ease than when she had been the epitome of beauty, and although her formerly svelte body had unavoidably thickened somewhat, there were merely a few finely drawn lines around her eyes, and hardly more than a fleck of grey in her wavy, silky hair. Deciding it was time to heed my mother's advice and move on from the past, I went in and sat down beside her on the sofa in the green drawing room.

There, after they had left, she told me about her relationship with the doctor. 'It all started really dramatically,' she began. 'I'd just got to know Chris when he told me he'd taken a job in Bolivia, beginning in a week's time, before he said he'd bought two plane tickets, one for him and one for me, and gave me twenty-four hours to decide if I wanted to join him. Not surprisingly, I was bowled over, and it was a major decision for me to make, especially as I'd had such a sheltered upbringing in North Berwick.'

After mulling it over all night, she had accepted his offer the next morning. For a year, they had lived in La Paz, where she had kept house while he was the doctor for remote villages in the Andes. Then, two years afterwards, she had gone with him to Africa, where he had been posted to an isolated village in south-west Kenya. When they got back to Britain, she had had Sophie. She would have liked to get married, as she believed it would give her and her daughter security, but he wouldn't hear of it, and he began being unpleasant towards her. She had hoped that he would change, so she had persevered for the last few years. But he hadn't, so they were going to separate. However, they still lived together in a village outside Milton Keynes, where she worked as a course administrator for Buckingham University.

At last, she laughed. 'So I'm free again! Now tell me about you.'

As I recounted to her in turn what had happened in my life the years rolled away, and it was as if we had just met. An hour later, we lay on the carpet in front of the dying fire and I did what I had wanted to do ever since I had first laid eyes on her – make love to her. After such a long wait, maybe it was inevitable that the experience was somewhat disappointing. Nonetheless, as I inhaled the warmth of her hair and caressed her still curvaceous, naked, lily-white body, I marvelled how unpredictable life was; never in my wildest flights of fantasy did I ever conceive that history would repeat itself and two decades later I would be at the start of another relationship with my teenage sweetheart.

Soon, while Chris took Sophie to stay with his new partner for the weekend, I started going down by train to visit her in their house. There, she introduced me to Sophie. A fresh-faced, nine-year-old girl with a pointed chin, freckles and long legs, she was without doubt going to inherit her mother's beauty, although Julia was disheartened by her tantrums and the way she stomped histrionically about the house. All the same, I was relieved to discover that, unlike in my relationship with Penny's son, we took to each other on the spot. She amused me because she was quite precocious; she was intrigued to see Julia with her first love and someone who, in contrast to Chris, treated her mother with respect.

Initially, as Julia wanted to avoid destabilising Sophie, we refrained from touching each other in her presence, and every night I slept in the spare bed. However, Julia and I felt increasingly uneasy about my being in their house, so instead she began coming up to Edinburgh every month. Then, after friends began hinting she shouldn't be spending so much time away from Sophie, she brought her up, too. After Sophie had gone to sleep, we would make love in the sitting room of my new flat, still totally empty apart from two chocolate-coloured beanbags and a television set, or on my moth-eaten mattress on the bedroom floor. Every once in a while, Julia lunched with my mother, who, predictably, was thrilled to see us together again.

Often, we called in on Julia's parents in North Berwick. As before, I got on well with them, although her father fretted about Julia becoming embroiled with another man so soon after her relationship with Chris had broken up. Julia relished being back in Scotland, and once again we sat at dusk on rocks beyond the outdoor swimming pool, watching the sun dissolve into the vermilion sea. We regularly drove down to the Borders, which we both loved. Once, while Julia's parents took care of Sophie, we hired a car and took a ferry to Harris in the Outer Hebrides, where we roamed along pristine white beaches and made love by the side of glittering peaty lochans.

For six months, she played with the idea of returning to live in Scotland, until she decided against it, as she was settled in England with a good job and Sophie was happy at the local school.

Instead she bought a little cottage with the alimony Chris gave her. In a honey-coloured row off the main street of a cheerful market town, it looked idyllic, with roses climbing outside latticed windows and a pocket-sized back garden. Now it was much easier for me to go down and stay with her. At midday, we met in her office on the campus of Buckingham University for lunch, before, because I hadn't wholly given up writing, I wrote my diary in its library. She introduced me to her friends. They were all well-educated, middle-class professionals from the Home Counties, and they were welcoming and hospitable, if somewhat conventional. She took me to a party in Milton Keynes, where she introduced me to Chris.

To my surprise, given how disparagingly my mother had spoken about him, I liked him and his new partner. Julia enjoyed cooking, and every evening she served up gourmet, three-course meals for the three of us. At weekends, while Sophie stayed with her friend, Julia and I drove to black-and-white timbered pubs in adjacent villages. She loved wandering about medieval churches and moss-encrusted graveyards, and that autumn we spent the weekend visiting thatched hamlets in Suffolk, after which we frequently paused to make love in golden wheat fields.

Then, almost indiscernibly, cracks started to creep into our relationship. When I was at the cottage, I felt more and more like a cornered animal. At the time, 1986, tension was running high in Western Europe, where the United States was planning to install cruise missiles against the 'threat' from the Soviet Union, and, once again, as with the Cuban missile crisis, there was a threat of nuclear Armageddon. With nothing to occupy me all day other than write my diary and watch F-16s from a nearby American air force base circle incessantly in the sky, I was aware that sometime or other, as had happened with Marie, something would have to give. I couldn't envisage myself living in a cramped cottage outside Milton Keynes, a soulless modern town that encapsulated everything I hated about contemporary architecture. And even though I had longed for stability, I was having a change of heart about whether I was suited for family life. Regardless, unable to stomach the idea of yet another love affair breaking up, I told myself to enjoy it while it lasted.

Once, to escape from my never-ending indecision and procrastination about what to do, I travelled with Alistair to Italy. There, we split up for a week, as he intended to stay with an affluent American friend who lived in a small, fortified keep within spitting distance of Florence. While I was waiting for him, I hitchhiked down dreamy country roads in Tuscany. In the afternoon, I paused for a cappuccino or an ice cream in tranquil village squares on top of the rolling hills. In the coolness of the evening, church bells tolled, and stooped septuagenarians congregated around gushing fountains.

After Alistair and I met in Sienna, with its sea of terracotta-tiled roofs and high-spirited, chattering Italians parading in the grand piazza, we took the train to Naples, where we stayed in the apartment of another of Alistair's wealthy Italian friends. A minor Neapolitan prince who lived high up in the backstreets, he was in Paris at the time and had agreed to let us use his apartment. Commanding sensational vistas of the bay, it was impeccably furnished with priceless-looking Louis the Fourteenth chairs, cinquecento commodes, black lacquer cabinets, rich tapestries and paintings in frames of golden arabesque. Every day, we traipsed round the city's jaw-dropping array of palaces and museums until we took a ship to the island of Stromboli, Alistair's closely guarded 'hideaway' where he had several times gone to write.

In the semi-abandoned, crumbling village of Ginostra, he took his customary room in the ramshackle house at the base of the island's soaring active volcano and I found one further down nearer the water.

Ginostra was everything he had claimed it to be. The first afternoon he led me through the white, ghostly ruined houses to the cemetery. Overshadowed by a solitary poplar tree, generations of families, most of whose successors had emigrated to America, were buried in disintegrating graves, with photographs of loved ones encased in alabaster on their tombstones. We swiftly settled into our individual routine. When we had finished breakfast, we trekked along a path that twisted and turned along the top of cliffs and wound down to black rocks by the sea. There, a sprinkling of naked Italians and I would sunbathe or swim; he shut himself off on a peninsula further along. I assumed he wished to be alone, but, as he confessed afterwards, he was in reality dispirited and paranoid. He was paranoid about the future of the bookshop. He was paranoid about the Dutch tax authorities, whose demands over the years had made his life a misery and who were beginning to harass him again. He was even paranoid about swimming in the sea, where he was convinced that sharks or eels would attack him.

Unaware of his mental turmoil, I rarely caught sight of him during the day, but we met up in the evening, when he would prepare his usual gourmet suppers in his cavernous, candlelit room. There we sat listening to the volcano thunder above our heads. We also laughed a great deal, as we invariably did, although the friction that essentially underlies all friendships periodically bubbled to the surface. Once, in an impassioned exchange of words, he burst out, 'You're simply fooling yourself you're a writer! You say you're going to write, but the minute the sun appears you drop everything. Patrick, one day you'll have to decide whether you want to be a writer or a sun-worshipper!'

Stung to the quick, I rounded on him for being immature and pretentious. All the same, we discussed the other's accusations, because we recognised that substantial elements of what the other said were – however unpalatable – true. I didn't need him to warn me I was becoming an incurable vacillator, incapable of committing myself to anything, anybody or anywhere; he admitted that he tried to be someone he didn't feel himself to be. For nearly two decades he had been in perpetual crisis, because he perceived himself as being unlovable and an irredeemable failure. It was no wonder, therefore, that he sought to present himself as worldly wise beyond his years, a self-image he felt he had to live up to.

One balmy evening we decided to climb the brooding volcano. Steering around thorny cacti, we laboured up its flanks of black ash until, two hours later, just below the summit, we reached a surreal lunar plateau which we traversed until we were only fifty feet from the rim. There, trying to dodge falling embers, we crouched cautiously watching the eruptions. These are amongst the most predictable on the planet, so, aware we had ten minutes before the next one, we inched towards the edge and peered dizzily down into the mouth itself. It was a stupendous sight. As the giant, bottomless yawning orifice sucked and gurgled greedily, it was like watching a monstrous, breathing elemental being as it retched huge puffs of ashen, sulphurous smoke and sent molten lava whooshing hundreds of feet into the atmosphere.

Soon it was autumn and, once violent rainstorms started galloping like racehorses towards Stromboli across the sea to the west, we felt it was time to return to Amsterdam and Britain respectively. There, deceiving myself that I was merely living for the moment, I carried on going down to visit Julia. As the months tripped past, she, understandably, had begun to sense something was badly wrong, and now she several times accused me of not being honest with her. Feeling increasingly guilty, I knew she was right, and that I was doing to her what Penny had done to me; just as I had never known where I was with Penny, now Julia never knew where she was with me. And just as Penny had been seized with a desire to do one thing one minute and the opposite the next, now it was Julia who was at the mercy of my whims. But although she remained immensely loving, she was also becoming ever more critical of me.

'How could you have allowed the whole Amsterdam thing go on for so long?' she cried one Saturday. 'You're just a dilettante. At least Chris as a doctor does some good in his life! All you want is a woman who makes things as difficult as possible for you!'

On another occasion, after she phoned me in Edinburgh at 9 p.m. and I was short with her, the phone rang again at midnight. 'You arrogant little shit!' she yelled and banged down the receiver.

Then came that fateful January. In the midst of my rapidly deteriorating relationship with Julia, I travelled over to Amsterdam to meet an official from the city council to discuss their offer of accommodation, as I was toying with the idea of either using it as a base or sub-letting it. At the time, Europe was in the grip of a Siberian winter, and because it was impossible to sleep in the garret, where there was no gas or water and the chemical toilet had frozen solid, I slept on Alistair's floor. It was his thirty-fourth birthday and, as his love affair with Willem looked to be going well for once, bizarrely enough – given what was about to come – he struck me as being happier than I had seen him for some time.

The day after I arrived, we meandered through the Vondelpark to the Zuiderbad, a stunning art deco swimming pool just off the Kalverstraat, where I had used to go for a swim. After I swam thirty lengths while he pottered about in the shallow end, we strolled to the Café Américain. We had no sooner ensconced ourselves in a secluded alcove overlooking the Stadtsschowburg than he looked me straight in the eyes.

'Patrick, four days ago I discovered I'm HIV-positive,' he announced almost casually. 'But it's all right. I've always believed I'd die before I was forty, and I'd prefer to have lived dangerously and die young than become a tiresome old fart.'

He seemed so unperturbed, in fact, that at first I thought he was joking. Then, for a moment, it flashed through my mind that I might have caught the virus from him, until I banished the thought just as swiftly – by now it was generally recognised that AIDS was transmitted solely by the exchange of body fluids. All at once, it dawned on me that my best friend and soulmate, whom I had assumed would be with me all my life, was going to die on me, and sooner rather than later.

'How did you find out?' I asked.

'Conrad told me.'

'Conrad?'

'Yes.'

'How did he know?'

'Because he gave it to me.'

'What?'

Staggered, I listened as he continued.

'Apparently, I've got about a one-in-five chance of developing AIDS. Still, like a lot of gay men who've been diagnosed as HIV-positive, I don't regard it as a death sentence. Instead, I want to look at it as a wake-up call. Now I want to start living as if every day's my last. Obviously, I'd rather have learned that lesson without testing HIV-positive, but what's happened has happened, and I need to accept it.'

To my astonishment, he didn't blame Conrad.

'The thing is, if I hadn't got it from him I would probably have got it from somebody else,' he declared philosophically.

He was right. In the 1970s and early 1980s, Amsterdam had been the gay capital of Europe, and, like numerous homosexuals there, and myself, Alistair had been exceedingly promiscuous. For a long time, he had dissipated most of his free nights in a gay club off the Leidsestraat and, although I had never taken up his offer to accompany him, even I, who considered myself unusually broad-minded, had been shocked to the core when he had described what went on there. That, though, had been before the onset of the AIDS epidemic and people knew how risky unprotected sex was between gay

men. Now the damage had been done, and for many of them the new awareness had come too late.

That evening, as if it were any other ordinary day, he and I cycled to
a film – one of Bertolucci's if I remember correctly. To all appearances, he
seemed to enjoy it, and afterwards we played chess in the Van Lennepkade
before we nodded off at 5 a.m. The following day, he invited me to his
favourite Italian café in a side street off the Leidseplein. He had arranged to
meet Willem, who had flown to Amsterdam at short notice to discuss the
implications of Alistair's diagnosis. To my surprise, given Alistair's derogatory
comments about him, I couldn't help liking him; he was a small, surprisingly mature man with puckish, clown-like features. Even so, although he
was interesting and easy to chat to, I rapidly tired of his ceaseless analysis of
Alistair's reactions and demeanour. Alistair, undaunted and still hopelessly in
love with him, divulged that he was about to sell the bookshop and go with
him to his chateau in France, and then to New Zealand, where Willem was
due to give a series of talks.

Back in Britain, my love affair with Julia was as good as over. Now, whenever
she came up to Edinburgh, I retreated into ever-longer silences, and when
I waved her off on the platform of Waverley Station on the train south,
she reciprocated sadly, as if she was aware how relieved I was to see her go.
Then, a month after we had last seen one other, I received a letter from her.
In it, she divulged that she had become acquainted with a forty-year-old
Australian. Originally, he had been purely a friend with whom she could
discuss her problems, including those she had with me. Now, despairing of
our relationship, she had started having one with him. That night, as I lay in
bed, the ramifications of what I had done dawned on me, and the familiar
black void opened up in front of me. Yet again, I had squandered the love
of a good, gentle, loving woman. Now, with no job other than sporadically
teaching English part-time to foreigners in a private language school, along
with my never-ending uncertainty about where to live, the only person that
had given my life meaning was gone.

Wracked by inner confusion, for six days I agonised over how to end
my crises. In the end, knowing the solution was to start committing myself,

once and for all, to either a person or a place, I hit on what to do – absurd though it sounds, I would ask Julia to marry me. Even at that time it struck me as unpardonable folly. Had I not just allowed our relationship to wither away like a grape on the vine? Had I not come to the ineluctable conclusion that she didn't stimulate me intellectually? Had I not decided that domesticity wasn't for me? On the other hand, she was what every man dreamed of. She was caring, understanding and supportive. She was beautiful, mature, and interested in books, films and art. She was well travelled and cosmopolitan. Wasn't I being incredibly selfish, even thinking of solving my apparently insuperable problems at her expense? If I genuinely wished her happiness, shouldn't I leave her alone?

Desperate for guidance, I asked my mother to go with me on a drive to the Borders. Just before the village of Eddlestone we drew up at a roadside café. There, I bared my soul to her as I had never done before. I divulged my crises with women over the years and the blackness threatening to overwhelm me. I revealed my need to find a purpose in life. I disclosed everything about my love affair with Julia – everything except that, only the previous month, I had decided to end it.

'So what d'you think I should do?' I said despairingly. 'Should I try to win her back?'

She hesitated. 'You can try,' she responded, looking doubtful, 'but the situation's now most likely out of your hands.'

Besides seeking her opinion, I was constantly on the telephone to Alistair. Although he warned me not to hand responsibility for my happiness over to someone else, he thought my idea of marrying Julia was terrific, because it would provide me with a new goal. So, two nights later, after vacillating wildly, I phoned Julia and asked her to marry me.

For ten minutes she listened, aghast, as I apologised for my confusing conduct over the last six months.

At length, she spoke. 'Patrick,' she began, 'I've weaned myself off you. I loved you and I put so much into our relationship, only for you to slam the door in my face time and time again. Now I'm free of you. But we can't finish things over the phone. Why don't you come down for the day and we'll talk about it?'

Still hoping against hope I could persuade her to change her mind, a week afterwards I took the train down to Peterborough. As the train streaked past North Berwick, all the indelible memories of being there with her when I was seventeen, and again when I was forty, flooded back, and a wave of grief swept over me. I couldn't bear the prospect of never again strolling with her on the beach, or to the rocks by the swimming pool to watch the sunset. I couldn't bear the thought of never again making love with her in the sitting room in St Stephen Street, or staying in her tiny cottage. I could no longer endure the loss, the loss of my youth, the loss of my innocence, the loss of hope, I was so, so weary of breaking up again and again and again, and the endless searching for happiness …

When she collected me at the station in her little Fiat, I had scarcely ever seen her look more beautiful and radiant. She wore pink trousers and a di-aphanous pink blouse speckled with viridian, her long wavy hair was silkier than ever, and her perfect teeth were as white as snow. After we drove back to her cottage, we took some wine and a rug out to the tiny back garden, where I again asked her to marry her.

'But why, Patrick?' she enquired, her brow furrowing in puzzlement.

'Because … because you mean so much to me.'

'But why for God's sake didn't you tell me before? I thought you were just playing games with me, so I had absolutely no inkling you felt like this!'

'Because I was so mixed-up!' I blundered on. 'Think about it. If you say yes, you'd have the security of being married, I could provide for you and Sophie, I've got a flat and, one day, when my parents die, I'll have no money worries. You could return to Scotland, where you'd be close to the hills and rivers of the Borders, which you love so much. You'd be near to your parents and your sister. We could start a small business, for instance a coffee shop or a …'

'But this sounds more like a business proposition than a marriage offer!' she butted in, laughing. Then her face clouded over. 'Look, after ten years with Chris, I don't want another complicated relationship,' she said pensively. 'Now I'm happy with my new partner. He values me, he's got children as well, and we can talk frankly and honestly with each other. I also think I'm in love with him. So the answer's no.'

For a while I wept uncontrollably, and she put her arm comfortingly around my shoulder. She was bright-eyed and animated, but troubled at see-ing my anguish. After the sun dipped down, we went upstairs, where I asked her to sit beside me on the sofa. Beguiled as ever by her heart-breaking grace and beauty, and my head addled by alcohol, I quickly became aroused and I ached to make love to her. Before long, I started to play with her earrings and caress her milky-white, satin skin, before I kissed her neck, which smelled of almonds. She was flushed as she too had drunk several glasses of wine and for several minutes she stroked my hair as I kissed her soft, cool lips. Then abruptly, at 11 p.m., at the exact moment I was beginning to think anything was possible, she rose to her feet.

'Patrick, you'll forever have a special place in my heart, but the answer's again no,' she declared decisively, as if she had just realised what she was doing. 'Now it's best you go.'

As it was too late to catch a bus or train back to Edinburgh, as we had agreed, I slept the night, completely drunk, at the house of a friend of hers. The next morning Julia drove me to the station at Peterborough and waved me off on the London to Edinburgh express. As it hurtled north, I stood by the door of the carriage, where I toyed with opening it and throwing myself out. The following four months, when I was smoking non-stop and was even more befuddled by alcohol than when I had split up with Hannah, was the blackest period of my life. Now, with possibly two homes in two towns in two countries, I knew how a schizophrenic felt. One lunchtime, I stood on the small stone bridge over the Water of Leith and, for the first time in my life, I could find no reason to turn left or to turn right. Bewildered and disoriented, I stumbled back to the flat in St Stephen Street, where I put my head in the oven and for two long, long minutes considered turning on the gas, before I realised I was too much of a coward to kill myself.

Appalled, and acutely aware I couldn't sink any lower, I knew I had to act to save myself. There and then, I resolved never again to make my reason for existing dependent on another human being. Simultaneously, I made up my mind to go to the Netherlands and clear out the garret once and for all. A month later, I notified Amsterdam city council that I was declining their offer to rehouse me, and travelled in the Volkswagen to Hull, where I took the ferry to Rotterdam and drove to the Kerkstraat. There, the oh-so-familiar house was a mere shell of its former self. Christos had been arrested for dealing cocaine, and was serving a six-year sentence in the Bijlmerbajes, the grim prison on the outskirts of Amsterdam. Aileen had long since left him and vanished.

The only person remaining was André, who, after eleven years – unbelievably – was still a student. On the verge of tears, I loaded all my books and records into the Volkswagen and took photographs of my beloved garret. Then, after saying goodbye to André and embracing Alistair, who had come to say farewell, I left the Netherlands for ever.

Journeying through Grief

To my dismay, hardly anything had changed in the family. My attempts to get my father and sister to cease treating my mother as the butt of the family's humour had failed dismally. He continued to attack her for not dieting; my sister, when she was over from Germany, told her that she had been eating the wrong food all her life and implied it was her fault she had contracted cancer. After her operation her arm had remained painfully swollen, although she had congratulated herself she had survived for more than five years, after which the odds against a relapse are substantially smaller. Now, a year after I had first run into Julia, came the tragic news during my mother's yearly check-up that a malignant lump had been found in her lung and she had to have scans to ascertain if metastases had spread into her liver and bones. She was inconsolable, and she, my father and I found waiting for the results almost unbearable. Every time the telephone rang, she rushed to pick up the receiver, only to discover that the caller was one of her friends wishing her well. Mercifully, when the results came a week later they were negative, and she was notified that the surgeons were going to attempt to remove the lump before they put her on a new cocktail of drugs. However, she was so mutilated and scarred by the mastectomy and radiation that they would have to operate through her back, and even then there was no guarantee they could remove the lump.

Because we were so close, and I was the one person in the family with whom she could discuss her health, we had long talks in their kitchen.

'What'll happen if the latest drugs don't work and it spreads?' she would plead.

'Don't worry, they'll work,' I would say reassuringly.

'But what if they don't?'

'They'll try other ones.'

'And if they don't work, what'll they do?'

'They've always got something up their sleeve,' I would reply. 'Anyway, they're coming up with something new the whole time.'

'Well, I won't go quietly!' she cried defiantly. 'As Dylan Thomas said, "Rage, rage, against the dying of the light!"'

For several months, after the lump was removed, her new medication appeared to be working. Determined to see as much of her as possible, every other day I went up to visit her in Howe Street or we would meet for a coffee in a café opposite. At the weekend, I took her and my father for a drive to the Borders, although I found his bad-tempered presence so inhibiting that I frequently turned the mirror in order not to see him in the back seat. Every now and again, during our talks in the kitchen, she disclosed details of her marriage, some so intimate that I felt they went beyond the bounds of propriety. Eventually, the burden of being her counsellor, advisor, priest and confessor became too much for me, and I cajoled her into going with me to a voluntary organisation that offered free counselling to the dying and their carers. After attending two group sessions, however, she told me she found them of no benefit and we stopped going.

At the time, I had been caught up in my relationship with Julia, effectively my sole outlet for switching off from the tragedy unfolding in front of me. One day, when Julia was in Edinburgh, I had phoned my mother to say I wouldn't be up to their house for a day or two. Half an hour afterwards, the phone rang.

'You inconsiderate bastard! How you have the audacity to leave your father to cope all alone!' she shouted, and slammed down the receiver.

Stressed and resentful of the extent to which my mother was monopolising my everyday existence, I was so outraged that for two months I saw comparatively little of her. Then, in January, after my relationship with Julia had collapsed, she rang me to say she had been told that the cancer had metastasised into both her lungs, and that instead of operating on her they were going to put her on a groundbreaking course of chemotherapy.

Naturally, I went straight up to see her, where, for a while, she sat in the kitchen and wept inconsolably.

'I can't believe it!' she burst out, mascara running down her cheeks. 'I'm finished! How am I going to live with it all? It's so cruel. I was all ready for the hospital, and now it's fallen through at the last hurdle. My hair's going to drop out, and I'm going to be sick, yet everybody says I look so well! How I wished I'd never loved life so much …'

'No,' I replied, putting my arm around her, and cradling her head on my shoulder, 'that was the best thing you've ever done.'

The effects of the chemotherapy were heartbreaking to behold. All her hair fell out, and she started wearing a wig that was far too black for a seventy-one-year-old woman. Her body ballooned more than ever, she was vomiting incessantly from the medication, and she was more and more exhausted. Full of remorse about the distance I had allowed to develop between us, once again I saw her as much as possible. She appeared to be composed, as if she didn't believe what was happening to her, although I knew she was terrified. At last, I gave in to one of her greatest wishes – for the two of us to drive to the west coast of Scotland for a week or two.

Before we departed she said to me, 'Do you think this'll be our last trip? Answer truthfully, as you always do.'

'No,' I lied, 'of course not. I'm certain there'll be a lot more.'

It was autumn as we set off. The leaves on the trees were beginning to turn, and the fields were full of sheaves of yellow, ripening barley. In the Highlands, the moors were violet and the hedgerows were awash with purple lupins. It was a drowsy, cloudless day, and we picnicked by the shore of Loch Awe, but she had deteriorated so rapidly she could hardly walk a hundred yards. When we arrived in Oban, we stayed in the Victorian hotel where her mother had used to stay. Then, it had been a stately pile, but now it was down-at-heel and catered for bus parties and old-age pensioners. A few days later, we left the mountains behind and took the ferry to Mull. There, we drove through the island's unending moors to the north, and, as we did, she talked. She talked about how she had loved her Irish forbears and her father. She talked about my father, his lack of affection towards her and why they had quarrelled so much. She talked about how much she regretted having been unable to discuss things with my sister and father, and their inability to deal openly with their emotions.

We found a cosy, intimate hotel in the tiny town of Tobermory, where I took the room next to her. Every night for a week, through the paper-thin wall, I could hear her coughing and gasping for breath. At times, I was even afraid she wouldn't last the night, yet, at 8 a.m., there she was at the breakfast table, and it was as if my fears had merely been part of a nightmare. Afterwards, we strolled arm in arm past the blue, pink and yellow houses to the harbour, which was full of bobbing yachts. Now, I could only hug her and tell her how much I loved her. Now, there was no more time to be irritated by her mannerisms that had annoyed me for so long – the noise she made when she drank her tea, her impatience with shopkeepers, and her some-times stentorian voice in public places …

A week later, it was time to return home. During the long, tiring drive back down south, we drew up by the side of lochs and took photographs of each other leaning against the van, as if we were trying to freeze time. But she had lost her faith. 'Why me?' she would cry plaintively. 'I'm only seventy-one, and nearly all my friends are far older! And how can I die when I've so much to live for? There's the new house to enjoy. I want to see you settled, the grandchildren grow up. Oh, there're so many loose ends that I don't have time to die …'

When we arrived back in Edinburgh, I felt glad I had become so close to her again, and I prayed there would be more time remaining. Most of all, I wanted to make amends for the way I had never shared my private life with her. Since I was a teenager, I, unlike my sister, had kept my friends away from her, because I had been perturbed that she would take them over, as she had Julia. That wasn't the sole reason. I had also been afraid that she would inter-fere as she had done, albeit with the best of intentions, over and over, and see me as the muddled and confused person I at times perceived myself to be. How hurtful my behaviour must have been to her! What a cause for worry, anxiety and despair I must have been – at the age of forty, still unsettled and restless, still with no work and undecided what I was going to do, and where and with whom I was going to do it! For all that, even though I had excluded her from my life and given her so little cause for pride, she had loved me unconditionally and would have done anything for me …

But in no time at all, before my very eyes, the prodigiously warm, big-hearted, irrepressible person I had known all my life had became a hunched, breathless old woman. One afternoon, I caught sight of her and my father walking laboriously up the street fifty yards from Howe Street. He had even allowed her to take his arm – practically the first time I had ever seen that happen – and for once they could have been any elderly loving couple. Shortly afterwards, I invited them to tea on Saturday to St Stephen Street, as I had done since returning to Edinburgh from Amsterdam, and, determined to come one last time, she had to crawl on all fours up the last few stairs. In July, gravely ill, she was admitted to hospital, although even there, notwithstand-ing her condition, she retained her unconquerable spirit and undiminished courage. Once, after nurses had finished attending to her, some of her closest friends smuggled a bottle of champagne into her room. The minute she laid eyes on them, her eyes lit up and, for an hour, trying hard to restrain their uproarious laughter, they had a party, and she once again became the larger-than-life woman that she had always been.

Two weeks later, doctors in the corridor notified my father and me that the tumour had gone into her brain and there was nothing further they could do. Because she had said she didn't want to die in hospital, my father and I took her home. For the next two months, she lay in their bedroom overlooking the Firth of Forth, where she lapsed imperceptibly into an ever-deeper coma. My sister came over from West Germany, although she had a young family to look after. I requested compassionate leave from my summer post as a teacher of English to foreigners. As we busied ourselves about her bedside, a remarkable transformation occurred in the family. At long last, my father, no longer moody and irritable, reverted to being the selfless, dedicated husband he had been in Sussex. With the efficiency of the cowman he had once been, he lovingly dished up food for her and helped her, whimpering pitifully and clinging to his belt, from the bed-room they still shared to the adjoining lavatory on the first floor. My sister, no longer the hectoring, quarrelsome daughter, affectionately combed her hair and sliced slivers of fruit for her to nibble on. I for my part, no longer the whimsical, mercurial son, propped her tenderly up in bed and rear-ranged her pillows. It was almost as if she had had to get cancer to obtain the love she was now receiving.

In addition, a district nurse arrived to assist us. After she had washed her, my mother looked much better. From afar, with her pearly-grey hair neatly brushed back, she again had the features of the dignified woman she had been little more than a year ago. But it was an illusion. The closer you approached, the more you could distinguish pain lines and the outline of death etched on her face, now as white as snow. Day after day, I sat in the wickerwork chair in the bay window, wondering how long this could go on. On the other side of her bed, my father sat reading his newspaper and my sister leafed through magazines. I was astonished at how matter of fact they appeared to be about what was happening, yet, in their own way, they were as present as I was, and this was how they dealt with her dying.

During her illness, I had read several books by Elisabeth Kübler-Ross, one of the world's experts on dying. Now, believing honesty was the best policy, I felt it was time to discuss dying with her. It was a mistake; all she wanted was reassurance that her life's work – her family – had been a success.

Every now and then, she awoke to say how sick she felt. At other times, she was confused.

'Where do I have to go today?' she would ask, or 'How am I going to get there with so many stairs to climb?'

But for the most part there was silence, cut short only by the sound of pages turning and the creak of our wickerwork chairs. Now and again, I marvelled at how speedily human beings adjust, as if this were how things had been, and would be, evermore. It wasn't long until she had to wear an oxygen mask and my father had to wheel her to the toilet in a wheelchair. When my father and sister weren't in the room, I lay on the bed and stroked her hair until, in the end, I didn't care if they were there or not; I wanted to demonstrate that I could display love for her.

Once, she began murmuring in my ear so feebly that I could scarcely hear her. 'I never expected it to be like this,' she whispered. 'I thought it'd be sudden, but it's not like that at all.'

To be near her, I moved into the family house. Every night, I lay in my bedroom in the mammoth, echoing, creaking flat, listening to the wind moan and rattle the windowpanes. At the same time, I wondered how I could continue without her. For forty years she had been the centre of my world, yet shortly she would be gone, leaving behind her a hole of monumental proportions …

Then, one day, after she asked to hold my hands and those of my sister, she seemed to be making her last confession.

'I want you to know what a good son and daughter you've been,' she breathed in a barely audible voice. 'The greatest pleasure in my life has been my family. You've both made me so happy. So has your father, who has been such a fantastic husband. Promise me you'll look after him.'

Two days afterwards – it was a Friday – I went in to see her immediately I awoke. To my surprise, my father and sister were already by her bedside, holding her hand underneath the rose-coloured duvet. It had been twenty-four hours since she had last spoken or asked for water, and she looked in distress, as she was breathing heavily and she kept turning her head painfully from side to side. After they made space for me, they went to the kitchen downstairs, so I lay alone with her with my head on her chest. It was a bizarre feeling. For the past four months she had been the infant while I had fed her spoonfuls of soup and lifted a water beaker to her mouth; now, with my head resting on the scarred space where I had once suckled at her breast, I was again the infant.

Suddenly, it felt as if all this had a meaning and the will of a higher force was being played out. There was no denying that her dying had been a horrible, protracted experience, accompanied by incalculable mental anguish and unimaginable physical suffering. Her body had betrayed her, and she had merely been able to look on helplessly as cancer ravaged her from within. But she had lived to the age of seventy-two, she had had countless friends and she had loved and been loved. She had married, given birth to two children, and had had the pleasure of seeing her grandchildren. She had spent many enjoyable years travelling to Spain and Greece and, for the last seven, had enjoyed appreciable wealth and the majestic home where now, embraced by her family, she was dying in her own bed.

Before the nurse left at midday, she requested that one of us take a pre-scription for morphine to the chemist. I volunteered, although I wanted to avoid being away too long in case she died while I was absent. When I got to the local chemist, he informed me he had no morphine and that, as all the other chemists were closed for the weekend, the only place I could find it was at a twenty-four hour pharmacy in the West End. Dismayed, I sped up the steep cobbled lane to Moray Place and past the grand Geor-gian house where she had been born. It was a crisp autumn afternoon and gossamer clouds sailed high in an unearthly cerulean sky. From the gardens in the middle of the square, where a gardener was raking leaves, came the odour of damp, rich soil, along with the haunting call of blackbirds. I cut up to Melville Street, where her family had lived after they had moved out of Moray Place. There, I turned into the street where, during our teenage years, my sister and I had gone with her to the Quaker meeting house.

After I collected the morphine, I sprinted along George Street to a bookshop, where I purchased a copy of *Myself and Michael Innes*, the recently published autobiography of J.I.M. Stewart – probably, of course, her first lover – who had never failed to send her a Christmas card every year and a copy of his latest book. Now, aware of the almost spiritual bond between them, I intended to give it to her as a final parting present.

Before the book was gift-wrapped, I wrote inside:

'To my beloved mother, for your journey, until we meet again,
Your ever loving son.'

By the time I got back to the house, there had been a dramatic deterioration in her condition, as her face was anaemic and drawn and her pupils were frosty. I laid the book on her bedside cabinet; in the meantime, my father, manifestly impervious to the change, sat in his chair reading the newspaper. After he had gone to prepare food in the kitchen downstairs, I lay on the bed. Suddenly, her tiny breaths started coming faster and faster, as if she was working up to something.

It was only then it dawned on me her moment had come.

'Go on!' I whispered encouragingly in her ear, as I took her cold, limp hand and stroked her forehead. 'There's no need to wait any more. Go on, God's with you, and there's nothing to be afraid of.'

For a few seconds, her breath ceased altogether, as though she were listening, until the breaths began again. 'Go on,' I repeated. 'You've had a good life, and now it's time to go.' Two minutes elapsed, and her breath came back once, twice and ceased. I waited one minute, two minutes, three minutes, four minutes.

She was dead.

For ten minutes I lay there, with tears streaming down my cheeks. Without warning, I was unaccountably swept by a wave of euphoria. It was the first time I had witnessed death, and I couldn't believe I had been at that of my own mother, as I had so desperately wanted. It was almost as if some higher power had ordained it. She had given me the inestimable gift of waiting for me to return before she chose to die. Convinced, as the *Tibetan Book of the Dead* contends, that the retreating soul can hear from the beyond, I continued whispering in her ear, before I closed her lifeless eyes. It was 6.51 p.m. Downstairs, I could hear my sister and my father moving around in the kitchen. At last, I shouted for them to come and they raced upstairs. For thirty seconds, my father stood by her dressing table, looking at her, until, for the first time in my life, I saw him burst into tears, and my sister sat sobbing quietly at the foot of her bed. For several minutes, I lingered at the door, where I mused how odd it would be now that there were only us three. Then

I kissed her brow before I crossed to my bedroom, where I knelt down and thanked God for having granted me the opportunity to ease her into the beyond, eternity, call it what you will. Through the window, the sun, which had set at the instant she had died, was sinking over Corstorphine Hill, tinting clouds chrysanthemum and gold.

Three hours later, the doctor came to issue a death certificate, closely followed by two undertakers. While they were attending to her, I went into the brown drawing room and proposed that we open a bottle of wine and toast her.

'To a wonderful mother!' I exclaimed, as we clinked our glasses.

When the men had finished, they struggled with the coffin down the spiral stairs to the green drawing room. There, we had elected, knowing how much she identified with the Irish, to hold a vigil for her, rather than have her removed to the undertaker's parlour, which we knew she would have loathed. For the next three days, I from time to time went in to look at her. She lay with her hands folded across her chest in an oak coffin partly covered with white silk covers. Dressed in an orchid nightdress flecked with cherry roses, her waxen cheeks were as smooth as porcelain and she looked serene. In the muted light of the two Victorian wall lamps, the green room, with its claret carpet, burgundy draped curtains, and flowery sofa and chairs, was like a shrine.

Once, I fetched scissors and snipped off a locket of her silver hair. Beside the coffin, on top of a polished mahogany table, was a cluster of family photographs in silver mounts. One of them showed her, aged five, gazing into the camera and, with her chubby features framed by curly ringlets and smiling brown eyes so big that you could get lost in them, she could have been a cherub or seraph floating on a cotton-wool cloud. Beside it was a photograph of my sister wearing a Tyrolean dress, a photograph of me in Amsterdam, and a photograph of the grandchildren, so I placed them on her chest.

Three days later, it was time for the funeral. As her coffin was being carried out of the green drawing room and through the front door, for the second time in my life I saw my father dissolve into tears.

'Don't take her away, don't take her away!' he cried.

My father, sister and I followed the hearse by taxi down to Warriston, a crematorium a mile away, where we had requested that everyone wear colourful clothes. Inside, a senior Quaker we had asked to conduct the service read a short piece. Battling to control my emotions, I recited one of her favourite poems by Yeats. When I had finished, a deeply spiritual Roman Catholic friend of the family asked everybody to hold hands and stand in silence in a circle around the coffin for five minutes. After the service was over, my father, my sister and I lined up outside the door of the crematorium, where, as they filed past, offering their condolences, we shook everyone's hand. Then, that evening, we held a wake in the house, where, once more, the long pine kitchen table was groaning with food and both drawing rooms resounded to the babble and laughter of friends of my mother and sister.

A few days afterwards, I drove my father and sister down to the Meldon Hills in the Borders to scatter the ashes. The spot we had chosen was by a stream in a tranquil, heather-clad valley where she and my father had often gone for a Sunday drive and, later, taken the grandchildren for a picnic. It was a leaden, overcast day and there was a deafening silence apart from the sound of the gurgling stream. As I scattered half the ashes in the clear, peat-coloured water and the other half over nearby clumps of lilac heather, I looked up and prayed the sun would burst through. All of a sudden, the clouds parted and rays of numinous light suffused the valley and for one fleeting moment it seemed as if my request for some transcendental sign had been granted; at the climax of the most emotional week of my life, I told myself that it was far more than a coincidence, and it confirmed my belief that there was some omnipotent, universal intelligence in the world.

After the collapse of my calamitous love affair with Julia, along with my decision to return to Scotland and the death of my mother, my life underwent a startling transformation. Although I had left Amsterdam for good, its sublime beauty had permanently moulded my sense of aesthetics, and its liberal, progressive values and nonconformity would continue to shape me for the rest of my life. As anticipated, I missed my mother dreadfully and, despite our turbulent relationship, I often wept at the thought of her. But after the trauma of the last four months, her death had come as a colossal relief to my sister and me, and I comforted myself with the belief that she would always be there to guide me. Now, in a sudden burst of activity, I settled into my flat. I bought pine bookshelves for the sitting room, where I had a carpet fitted, and a marble mantelpiece and a coal-effect gas fire installed. I replaced the discoloured coffee-coloured velvet curtains in the bedroom – the last remaining trace of the garret – with new cream ones. I threw out my sister's discarded moth-eaten mattress on which I had slept on the floor, and bought a new double bed. I bought plants, and decorated the walls of every room with pictures.

Meanwhile, things in Amsterdam had likewise changed drastically for Alistair. Over the following months, in a series of ten-page letters and telephone calls to me in Edinburgh, he described what had happened to him since I had last seen him. To begin with, he had been flattered to find himself Willem's favourite. But when he visited him in his chateau in France, surrounded by a clique of well-heeled acolytes, he kept on criticising him, although maintaining that he wanted purely to help him 'grow'. With his self-confidence at an all-time low, Alistair decided to give the bookshop one last go, and flung himself into his work there. He hadn't written anything for two years, and he was progressively losing interest in Amsterdam where, providing Conrad wasn't there, he saw nobody apart from Fritz.

Then, even that friendship had threatened to crumble, as Fritz, a chain smoker, had had to undergo a heart bypass and almost died on the operating table. Alistair had been shaken to the core and found the prospect of living in Amsterdam without him or myself didn't bear thinking about. Now, as the bottom fell out of his world, and despite his remarkable acceptance of his diagnosis, he was sick of everything. He was sick of slaving away for twelve hours a day, six days a week. He was sick of being unable to afford even a cheap, second-hand car. He was sick of living in rotting houses. Worst of all, he acknowledged he was indeed no longer 'growing', as Willem had contended, and he pined for his long-gone sense of adventure.

Two months afterwards, in a perilously unstable frame of mind, Alistair sold the bookshop for a pittance and fled Amsterdam. First he travelled to the south of France, where he planned to complete Willem's course. To his consternation, Willem continued to harangue him so relentlessly that he ended their relationship and withdrew from his course. For a week, he hung on in the chateau, as he felt that beyond lay merely 'the abyss'. Then he headed for Italy, where he intended to look up his friend the prince in Naples, before he earned some much-needed money by working on the grape harvest. Unfortunately, the prince was away, so, unable to confront the physical rigours of the harvest, he took the ship once again to Stromboli.

There, as usual, he rented his room in the ramshackle house in Ginostra, at the foot of the volcano. In a series of lengthy, remarkably poetic letters to me, he described how he sat every night at a candlelit wooden table, watching 'shadows gambol on crumbling walls' and trying to write, until he slumped demoralised over a bottle of grappa. Overwhelmed with uncertainty one minute and laughing hysterically the next, he was having uncontrollable mood swings, which he attributed to homeopathic pills he had been taking since his diagnosis. However he hadn't lost his offbeat sense of humour, as he recounted various ways he had contemplated committing suicide, which ranged from scaling Stromboli's volcano and plunging headfirst with his journals into the crater, to jumping with his rucksack and typewriter off the ship back to Naples. Then he spelled out why he hadn't been able to do it; he would chicken out at the volcano's rim and have to walk the whole way back down to Ginostra or, if he jumped overboard from the ship, he would most likely be washed up alive on some Calabrian beach, before he needed to find a telephone box. In the end, he had elected to look up his American friend who had the little castle in Tuscany with a view to living in Italy and, if that wasn't successful, he planned to return to Amsterdam.

I wrote back, suggesting that, rather than relapse into his former life, he leave the Netherlands for good and, like myself, come to Scotland to make a fresh start. I never believed that he would, as for years he had maintained it was the last place he would return to, and he had always recoiled at the very thought of its 'provincialism' and 'appalling climate'. Nevertheless, in July, a year after my mother died, he telephoned from Fritz's house to say that he was coming to Edinburgh to do precisely that. He gave several reasons. He intended to wean himself off the sex, alcohol, cigarettes and cocaine to which he had become addicted in Amsterdam. He had given up the notion of try-ing to settle in Italy and, weary of being a perpetual outsider, he wanted to have the security of Britain's National Health Service in case his condition worsened. Above all, he longed to develop a closer relationship with his father while there was still time, but if his plan to settle in Scotland didn't work out, he would use his fast-dwindling funds to go travelling to Mada-gascar, Sri Lanka or the Philippines. Beyond that, he didn't have the remotest clue.

At the beginning, I envisaged him destitute or living from hand to mouth in some dreary flat. He didn't take long to prove that I was profoundly mis-

taken. For six months he stayed in my father's pied-à-terre, before he found
a self-contained little wing in an elegant Georgian manse in Saxe-Coburg
Square. Situated less than two minutes round the corner from my flat, it
was owned by an affluent woman who had contacts at Wellspring, a highly
respected psychotherapy centre in Edinburgh. Within weeks, he had a part-
time job there and, even though he was merely the receptionist, he soon
became irreplaceable thanks to his engaging personality and the administrative skills he had learned in the bookshop.

   But all this was secondary to his new passion in life – photography. For a
long time, he had taken snapshots during his travels in India and South-east
Asia, although they showed no particular promise. Now, every weekend, I
borrowed my parents' Mini and drove him to gardens of country mansions
in Perthshire and the Borders, and the windswept Tyninghame beach in East
Lothian, where he photographed mossy benches, knotted tree trunks and
rock pools. At the time, I assumed his interest in photography was only his
latest hobby, but the results were both eye-catching and deeply spiritual.

   It wasn't long before he was mounting mini exhibitions in arty cafés and
the New Town houses of prosperous Wellspring patrons with whom he had
become friendly. When his work at the psychotherapy centre was finished

for the day, he spent his evenings at home, where, after we had eaten another of his gourmet meals, we whiled away hours choosing those of 'exhibition quality'.

All at once, doors opened for him. A year after he took up photography, I helped him mount his first solo exhibition at Edinburgh's premier art-house cinema. Sponsored in part by Kodak, it was evocatively titled 'Stone Song. Images of stone, sand, water surfaces, tree-bark, leaves, flowers and forest. What may appear to be mute is not necessarily silent.' In no time at all, at his first attempt, he received a grant from a national arts foundation and with the money he purchased a second-hand moped to carry out his project, photographing nature reserves. Now he was no longer dependent on me for transport and, that winter, when I took the car for a Sunday drive along deserted country roads in the Borders, I sometimes glimpsed his familiar figure hunched over the handlebars of his moped, with his camera slung around his shoulders and a scarf muffling his mouth against the icy blasts.

The following July, Fritz and I gave him money to mount his second exhibition in the Filmhouse, which he also scheduled to tour four major botanical gardens in the Netherlands. In August, a local BBC radio station interviewed him about his photography, and in September the Dutch photography magazine *Foto* assigned its centre pages to his work, accompanied by an article comparing him to the illustrious American landscape photographer Edward Weston. As might be expected, it was music to his ears; finally he was receiving the acclaim he had craved for so long, even if it was for his photography rather than his writing.

That year was, in all probability, the happiest of his life. He had achieved most of the goals he had set himself when he returned to Scotland. He had settled down in his pocket-sized wing of the manse, and he had a satisfying, part-time job at the psychotherapy centre that provided him with enough money to live on. In Findhorn, he had embarked on a course in reflexology with Barbara, an eighty-five-year-old woman who had become his mentor, and he had given up alcohol, cigarettes, cocaine and sex. His friendships were similarly fulfilling. He was no longer even interested in sex, and he had become friends with several of the psychotherapists, above all its director, Di Bates. A profoundly spiritual woman, she was the daughter of the founder, the distinguished Jungian psychoanalyst Winifred Rushforth, and the two of them sometimes went for long Sunday walks along the Fife coast, where they had deep, meaningful conversations about death.

But by far the most crucial of his new relationships was with his mother and father in Perth. His mother, predictably, was overjoyed at having her son close at hand, and his father had eventually come round to accepting his son's homosexuality. In addition, he had got to know my own father, whom he sometimes took for a drive to the Borders. He had even got to know my sister and her family, as, once, when I had taken him down to meet Marie in Strasbourg, we had stopped off at my sister's house in Germany. There, she and her children had loved him and his hilarious laugh, and now, whenever they came over to Edinburgh, he got on so famously with them that I became jealous. Still, we discussed it, and he learned, sensitive as ever, when to keep his distance.

And I, of course, lived just round the corner. On sunny summer afternoons we frequently reclined in deck chairs under a spreading chestnut tree in the manse's walled garden. And we went for drives. We drove down to the annual funfair on the seashore just outside Edinburgh or in Fife, where we laughed uproariously on merry-go-rounds or dodgem cars. If the weather was favourable, we drove to outdoor swimming pools at Port Seton or North Berwick, where we careered down chutes and larked about in the icy water. Often, we drove down to the Borders, and on the return journey we paused on a quiet road in the middle of treeless moors to the south of Edinburgh. There, we stood under a row of stark, solitary, windswept trees and had fun betting, as we had done for close upon a decade, about everything and anything that moved: what time the sun would sink behind the Pentland Hills, when the next cloud would appear, and how long it would take for the first car to appear ...

Indeed Alistair's health seemed so stable that, for the first time since I had been to Africa, six years previously, I resolved to go travelling again. So he and my sister's twin boys waved me off at Waverley Station on the express to London, from where I flew to Moscow to take the Trans-Siberian Railway to Lake Baikal in Siberia. When I got back to Britain, he was in a quandary about whether to do a course in dream therapy, which he felt would help him come to terms with his diagnosis. Based on the work of a distinguished American, one of the world's leading authorities in the field, it was a major decision to take because it would last eight months and swallow a sizeable amount of his hard-earned savings. After we had weighed the pros and cons, he took the plunge and decided to go ahead, as the American would himself be visiting Edinburgh every month to take the course, which Alistair regarded as a vital way of coming to terms with his illness.

Once the course commenced, he found it invigorating, even though he, like most of the students, was alienated by how the American kept arriving halfway through the session before informing them, when someone objected, that it was their problem, not his. When the course was over, he invited me to see the show in a draughty church hall in Morningside where the participants exhibited their work. To my surprise, his paintings, the lion's share of which figured his father, were alarmingly violent, although, in retrospect, given his inner torment caused by having to hide his sexuality from his parents for years, that wasn't surprising.

But storm clouds were gathering. Since he had arrived in Edinburgh, he had been leading a double life. Fearful that his landlady or the psychotherapy centre would discover he was HIV-positive and he would be ejected on to the street or lose his job, every month he travelled to a hospital in Glasgow to be treated under a false name. But it put him under almost unbearable stress, and we had interminable discussions about whom to inform and when to do it. Regardless, to my shame, I still didn't believe what was happening to him; on the return from outings to country house gardens in the Highlands, I would go for a run on deserted roads halfway up Schiehallion, and when he picked me up in the van, I would exclaim, 'Come on, Grandpa, hurry up!'

But instead of complaining he simply laughed and suffered stoically, although once, in his little wing in the manse, he wept on my shoulder.

Then, because he had developed full-blown AIDS, he began losing weight. His blood counts plummeted, and he was put on highly toxic drugs. He found going to the psychotherapy centre increasingly taxing, and he could scarcely do three hours' work before he had to return home to bed. In addition, the painful injections and headaches induced by the medication tested him sorely. After a while, his condition could no longer be disguised, and we agreed that he had to divulge his diagnosis to the owner of the manse and the psychotherapy centre. To our immeasurable relief, both were enormously supportive. His landlady divulged subsequently that she had speculated from day one that he had AIDS, but that it made no difference to her; the psychotherapy centre were equally understanding and assured him that he could take as much paid leave as he wished.

For a few months, his condition stabilised, and he started talking about going on holiday to Italy, for which Fritz generously offered to pay, as it looked as if he had hardly any time remaining to benefit from the inheritance that he, Fritz, planned to leave him. So I determined to go travelling again, this time to Japan and China; after all, I told myself, I had my own life to lead, and Alistair seemed to be back on his feet. Initially daunted by the prospect of travelling alone in China, which at that time was about as alien as the moon to Westerners, I made a half-hearted effort to persuade Michel into going with me. Although I hadn't laid eyes on him for six years, I had heard that he had bought a tumbledown farmhouse in an obscure part of southern Portugal. When I did, he let slip that he had never regarded me as a close friend. In reality he was right. We had had nothing in common, of course, other than being two footloose and fancy-free rolling stones who it suited to travel together. Now, when I eventually tracked down his telephone number, he declined my offer, as he was renovating the cottage in the cherished hope of persuading the German woman, the love of his life, to come and live with him.

Throughout January, staying in Buddhist monasteries in northern Japan, I waded through two-foot snowdrifts before I flew to Hong Kong, travelled on to remote south-west China and sailed down the River Yangtze.

Two months later, on my return to Britain, I was appalled to see how emaciated Alistair had become. He welcomed me back with open arms, of course, but I reproached myself bitterly for having left him in the first place. He was, however, distressed not by my absence but because, after he had been to Utrecht for the triumphant opening of his photography exhibition, the remaining Dutch botanical gardens had, pleading cutbacks in subsidies, scrapped his tour.

The following weekend, he asked me to accompany him to the west coast of Scotland, after which he planned to go to Findhorn to look up Barbara, his beloved mentor and reflexology teacher. For some reason, I couldn't go. It was a decision I will rue until the day I die. Heavy-hearted, he set off by himself. First he broke his journey in Perth to call in on his parents, who revealed subsequently that, with hindsight, they were certain he had come to say goodbye. After that, he hitchhiked to the west coast before he arrived in Findhorn, only to learn that Barbara's body had just been found in the neighbouring eponymous river. Naturally, he was heartbroken, even though he was convinced that, given she had been found with a peaceful expression on her face, she had felt it was time to 'move on'. The community in Findhorn, on the other hand, believed she had been washed away by a freak wave. At all events, it was most likely her death that tipped him over the edge, although Fritz argued later that it was caused by his toxic medication, and the doctors maintained that it was because the AIDS virus had reached his brain.

While it may have been a combination of all three, what is beyond doubt is that, three days after he left Edinburgh, I received an urgent telephone call from his mother.

'Patrick,' she cried, 'Alistair's been arrested by the police in Findhorn for causing a public disturbance! They say he's in such a state that he's been sectioned under the Mental Health Act and sent to some psychiatric hospital!'

I knew instantly, of course, that something was horribly wrong, as he was one of the most peace-loving people I had ever met. As it was a public holiday and I wasn't teaching at the language school where I was employed for the summer, I promised her I would drive up to see him without delay. When I arrived, I found him in a cramped room off a ward in a grim, time-worn Victorian hospital and that he was, indeed, extremely agitated. He was also acutely paranoid.

'Patrick, they're out to get me!' he breathed conspiratorially, as I strove to stop him getting dressed and clambering out of the window. 'Please get me out of here!'

I was mystified. Superficially, that struck me as a reasonable request. On several occasions, he had told me how much he hated authority, and although he had no history of mental illness, he had spoken of his nightmares about precisely this kind of scenario. Moreover, I was alarmed to find him pumped so full of drugs, and had I been him, I too would have been itching to escape from there. But there had to be more to it than that, as there was little doubt that he was hallucinating.

'Patrick, Patrick, people are coming out the wall!' he blurted out, gesticulating to the mirror above the sink.

'OK, OK!' I exclaimed, trying to steer him back into bed. 'Look, if you play their game and behave, I swear I'll get you out of here.'

When I arrived back in Edinburgh, Di Bates and I tried desperately to have him transferred to a mental hospital there, where it would be easier for his parents and me to visit him. But our efforts were futile, as the psychiatric hospital was adamant he was too fragile to withstand the long journey south. To my huge regret, I had to teach for the next three days, but his mother kept me up to date by telephone. Two days afterwards, the authorities unearthed his medical history, and he was transferred to the Royal Infirmary of Aberdeen.

I had been planning to drive up to see him at the weekend, when at lunchtime on Friday the course director informed me I had an urgent telephone call. It was his mother, who, unable to restrain her tears, told me the hospital had advised her that his condition had worsened dramatically and he wasn't expected to last the night. After coming to grips with the shock, I asked for the afternoon off. Then I borrowed my parents' Mini and set off for the final time on the three-hour journey north. To the west, sullen black clouds boiled in a portentous-looking sky and, aware that the second most momentous event in my life was imminent, I felt an overwhelming sense of trepidation.

The minute I arrived, I waylaid a doctor in the corridor, who told me that Alistair had advanced pneumonia. When I joined his parents at his bedside, he looked dreadful. Unconscious and on a respirator, he was gasping for breath, and underneath the sheets his body was so wasted that he was merely skin and bone. For an hour, the three of us sat there until, knowing how inseparable he and I had been, his parents left us alone. After the door was closed, I leaned over and held his atrophied hand.

'It's OK,' I said softly, 'I'm here with you.'

I felt certain he could hear me because, at intermittent intervals, his frantic gasps for oxygen petered out and there was a protracted, drawn-out silence, as if he were listening. As the night progressed, his parents and I took it in turns to stay with him, and when I was again by myself with him, I stroked his hair.

'It's OK,' I whispered again in his ear reassuringly. Then, using the same words as I had used with my mother, 'There's no need to be afraid. You can go any time you want.'

As I sat there, time seemed to stretch interminably and I can still recollect wondering, as I had with my mother's death, how long this could continue. Then, at 4 a.m., while his parents were getting fresh air in the hospital grounds and I was in the corridor having a break, a nurse ran out of his room. 'Come quickly!' she shouted. But by the time I arrived he was dead.

After the nurse hastened to fetch the doctor and his parents, I sat alone by his bedside. Engulfed by contradictory feelings, I was devastated that, on the one hand, I hadn't been holding his hand when he died. On the other, for the second time I felt an indescribable sense of awe at being in the presence of death and that, again as with my mother, he seemed to have waited for me to be at his bedside before he allowed me to talk him into the beyond.

The funeral was held in a drab Presbyterian church near Perth where joyless bells tolled. It was the last thing Alistair would have wanted, because he had hated Western religions for what he, like myself, judged as their bloody past. In spite of telephone calls from Di Bates and myself beseeching them to think it over, his parents, who were frightened of scandal and had maintained to their friends and relatives that he had died of pneumonia, wouldn't give their consent to the humanist ceremony that Di and I proposed. The church was thronged with people, including Di Bates, the therapists from the psychotherapy centre, his new friends from Edinburgh, and Fritz and other friends from Amsterdam. After a clichéd sermon and a dry eulogy by the sanctimonious minister, who hadn't even known him, I read out a piece I had written celebrating his life. Once again, as at my mother's funeral, I felt highly emotional, although I succeeded in getting through it without breaking down. I ended it with the words he had used to sign off the letter he had posted to me in China: "'Dear friend, may your journeys be protected and your rest assured.'"

After the service, his closest friends drove in a convoy to the farm in Fife of Di Bates, a short distance away, where half of his ashes were scattered over a copper beech sapling, his favourite tree, which we planted in his memory. When the ceremony was finished, there was a reception and dancing to a band in the barn. A few days later, I drove to Dawyck Gardens, which he had loved, in the Borders to scatter the remainder. With me was Maureen, a warm-hearted Glaswegian who was one of our closest friends, and her eight-year-old blond, blue-eyed son whom Alistair had doted on. We found a knoll overlooking dreamlike Stobo Valley, where she unclasped her handbag, inside which was the urn containing his ashes. Suddenly, as she peered inside, her face fell.

'Oh God, the lid's come off and they've all spilled out!' she exclaimed. Then she roared unexpectedly with laughter. 'Alistair would've rolled in the aisles!' she chortled, whereupon we emptied a cloud of white powder over a beech sapling.

Going with his younger brother to the manse to clear out his belongings was a distressing experience. Alistair had had pathetically few possessions apart from his beloved moped, which he bequeathed to his brother, and his books, photographs and writings, which he bequeathed to me. But he left behind far more important legacies. Apart from teaching me to appreciate how soft, gentle and non-aggressive many gay men are compared to their heterosexual counterparts, he gave me the gift of the greatest friendship it is possible for one man to have with another. For three years I kept coming across people who, although I had no idea they had even met him, told me how much he had touched their hearts. Each encounter stopped me in my tracks, as I had believed I knew everything about him. But, like numerous gay men, he had divided his life into compartments, and hardly any people in one knew about the existence of those in the other. After his death, his parents were equally amazed at how many passers-by in the street in Perth complimented them on what a 'charming and charismatic' son they had had. For all that, few people apart from myself realised to what extent, behind his infectious laugh and pleasure-seeking façade, he had been tormented by his inner demons since he had been a teenager, before he died at the cruelly young age of thirty-seven.

Landfall

B ut long before Alistair died, I was beginning to accept Edinburgh and living in Scotland. By now I had grown to love the capital's compact centre, the unsurpassed vistas down to the sea, and the barren Pentland Hills that began almost immediately to the south. I loved its leisurely pace of life, and its remoteness from the creeping conurbations, congested motorways and tower-blocks of England. I loved gazing up at the awe-inspiring castle perched high on its rock. I loved letting my eye follow the plunging cobbled streets of the medieval Old Town down to the sea, or trace the elegant lines of Georgian New Town. And I had come to respect the honest, humble Scots; by joining two mountaineering clubs and going climbing in the Highlands, less than an hour to the north, I had not only come to terms with the climate, but, on the mountains, also come to savour the exhilarating, dynamic skies, bracing winds and squalls gusting in from the west.

The change wasn't merely external. Now I was no longer oscillating chronically about where to live, and the conflict that had torn me apart for so many years was over. Even the recurring nightmare I'd had for a decade – I was in the garret as it increasingly swayed from side to side until it slowly toppled over – was gradually receding. But even more fundamental was my realisation that my biggest mistake had been to believe that, in the absence of my having a career, a woman could provide my existence with meaning. Of course, I had sometimes used women for sex, but, far more important, I had perennially hoped I could meet a woman who could do precisely that. Now I knew that the answer lay within myself. And I had learned other things as well, such as how to do things for their own sake, rather than to achieve an end. I had learned not to care what people thought of me. I had also had the privilege of being present at the death of my mother, the most spiritual experience of my life. I had even had the greatest friendship it is possible for a heterosexual man to have with a gay man. Now I knew what I wanted to do – continue travelling to far-off parts of the world and, for the first time, write to be published.

So, once again, I set off. This time I followed the Silk Road across north-west China and down the Karakoram Highway in Pakistan. Then, when I returned, and only a month after Alistair died, I started doing an evening class at university in German, which, seeing that my sister and her family still lived in Nord Rhine-Westphalia, I wanted to maintain. The teacher was an attractive thirty-year-old German from Göttingen called Gabriella. Willowy, with slender legs, shoulder-length fair hair and delicate fingers, she wore a thin gauze blouse that barely concealed her shapely body, and her classes were light-hearted as well as instructive. One evening, in the coffee queue during the break, she told me that she was struggling with not having a proper job and income. She had studied at university and then trained in Sussex to be a Rudolf Steiner schoolteacher before she had come to Edinburgh; now she had the income of only three classes a week at the university to live on.

Afraid that she was disclosing too much personal information to someone she hardly knew, thereafter, for a while, I took care to put distance between us. After Christmas, however, when her class had fallen through because of lack of numbers, she telephoned me to ask if I wanted to join a private class she was organising. I replied that I couldn't, but as she had mentioned to me that she liked going to continental-style cafés, I decided to invite her to Café Florentin, at the time the only such café in town. There, I discovered we both liked travel, languages and classical music – she was an accomplished classical pianist – so the following week I invited her to lunch at a Danish restaurant off the Royal Mile.

By now I was definitely attracted to her and I was so on edge that I had to go to the lavatory four times. A week later, I invited her for a drive to the east coast. On the way, we stopped in Dirleton, a pretty village with a village green and a ruined castle. It was a mild spring day as we meandered through woods carpeted with snowdrops to the church, behind which we could see sand dunes and hear the roar of the sea. There, we found ourselves engaged

in a deep philosophical discussion about Nietzsche. It wasn't exactly what I had intended, but she was gentle and poetic – she was descended from the renowned nineteenth-century German poet Eduard Moerike – so that weekend I invited her to the fortieth birthday party of a friend of mine. It was being held in a subterranean basement in the Dungeons, a horror museum in the West End, and it was dim, claustrophobic and jam-packed. For an hour, trying to pluck up sufficient courage to put my arms around her, I gulped down umpteen beers until, on a whim, I pinned her against the bars of a cage full of skeletons and kissed her.

Little did I know I had found my life's partner and that I was on the threshold of a new existence ...

Gabriella was deeply spiritual, and later she revealed that, after studying at university and just before she began her teacher training in Sussex – by a bizarre coincidence only six miles from where I had been born – she had felt something pulling her towards Edinburgh.

'It was very strange, because, before I went there, the only thing I knew about it was the name and that it had a famous festival,' she said. 'Of course, I didn't have a job and I knew no one. But on my very first walk in the

Pentlands I had an incredible feeling of déjà vu. It was as if I was seeing the landscape of some dream deep inside me. Then, three years afterwards, I met you. It was as if we were destined to meet. Some would say it was a fluke, but I believe it was synchronicity. We were simply waiting for the time to be ripe, and I knew that, from the moment I caught sight of you in my class, I had found my soulmate.'

Her spirituality also chimed with my own. Not that I believed in a god, but it seemed to me that the number of factors that had to be precisely right for life to exist on earth was so enormous, and the simplicity that lay behind the mathematical laws of nature were so aesthetically exquisite, that there had to be some non-human intelligence at work.

So, secure in myself and the feeling I was loved, as well as now having a firm base in Edinburgh, I continued on my travels. Hitherto, I had travelled extensively through Buddhist countries, such as Burma, Nepal, Ladakh and Japan; now I added Mongolia and Tibet to the list.

For many years, it had seemed as though my travelling to such places was accidental, but suddenly it felt as if I had, in fact, been unconsciously lured to them. For the first time, I could identify with those sculptors and writers who maintain, after they complete a piece of work, that the sculpture or novel is merely waiting to be uncovered; now I had fitted together the jigsaw puzzle that had constituted my past, and it felt as if there had been a pattern all along.

One day, that past caught up with me. I was browsing in the basement of a musty antiquarian bookshop in Edinburgh's West Port. All of a sudden, a man with his head bent over books glanced up and, to my amazement, I realised it was Jonathan, with whom I had been so friendly in Amsterdam. Although he had hollow cheeks and sunken temples, he was still handsome in a ravaged sort of way and, when we went for a coffee, he recounted what had happened to him. In England he had fallen madly in love with his college lecturer. For a year, she had been the love of his life before she had been tragically killed in a car crash. Devastated, he had withdrawn from his course and gone to live on a friend's farm on a remote hillside in Wales. After he had managed to come to terms with his grief, for a few years he lived on an estate in Devon that belonged to a famous rock musician he had run into. Then he had drifted up to a squat in a rambling manor house twenty miles south of Edinburgh. There, unknown to all his former friends in Scotland, he had been unobtrusively living and working in the garden for nine years. The house, which, sooner or later, was going to be repossessed and converted into an old people's home, was awash with would-be filmmakers, artists and un-employed musicians, and here he met a beautiful clinical psychologist called Elaine. For some reason that I never fully comprehended she had been un-able to find anywhere to live after her marriage had foundered, even though she had a highly paid job in a nursing home in Edinburgh. Now, although she was twenty-five years younger than him, they were having a very pas-sionate relationship.

That summer my friendship with Jonathan once again blossomed like a flower. Two months later, after word came that everyone in the country house was finally about be evicted, he revealed that he had applied to do a course in Somerset on Buddhism, which he professed to have been interest-ed in for years. Nonetheless, he didn't seem to have digested its teachings, as his speech was peppered with angry expletives, and he seemed to be perma-nently at loggerheads with the world. Furthermore, he appeared to believe – wrongly – that the rudimentary Buddhist tenet of non-attachment meant that every few years he had to sever all ties with his past, which clarified why we had lost touch after he left Amsterdam. Then, several weeks before he was due to leave, he invited me to join him and the psychologist for the weekend in north-west Scotland. He was staying in a country house which, part of a tiny bohemian community on the virtually uninhabited, mountainous Sco-raig peninsula, was about to converted into a yoga centre.

The following Friday I made the tiring four-hour journey by car up to Little Loch Broom, the prearranged rendezvous, where a youth in a rowing boat was waiting for me at a lonely landing stage. It was a windless, sunny day and he had his head protected by a beekeeper's mask against hosts of midges. Within minutes I found myself being rowed across the smooth, silky loch, and twenty minutes later we landed at a two-storey white house whose gardens were gradually being strangled by wild rhododendrons. For the next two days I hardly caught a glimpse of Jonathan or Elaine, as they were both interested in Tantric sex and spent all their time in their bedroom. However, once, when she was alone, I bumped into her, and she confided in me how much she dreaded him leaving for Somerset, as she feared she would never see him again. Her intuition proved to be correct; after we got back to Edinburgh, Jonathan and I embraced each other, before he once more cut all ties with me and everybody else who knew him, and disappeared forever from our lives.

After my mother's death, my sister and I had been very worried that our father, married to her for the greatest part of fifty years, would go to pieces. She had been his world. She had cleaned the house, washed his dishes and ironed his clothes. She had prepared all his meals and done the shopping. With her huge circle of friends, she had provided all his social needs; as he had never learned to drive, she had even continued to chauffeur him every year thousands of miles to the south of Spain and back.

Now, for several years, he did indeed fall into the blackest of depressions, and it looked as if our fears were well founded. Then, out of compassion, a handful of my mother's loyal female friends took him under their wing. The most prominent of these was Brenda, one of my mother's closest friends. He liked her because she was large, jovial and hospitable – she perhaps reminded him of my mother – and she amused him. She for her part liked him because she, like my mother, found him a challenge. She also liked having a man around, although she had taken a vow of celibacy after her husband, a chief inspector of schools, had died of a heart attack when she was barely forty-nine.

For the next twenty years they developed a remarkably enduring friendship. The first real friend he had ever had, she took him here, there and everywhere. She took him to parties and she took him to the cinema. She took him to the theatre, book openings and her arts club. Every day, he walked down the hill to her elegant Georgian flat in nearby Saxe-Coburg Square, where she cooked him meals and they played Scrabble, at which they both excelled. Together, they briefly started attending Italian classes, as they occasionally stayed in a small, fourteenth-century keep in Tuscany which belonged to a friend of mine. For a while, she even succeeded in taking him – a major achievement considering that he was a confirmed atheist – to her church, the Seventh-day Adventists, whose values symbolised everything he loathed.

Though he had no geographical sense of direction – every so often he would even get lost going up to Princes Street – for years, after my mother died, he even managed to travel by himself back to Sifnos in Greece, where they had often gone together. With my help, he began to learn to drive and, after three attempts, at the age of eighty-two, passed his driving test. For several years he drove around in a surprisingly sporty little second-hand car that he bought. He didn't find driving easy, however, and, as he time and again unwittingly drove through red traffic lights, he was a constant hazard on the roads. Then, one winter's day, blinded by the low sun sinking to the west, he drove head-on into a skip parked in Longniddry, a coastal village in East Lothian. Luckily, he only suffered bruising, although the impact was so severe that the corner of the skip concertinaed the passenger seat into the boot. Traumatised, he reluctantly heeded my advice not to press his luck any further, and thereafter Brenda chauffeured him around instead.

From time to time, they travelled to the west coast, where he invited her to a luxury timeshare that he had bought. Of course, because I had sworn to my mother that I would look after him – and he was, after all, my father – I continued to invite him down to Saturday afternoon tea. They weren't particularly pleasurable occasions. After he had wanted to throw me out of the house all those years ago, I had told him that I wouldn't discuss politics or any controversial subject with him. Instead, although he persisted in trying to provoke me, I encouraged him to talk about himself. I found that immensely difficult, as he was such a diffident, unforthcoming man. Nonetheless, I managed to get him to reminisce about life in Sussex and his parents, although – almost as if our loss was too incalculable to bear

– he and I hardly ever mentioned my mother. Nor could I bear to visit him in Howe Street, and even then I saw him only in the kitchen, as I found it too distressing to sit with him in the drawing rooms, which reminded me so much of her.

After a few years, he and Brenda started going to the Canary Islands. Then, because they loved its warm, sunny winters, he bought a holiday apartment in Playa Blanca in the south of Lanzarote, where he once more invited her to stay. Looking down to the glittering sea and the distant mountains of the island of Fuerteventura, it was very appealing. Like all the island's other houses, which were designed by César Manrique – the local, internationally acclaimed architect responsible for Lanzarote having avoided the high-rise development so characteristic of the Canaries – it was white, with green doors, green windows and a green balcony, and overlooked a square built round a pale blue artificial football pitch.

A year later, Brenda also bought a small holiday apartment in Playa Blanca. Further down the same street, and nearer the sea, it was so close to his that he could practically see her on her balcony. Now, instead of walking two hundred yards down to her flat in Edinburgh, he walked two hundred yards down to her apartment in Playa Blanca. There, she once again cooked him three-course meals, and every day they met for coffee in a café off the pedestrianised main street, while at weekends she chauffeured him in his little second-hand car to Arrecife, the island's small capital, twenty-six miles to the east.

Of course, when he was there, Gabriella and I and my sister and her family flew out to visit him. They all liked Lanzarote, where they went three times a year. By now her children were grown up, and not infrequently, after they had returned to Germany to work, she stayed on by herself for up to three months. However, because Gabriella and I disliked the tawdry amusement arcades, gaudy souvenir shops and raucous Irish pubs, we went only twice a year for a few days. He seemed contented enough, but when he phoned my sister and me from a nearby phone box – for several years he refused to have a telephone – we could tell from the way he slurred his words that he had been drinking, and it was obvious that he wasn't a happy man.

He strenuously denied it, of course, as he always denied having any feelings at all. But in his eighties, although he had cut down on his drinking, he became more irascible and argumentative than ever. Most of his sentences contained negative words such as 'no' and 'not'. No matter what anybody said he contradicted it with 'but'. His face was set in a perennial grimace, and there was hardly a time when he wasn't having an acrimonious battle with someone or other. In fact everyone who knew him concluded that it was being at loggerheads with the world that kept him alive. He looked daggers at his neighbours in the square, where he was detested. He had always hated tourists, even though he was one himself. He raged against the corruption in the town council in particular and Spain in general. He had become decidedly racist and he railed against African refugees who, at the time, were flooding into the Canary Islands.

'Throw them back into the sea!" he would rage.

Now and again, because Gabriella, who had retrained as a counsellor, had to work, I flew out to Lanzarote by myself. If my plane was delayed and I arrived later than expected he would unlock his door and greet me with a scowl.

'You're late!' he would exclaim accusingly.

All the same, he would invariably have set the table with his finest crockery before he served up his infamous chicken soup, followed by the only dish he could cook – chicken, roast potatoes, salad and spinach. During the meal, the conversation was invariably the same.

'How are you?' I would enquire.

'Fine.'

'What've you been doing lately?'

'Nothing!'

Admittedly, there wasn't much for him to relate, as every day he merely sat in the sun on his balcony, where he dozed or watered the miniature cactus garden which he had built up and which he nurtured like a baby. After we had depleted our standard stock of topics we would sit in silence, listening to the shouts of boys drift up from the football pitch below. Then, to try to relax us, I would open a bottle of wine and, after he had had several glasses, he would unleash such a vitriolic tirade against religion it was almost as if he harboured some deeply suppressed spiritual longing.

'It's the twenty-first century, but half the world still believes in God!' he would spit out. 'The human race is so stupid!'

The person he remained most respectful towards, apart from Gabriella – who kept her distance and therefore he never really got to know – was Brenda. However, occasionally he was abusive even to her; once, after an argument at his flat he told her he hoped she would be raped on her way home. Yet, after she wrote him a polite letter saying she wanted to be by herself for a while, he couldn't understand why, even when my sister or I explained to him what lay behind it.

'Oh, she's just very eccentric!' he would say.

Nevertheless, she persevered with him because she felt it was her duty as a Christian to look after him and, so she said subsequently, she never abandoned her friends. In addition, she found him so amusing – especially the way he threw down the board when she defeated him at Scrabble – that she from time to time had to laugh out loud. Then there were his barefaced lies, which she found equally hilarious. One day, when he was in her apartment, and he didn't know that she could see him from the upstairs landing, he dropped a vase. When she came down to help him pick up the pieces, she asked him what had happened.

'I don't know, it must have fallen down by itself,' he explained with an innocent face.

He also became extraordinarily miserly. This was all the more surprising because, although he still claimed to be a socialist, he had grown wealthy from his investments. In Edinburgh, he chose to freeze in the huge, now lifeless, family house in winter rather than pay to have central heating installed; to save electricity and keep warm he even retreated into the attic box room. He wore a pair of spectacles whose broken arms he was forever repairing with Sellotape. He let his beetling eyebrows run rampant, and he cut his own hair.

He was equally frugal with himself. In Lanzarote, he ate only a bowl of muesli in the morning and in the evening he merely picked at raw carrots, frozen spinach and cut-price chicken, along with the cheapest bread, ice cream and wine he could buy in the local supermarket. When the chicken was finished, he boiled up the leftovers and made it into soup. If, for a change, he ate out at night, he scoured Playa Blanca for the cheapest three-course meal. If he went out for a drink with Brenda, he would polish off the peanuts at the bar when he thought she wasn't watching. If he had a problem with his teeth, he wouldn't go to any of the town's dentists because they were private and he would have to pay.

'Why should I?' he would exclaim. 'I'll wait till I go back to Britain, when I can go to the dentist for free.'

But if anyone accused him of being tight-fisted, he would retort indignantly, 'Nonsense! I only want value for money!' Once, though, he admitted it. 'If I am thrifty,' he confessed, 'it goes back to the days on the farm, when we had only thirty shillings a week to live on.'

My sister and her children found his miserliness amusing, and were continually teasing him about it. For a long time, I did the same. Then, in his mid-eighties, after it had become almost pathological, I stopped laughing at it, as this only encouraged him. But, although he had long since lost the ability to laugh, there was no doubt that he had, at times, a deadpan sense of humour and was able to recognise his own perversity. 'If you can't be cantankerous when you're approaching ninety, when can you be?' he would exclaim with mock indignation.

He couldn't be defeated in a discussion, because, if he was, he merely shifted the goalposts. But at least he admitted that, linguistically, he was as slippery as a bar of soap. 'Like Humpty Dumpty, I believe that words should mean what you want them to mean,' he would say wryly. His hearing had deteriorated, but, because he wouldn't get a hearing aid, people had to shout when they spoke to him. He didn't care. 'Not being able to hear has its advantages, as there are few people worth listening to', he would say. 'Actually, I only hear what I want to hear.'

But, generally speaking, his idea of humour was to laugh at people. He delighted in Schadenfreude, and he would inevitably open our weekly telephone conversation by enquiring – although he already knew the answer – what the weather was like in Edinburgh.

'Freezing and drizzling as usual,' I would say.

'Oh, it's twenty-four degrees here,' he would reply, chortling.

As the compact town to which he had been first attracted expanded along the coast, he withdrew – apart from his trip to the supermarket for their special Monday offers – almost permanently to his balcony. There, he thought of nothing at all, or relived memories of his childhood and his life in Sussex. In the evenings, he whiled away hours watching news bulletins being repeated on television, along with the rate of exchange, with which he was obsessed. The only other programme he watched was the broadcast of traditional Canarian music every Sunday evening, which he loved.

Apart from Brenda, he spoke to no one in Playa Blanca or in Edinburgh, to which, aged ninety-two, he still returned three times a year. In fact the only people he ever spoke to were his family, who he enjoyed seeing – providing it wasn't for too long.

By now, before I had started having major health problems, I had travelled to even more remote corners of the planet. I had sailed down the River Niger to Timbuktu. I had tracked down eagle-hunters in Mongolia and made a pilgrimage to sacred Mount Kailash in Tibet. I had traversed the Pacific, explored shark-worshipping in the Solomon Islands, and retraced the steps of Robert Louis Stevenson to the island of Butaritari in Kiribati, arguably the most isolated place on the planet.

I had also written dozens of travel articles and had published *Reports from Beyond*, a book describing many of my journeys and adventures. Of course, I gave him a copy, and when I asked him what he thought of it, he said – to his credit – that he thought it was 'impressively produced'. But, later on, when I asked him if he had read it, all he said was, 'Oh, I'm not interested in travel books,' and thereafter he put it away in a drawer.

Then, in Lanzarote, when he was ninety-one, he snapped his Achilles tendon. He wouldn't hear of going to the local doctor, whose fees he considered extortionate. For weeks, he hobbled around with a walking stick – home-made, of course, to avoid having to buy one – but he increasingly talked about how he had had enough and wanted to die. Meanwhile, unknown to my sister and me, conditions in his apartment had rapidly deteriorated. The boiler no longer functioned and he had no hot water. The refrigerator, which didn't work – was stuffed with curdled milk and food weeks past its sell-by date. He was eating less than ever; he was so thin that the skin hung from his bones, and he frequently took to his bed for sixteen hours a day; sometimes, he didn't even get up at all.

A month later, shortly after he tripped on the pavement near his apartment, he had a massive stroke. It was the only thing he had ever said that he dreaded. Overnight, he lay unconscious on his bedroom floor before Brenda, worried that he hadn't answered the phone, let herself in the next morning and he was rushed by ambulance to hospital in Arrecife. My sister and I immediately flew out to see him. Overlooking the harbour, the hospital, with its pale blue doors and windows, was intimate and peaceful. Outside, at the foot of the steps to the entrance, was a circle of giant palm trees and, over a wall, sleek white cruise ships were berthed in the docks.

Every afternoon we drove to the hospital, where for hours on end we sat at his bedside. He was in a bright, clean room, and a soft breeze wafted through open windows in the corridor. He was in a coma and, as he had pneumonia, he wasn't expected to live more than several days. Two or three times I asked my sister to leave me alone with him. Then, feeling very emotional, I would lean over him; I had just spent two months in hospital, and now it felt as if I was also dealing with my own death. Although he was unconscious I felt sure he could hear me. With tears in my eyes, I evoked memories of his days in Sussex with my mother, which he had always said were the happiest of his life. Although I had often disliked him intensely, I also told him how much I loved him – which was true – and what a wonderful father he had been.

His granddaughter – his favourite grandchild – flew over from Germany for twenty-four hours, before she had to return to the school where she was a teacher. Then, two days after she had made her emotional farewell, he opened his eyes. It was like a miracle; even the nurses and doctors were flabbergasted. He could barely talk, he couldn't walk, he couldn't read, he couldn't write and most of his memory had gone, but at least he recognised us.

'Who's this?' I would say, pointing to my sister.

'Daughter.'

'And who am I?'

'Son.'

If we asked him to, he could wiggle his toes and lift a cup of water to his mouth. We would prop him up on his pillows, and my sister would show him a photograph album of her family that she had made for his ninetieth birthday. For decades, he had hated being photographed, and whenever anybody had tried he would hide his face with his hands. But now he delighted in looking at the photos she had managed to take of him and the grandchildren, and as she chatted away about her life he would nod his head and mumble 'mmm'. It was as if all the animosity of the past three decades had drained from him and now he looked like a newly born, innocent baby. For the first time in his life, he even allowed us to take his hand and stroke his wispy silver hair. One afternoon, when I asked him if he was comfortable, he nodded.

'Why?' I enquired.

'Because I'm Timmy,' he responded contentedly, using the affectionate name the grandchildren called him by.

Every afternoon, if we couldn't wake him, my sister and I went to a nearby café overlooking the harbour. One day, while we were having a coffee under its palm trees, I asked her why she had had such a difficult relationship with our mother.

'Well, when I was a child, I was terrified of her,' she said to my astonishment. 'She could be so overpowering! Don't you remember how she used to sit at our bedsides, and to get us to go to sleep say with that threatening look of hers, "I'll count to just five"? But what hurt the most was the way she so obviously preferred you when we were little.'

'What?' I said, astonished. I had always fondly believed that her favouritism hadn't been noticeable until we were in our twenties. 'When were you first aware of it?'

'Between ten and thirteen.' She paused. 'Anyway, don't worry. I don't blame you for being her favourite. It came from her. But Dad and I felt so excluded. And she was so controlling! She always wanted to know where I'd been, who I'd been with ...'

'But that was because he wouldn't take responsibility for our upbringing ...'

'Yes, but she was different with you. You were a boy. She was supposed to be unconventional, but she wasn't really.'

'Did you really dislike her that much?' I asked sadly.

She looked taken aback. 'Oh no! I loved and hated her at the same time. In fact I wish I'd appreciated her more. I took it for granted she'd always be here, but of course she wasn't. You know, our parents were the most diametrically opposed people I've ever come across ...' Her voice trailed away.

Before long, he was making such good progress that the nurses sat him in a bedside chair and then wheeled him downstairs to have physiotherapy. But his improvement placed my sister and me in an agonising dilemma. Although we could take turns to fly to Lanzarote to look after him, neither of us could stay there indefinitely. What if he recovered sufficiently to be discharged from hospital? We could of course put him in a home in Arrecife – but when we investigated it we found it to be sterile and depressing. We could take him back to Edinburgh – but he had always loathed its damp, chilly climate. We even toyed with converting my sister's garage in Germany into a bedroom for some medical auxiliary, who could care for him twenty-four hours a day. But he would not regain his memory and ...

Two days later, he fell out of his chair and hit his head on the floor. From then on, he deteriorated rapidly. He couldn't lift his arms, and every day he awoke for only two or three hours. When we arrived, he would be asleep, with his mouth hanging open, and his half-closed eyes would be white and glazed. Often he would be very agitated, and sometimes he stopped breathing for thirty seconds. When he did awake and he smiled, it was like seeing Death grinning in Ingmar Bergman's film *The Seventh Seal*. Yet whenever we came back from a break, there he still was ...

It was like being on an emotional roller coaster, and every night, when we drove back to Playa Blanca through the dark, we were exhausted. Two weeks became three, three became four, but still he couldn't die. Now he was eating and drinking only when we chivvied him awake, and he ate so little that the handsome young man with whom my mother had fallen in love had become a bag of bones. For a few days, we deliberated whether to stop trying to wake or feed him, until we concluded that it would be inhuman, and, anyway, neither of us could do it. However, after the doctor reassured me this could go on for months, I had to return to Britain for some urgent medical treatment of my own.

Then, two days after I left – and two days short of his ninety-third birthday – he died.

Once more, I flew to Lanzarote to join my sister, while his grandchildren flew out from Germany. Three days later, we drove to the funeral parlour in Arrecife. He had, of course, always been an atheist and, perhaps as a gesture of defiance to the world, he had always said he wanted his body to be put in a black plastic bag and dumped at sea. Naturally, that was unthinkable, and now, still dressed in the grubby apricot shirt and fawn trousers he had been wearing when he had had the stroke, he lay in the funeral parlour in the open coffin that I had requested. His hands were folded across his chest and, though his face looked severe, it was drained of tension. At first the grandchildren, who had never seen death before, were reluctant to go in to see him. But finally they entered the parlour, and his granddaughter, with tears in her eyes, sprinkled rose petals over his chest.

After an hour, we drove to the chapel at the crematorium. Just outside Arrecife, it was at the end of a long avenue of palm trees that ended at the foot of barren hills. There, we met up with two Canarian musicians whom, knowing how much he loved its music, I had arranged to play at the service. Then, after four pallbearers carried the hearse into a large white room with a tall ceiling, Brenda and the grandchildren formed a semi-circle around the coffin while my sister and I sat on either side.

I began by reading a eulogy about his life, for which I felt genuinely grateful. Through my mother, he had known love. Their marriage had lasted nearly five decades, together they had successfully reared a family, and together they had spent many enjoyable years travelling in Spain and the Greek islands. He had survived her death, and, with the help of his faithful friend Brenda, built up a new life for himself. He had enjoyed remarkably good health and outlived all his brothers and sisters – an achievement of which he had been very proud – not to mention the husbands of all my mother's friends. He had been able to spend time in his beloved Lanzarote, and he'd had the chance to see his grandchildren grow up. Last but not least, he had died in a small, peaceful hospital, where he had received exemplary care, suffered no pain, and we'd had ample time to say farewell to him.

After I had finished the eulogy, everybody held hands and stood in a circle for five minutes around the coffin. Then, when the ceremony was over, we drove back to the marina outside Playa Blanca, where my sister had booked three tables at an Italian restaurant. Overlooking scores of moored yachts, the tables were sheltered from the breeze, and, as the proprietor had put three of them together, we must have looked like some extended Italian family in a spaghetti advertisement.

After we had all ordered, I proposed a toast to my father. 'Here's to Tim!' I proclaimed, and we all raised our glasses.

During the meal, my sister and I got chatting. 'I know he was incredibly difficult, but, apart from Joseph, he was also the most interesting man I ever met,' she began.

'Really?' I replied. 'What did you find so interesting?'

'His history. His politics. His view on life – everything. Joseph felt the same. The two of them used to discuss things for hours.'

'You amaze me,' I said. 'All he wanted to do with me was argue.'

'But he was so full of stories!'

'Not with me, he wasn't.'

'But that was the father and son thing. He told me the only subject you'd talk to him about was the weather.'

Caught unawares, for a moment I profoundly regretted having chosen – unlike my sister and her family – not to accept him for what he was. But my pang of contrition didn't last long. I had done my best to fulfill my promise to my mother to look after him. I had helped him pass his driving test after she died. I had supported him for years in the protracted court case he had brought against the owner of the flat underneath him in Howe Street after they had been responsible for the building subsiding. I had helped him buy his apartment in Playa Blanca, and I had always made sure his refrigerator was full of groceries whenever he returned home from Lanzarote. For twenty years I had even invited him every Saturday afternoon down to Stephen Street for tea.

Now, as we sat there looking out on the gently swaying yachts, we ate and drank to our hearts' content.

As the effect of wine coursed through my veins, I felt the strain of the last month drain away. His death had been very sad, of course, but it was also an enormous relief for everyone, and my sister and I had been spared having to transport him to some anonymous nursing home in Lanzarote, Germany or Edinburgh, which he would have hated.

After two hours, we moved the tables into the shade, where we ordered yet more puddings, bottles of wine, liqueurs and coffee. At last, as the strength of the sun lessened, it was time to settle the bill. It was going to cost a small fortune, although Joseph was going to settle it with money he would reclaim from the estate.

'If Tim knew how much this was going to cost, he'd die!' Brenda joked absent-mindedly, whereupon – knowing how much he, with his black sense of humour, would have appreciated her slip of the tongue – we all burst out laughing.

Acknowledgements

With thanks above all to Jim Hutcheson, without whom I couldn't have done the book; Caroline Gorham, for her patient help in producing it; Tom Gorham, for his creative typesetting and layout; Séan Costello, for his conscientious editing; Alison Rae, for her meticulous proofreading; Max Edgar, for stoically enduring my computer crises; and my partner, Gabriella, for being there.

Also thanks to: Nigel Chadwick, Peter Church, Bundesarchiv, DVM, Lenka Vybiralova, Wolfgang Venohr, Wolfgang Morodor, Stephen Richards, Lindsay Kemp, Roddy Smith, Chmee 2, Kevin Rea, Nigel Mykura, ECH Adam, Jesper Schoen, Luis Miguel Sanchez, MD Carchives, Mig de Jong, Mtcv, S. Moller, Polygoon Hollands Niews, Sven Storbeck, Fabienkhan, Andreas Praefcke, Frank Vincentz, Chensiyuan, Daniel Case, Lee Kindness, Marcelo Noah, Dirkvd M, Albert Kok2, Daniel Case, bMA Amsterdam, David Ball, PD Art, Bert Kaufmann CCA, De Bijenkorf Amsterdam, Litterair Café Amsterdam, Jos Van Zetten, Eddie Woods, Muz Murray, Dave Spicer, Brian0324, PD ART, Hotel Guadalmina.

To find out more about the author's journeys, go to
www.reportsfrombeyond.com